PRIVATE FACES

PRIVATE FACES

The Autobiography

Siân Phillips

Hodder & Stoughton

Copyright © 1999 by Siân Phillips

First published in Great Britain in 1999
by Hodder and Stoughton
A division of Hodder Headline PLC

The right of Siân Phillips to be identified as the Author of the Work
has been asserted by her in accordance with
the Copyright, Designs and Patents Act 1988.

10 9 8 7 6 5 4 3 2 1

A CIP catalogue record for this title
is available from the British Library.

ISBN 0 340 71255 4

Orators by W.H. Auden reprinted with permission by Faber & Faber.

Map by ML Design

Typeset by Hewer Text Ltd, Edinburgh
Printed and bound in Great Britain by Clays Ltd. St Ives Plc

Hodder and Stoughton
A division of Hodder Headline PLC
388 Euston Road
London NW1 3BH

For Sally and Dai, my mother and father

Acknowledgments

My thanks to my agent Mark Lucas, without whom I wouldn't have started, and my editor Rowena Webb, without whom I wouldn't have finished the book.

I thank Gethin Lewis and Meriel Lewis for help with family history and Patricia Myers (registrar at RADA) for reminding me of the geography of RADA past.

Huge thanks to Nina Humm for dealing with my terrible handwriting and for being so patient and resourceful throughout.

Most especially my thanks to William Corlett for understanding the problems of a novice and for his constant guidance. To him and Bryn Ellis my thanks for refuge and light entertainment.

'Thank you' seems an inadequate expression of what is due to Thierry Harcourt and Fabi Waisbort for their daily, unfailing love and support.

Private faces in public places
are wiser and nicer
than public faces in private places

Orators by W.H. Auden

PRIVATE FACES

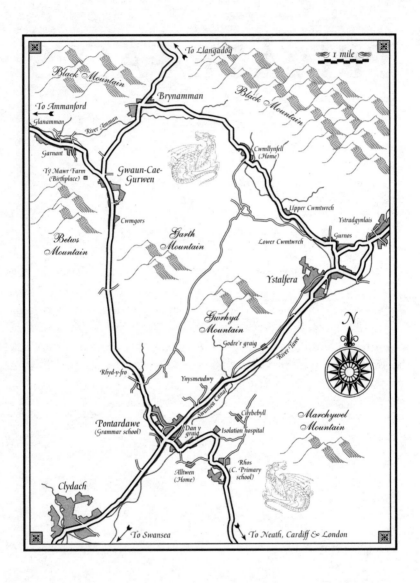

I was born on a farm on a windy mountain in South West Wales. Mountain? Some would call the Betws a hill. It is modest where it stands opposite the Black Mountain range. In the Valley between the big mountains and the little one lies Gwaun-Cae-Gurwen; (G.C.G. to even the most ardent Welsh speaker) a street or two of small granite houses, a few pubs, a chapel, a Miners' Welfare Hall doubling as a cinema and a coalmine. They say this place is wetter than Borneo and certainly the life into which I was born and which I thought would stay the same for ever is as curious and remote now as the lives of strange people, in an unknown country, far away.

Chapter One

I was almost out of the back door of Tŷ mawr, my grand-parents' farm where I was staying, when my grandmother, emerging from her cold, slate larder carrying a basin of milk, called 'Oi' in the firm but neutral tone she would use to address an errant beast. Jerking her head, she indicated the almost cold basin of washing water. I hated that tepid water with its pale blue soapy scum even more than I hated the face-flannel, cut from the tail of one of my grandfather's flannel shirts, striped and slimy with soap. Holding my breath, I dabbed at my nose and chin and, eyes tightly shut, reached for the towel. Brisk, capable hands lifted my face and scrubbed at my head and neck. I could feel water trickling down inside my jumper but knew better than to complain. She towelled me dry and reached for a comb, deftly undoing my plaits with one hand. Useless to say, 'Mammy lets me do my tangles first'. My hair was brushed, combed and plaited with the same calm speed with which cows were milked, dough kneaded and family discussions chaired around the large, black-leaded range with its gleaming brass fender.

I knew she wouldn't pause to look at me again when she was done and as she returned to her milk and flour and butter I stood on tiptoe to catch a quick glimpse of myself in the only looking-glass in the house which hung in the darkest corner of the kitchen. At six I could just glimpse my hair and my eyes. The little mirror was there for the men when they shaved, but

I sneaked regular looks so as not to miss the day when, as promised if I ate bread crusts, my hair would become thick and blonde and curly. Nothing doing today. Nondescript straight wisps. I looked back into the darkness of the big kitchen with its small window set deep in the far wall, the big settle and the little settle framing two sides of the scrubbed table, my grandfather's chair with its back to me, the grandfather clock in the corner and the fireplace with its overmantle serving as a filing cabinet; the yellow *Farmer's Weekly* and advertisements for cattle feed jammed behind the brass candlesticks. A larger window illuminated the long table where I had just been washed, at the far end of which my grandmother was now working. It was a thick slab of wood, scrubbed white, and on special days two men would turn it over to reveal a side polished like a conker.

I was thin and white and on the frail side and this exempted me from helping and I had never known my grandmother to delegate to anyone but, taking no chances, I gently backed away down the length of the table, past the larder, then whirling round I was out of the back door, across the clean scrubbed flagstones of the little yard, past the dairy then across the big, dirty yard skipping over the drying cow-pats and on down to the seclusion of the cow-sheds, cool and dim and at this hour of the morning empty and smelling more of disinfectant than cows and cow-dung. I loved the cows and knew them by name, but I found their personal habits hard to bear.

For a country child I was squeamish and ashamed of that and went to great pains to conceal it, having no wish to add to my list of oddities which my auntie Meriel, my mother's sister who lived at home on the farm, put down to my being a bit S-P-O-I-L-E-D. She mouthed this over my head by way of explaining why I read unsuitable books and why I politely but firmly rejected fresh eggs, milk warm from the cow, salty home-made butter and home-cured ham in favour of water, margarine and Spam. Her explanation of my behaviour as spoiled was just that – an explanation, uncritical and even tinged with humour. Behind an impassive face I wondered how she could imagine I couldn't hear her semi-spoken mouthing and how could she think I couldn't spell such a simple English word as 'spoiled' when I was already known as a GREAT READER. 'Go on – spell "epiglottis".'

Now, hauling myself into one of the enormous vats of dry cow-cake in the corner of the cow-shed, I wriggled into a comfortable position out of sight – just in case – and contemplated the limitless possibilities of the day. The only checks and hindrances would be meals. Adults were, without exception, obsessed with food; collecting it, slaughtering it, cooking it and never-endingly sitting down to eat it. How many times a day did my grandmother climb up on to the hedge near the spring calling people in to eat? Too many times, it seemed to me. Strangers passing through Tŷmawr land were corralled into the kitchen and urged to 'Eat! Eat!'. My grandmother brought out one of her three English sentences in the service of food. Addressing English itinerant labourers, she would call, 'Man, come to dinner!' – open vowels and a rolled 'r' at the end. John Dineen, the Irish itinerant who came to work on the farm each summer, was considered to be almost Welsh and was spoken to in Welsh and had to make the best of it. I shared his fondness for potatoes and ate such phenomenal amounts that I was referred to sarcastically (though never in John's presence) as 'the Irishman'.

Potatoes aside, I picked at food and my grandmother worried about my lack of appetite. She needn't have. I ate my way through the day and tasted everything I came across, knowing enough to avoid poisonous leaves and berries. Sitting unseen in the kitchen garden, I despatched spring onions, carrots and radishes straight out of the earth (a quick rub on my knicker leg got rid of most of the dirt). There was always something new to eat; peas in the pod, gooseberries, cooking apples, sorrel, dandelion leaves, nuts, even hawthorn berries weren't too bad and now, luxuriating in the huge feed bin, I nibbled a cow-cake; the size of a fingertip, brown and earthy tasting. Filling too. No one had ever said, 'Don't eat cow food', but I kept it to myself all the same.

Restored after the irritations of getting up, I lowered myself out of the feed bin and set off past the stables, making for the hen house. Most of the hens were scratching about outside but I knew that some of them would be perched inside. I longed to see a hen lay an egg and spent part of every day sitting on my heels in the hen house, watching and waiting, scarcely breathing, but the hens never forgot I was there. Heads tilted to one side then the other, they made comfortable noises that might have been the prelude to the laying of an egg but never was. After a bit, resigned, I straightened my stiff legs and left them to it. (This part of my day I never talked about.) How could animals be so patient? I would lie for hours in the field behind my parents' house in nearby Alltwen watching the skylark high in the sky, waiting for her to forget I was there and come down to her nest. She never, ever did and I always gave up first.

I was now working my way up the Betws mountain through a small wood at the back of the farmhouse. This was where we collected hazelnuts. Part of the wood was dark and sinister; the earth on the steep slope had leached away from the roots of the trees and they reached down in contorted rope-like shapes around the mouths of small hiding places, hardly big enough to be called caves. This place was always the setting I described when recounting the nastier parts of The Story – a rambling, on-going tale of adventure and death which I made up to tell my friends at infant school in Rhos, near Alltwen. It was along the lines of a 'Famous Five' adventure as told by Edgar Allen Poe. I loved *Tales of Mystery and Horror from Poe to Arlen* and borrowed plots to add to my own. There were few of my stories that didn't feature a ceiling or the roof of a cave that descended slowly and inexorably on a couple of trussed-up children dressed in blazers and wearing belts with snake buckles. Snakes! Speckled bands (deadly snakes) circled the heads of plucky girls with fresh complexions and naturally curly hair as they sat, not daring to move, until they were rescued by a boy in a blazer.

My young audience believed me only too completely and when one, then two, then three children were found crying with fright in their beds, there was a delegation of mothers to our house and a good deal of eye rolling and head shaking and whispering. My mother was unaccustomedly nonplussed by this unusual crime. She was all for originality; 'Go on, write a story! Use your imagination!' was an often-heard refrain in our house. Never before at a loss for words, she was now reduced to a rather feeble, 'RIGHT! Upstairs, and no coming down 'til I tell you.' The following day I was forbidden to tell any more stories until the fuss had died down and even then not to tell any that didn't have happy endings. 'Invent HAPPY things,' she said, at the end of her tether. Struggling through the dark, sinister undergrowth, I thought I wouldn't bother.

I reached the top of the Betws mountain and sat down, out of breath, and looked about. Down below was the farm with the lean-to washhouse and the long slope of the blue slate roof. Smoke rose steadily from the chimney. A long way below was the string of granite houses that made up the village of Gwaun-Cae-Gurwen. Carmel chapel was very big. The coalmine was so discreetly placed as to be scarcely visible. Reaching away to the horizon were the slopes of the Black Mountain, smooth like the flanks of an elephant and dun-coloured with the darker shadows of the few clouds, moving slowly today. One of these peaks I had selected as my Test. The Bible was very familiar to me – my grandmother seemed to know the whole of the Old Testament and few arguments at home were settled without a triumphant, apt quotation from it. My mother was more keen on the New Testament and I was already learning and reciting long pieces from that. Faith moving mountains had made a deep impression on me and I strained every nerve to move my chosen peak. I knew it would take a while and I wasn't even going to try today. It was something I did when I felt particularly 'holy' and ready to do battle with nature. Now I leaned back and did nothing.

Below and to the left smoke rises from Llwyncelyn which is a yellow house. My grandmother's house stands granite-dark and symmetrical and its outhouses are whitewashed. Llwyncelyn is smaller, more picturesque, maybe even prettier, but white seems more correct for a farmhouse than yellow. There is one farm I know which is outlandishly pink and some years when the mix goes wrong it becomes a vivid raspberry and when it rains, which is most of the time, it looks too bright by far. My grandmother's way in this, as in most things, is best. I sense that even my mother thinks this but at home in Alltwen we do things her way which is slightly, ever so slightly, different. I sit up and go on looking around, doing nothing. I spend a great deal of time here, in Tŷmawr. I hear people say I'm not 'the strongest'. I may not be the strongest but I feel fine and this life suits me fine. This is the countryside I know best and I like spending most of my time just looking at things. My mother comes over from Alltwen and nods approvingly at me but she looks anxious. She doesn't need to. On his day off my father comes as well and works on the farm. I love going home on the bus with them but sometimes they leave me here and we're all sad when we say goodbye but once they're out of sight I cheer up right away. I don't know why they call me 'delicate'.

When I can tell from the feel of the day that soon it will be time for the mid-day meal, I still have time to take the long, easier way down, entering the farmyard from below and stopping at the spring where we draw our water for the house. Very quietly I lift a few of the big mossy stones. The toad isn't there. There isn't anything there. The spring rises above a field of fairy rings and it seems to me reasonable that fairies would spend time around this very convenient, pleasant spot. Auntie Meriel made a face when I told her this but my mother didn't because she was in the house when I SAW a fairy, years ago when I was really small – maybe three or four years old. It wasn't a dragonfly and it wasn't a butterfly so what could it have been but a fairy? All the same I'm beginning to think that I'm never going to see another one. It's like the hens' eggs and the skylark.

My grandmother's metal-tipped boots are making a ringing sound on the flags as she moves quickly between the range and the work-table and the table where we eat. I slide into the little settle where I left my book last night. Life outside a village means life without electricity. My uncle Davy, the third of my grandparents' children, is a teacher and a councillor. He lives in a lovely white modern house called 'Pen-y-bryn' which he's built on a meadow below the farm and he is working hard on something called 'rural electrification' ('Go on, spell what Uncle Davy's doing'). He hasn't managed it yet and at night everything has to take place around the Tilly lamp in the kitchen and since Uncle Davy, when he was a student home from the university, set fire to himself, reading in bed, and my grandmother saved him and the house by throwing the burning mattress into the yard, there's been a strict rule against reading in bed by candlelight.

I read a bit now until all the places around the table are taken. It's cawl – Welsh stew – so that's all right. My grandmother ladles it into basins; lamb, carrots, swedes, potatoes, chopped leeks and great handfuls of parsley. The top is shiny with stars of fat. I pray there aren't too many bits of fat at the bottom of my basin. Tomorrow we'll eat the cawl again and it will taste even better. On day two it's called '*cawl aildwym*' – second-time-warm cawl. I hate Sunday food because there's always beef which has a lot of fat and the worst trial of all hangs above my head; a huge side of bacon which is nearly all fat with thin stripes of pink meat. I don't really like the Welsh cakes or the pancakes which are made on the bake-stone over the fire, nor do I care for my grandmother's famous pastry. What I like best is *siencyn* which the men eat after the first few hours of work, early in the morning. It's a basin of bread and butter, with sweet milky tea poured to the top of the basin and old cheese grated over it all. It's lovely.

The only members of the family not here are my mother who is in her house in Alltwen with my father, and her brother, Davy (the bed-burner) who is at school, teaching.

Daniel, my grandfather ('*Tadcu*' in Welsh), sits at the head of the table and is served first. He's a shadowy figure to me and I don't really like his moustache or his clothes which seem to have moulded themselves to his shape, but I do like his moleskin trousers – washed and washed until they are white – which make a 'whip, whip' sound as he walks. He is the son of Sali from Wernwgan farm – a 'hedge school teacher' who taught anywhere that was dry and convenient (did those teachers ever teach actually sitting in a hedge?), and the Welsh Bible was their only textbook. He looks fairer and much bigger than his mother, Sali, in the photograph of her in the parlour that shows a small, shrunken, beetle-like little woman, holding her Bible firmly between her and the world.

When he was younger, Daniel's passion was not farming but horses, and his dream was to breed a good racehorse. Needless to say he never succeeded in this and the failures were seconded to farm work for which they were completely unsuited. My mother, when she was a girl, lived in daily dread of entering the stable to put one of these high spirited, nervous monsters between the shafts of a hay-wain or a milk float. Their eyes rolled and they backed away from her, rearing up and lashing out with their hooves. 'Don't hurt that horse,' my grandfather would say as he passed the stable where my mother was trying to avoid serious injury to herself. Once the job was done and the float was backed out on to the yard, she had to fling herself aboard as the horse took off with a determination and speed never displayed in its earlier, racing life. They thundered down the stony dirt track to Gwaun-Cae-Gurwen, milk churns sliding perilously around her legs, only slowing to an exhausted, sulky trot as they took the sharp turn over the little river and began the steep climb up to the village.

Daniel's brother was a coal-miner and *his* dream was to find the big seam of anthracite which he was sure existed just outside the village. The little foothills of the Betws were pitted with small openings and shafts where he'd probed for his Big One. When he'd saved enough money he would stop working for the Mining Company and start his own dig again. The big strike was as elusive as his brother's champion horse but his dream was no impossible fantasy and after his death the big seam was found a few yards beyond one of his little shafts which had been discontinued for lack of funds. He enjoyed prospecting as much as my grandfather enjoyed playing with horseflesh; they weren't bitter in their disappointment and their wives only mildly (and silently) exasperated.

My grandmother, Elizabeth ('*Mamgu*'), was born in the room in Tŷ mawr where my uncle and aunt and my mother and now I had been born. Medium tall, medium slim, she was unremarkable save for her swift, athletic walk and the deftness and certainty of her gestures. Married to Daniel who loved to talk and linger down in the village, she was, above all, a skilful worker. Plain living and high thinking, was it a secret vanity that drove her, even after cold water had been piped through to the farm, to walk through the two farmyards to draw water from the spring to wash her face? Her feet, shod in laced-up boots, were as white and unblemished as a girl's. Her hands, gnarled as an old man's, didn't seem to belong to the unlined face and smooth feet. Her hair was scraped back under a faded cotton cap, elasticated behind and turned up at the front giving her a deceptively girlish air. She wore dark dresses and over them sleeveless overalls, small prints on black cotton. Indoors, over these she wore large clean light-coloured starched aprons and outdoors these were replaced by aprons made of clean sacking. There were 'day' clothes, then there were 'end of the day' clothes ('best' clothes past their best), which she would wear on weekdays to visit neighbours or receive visitors. 'Clothes of respect' were best clothes worn only to chapel and to weddings and funerals. All these were made by a relation, Syrviah, who along with her treadle sewing machine, would be met in the village and brought up to the farm on the horse-drawn milk float. She would stay for a week or two, making shirts and suits for the men and a sparse wardrobe of dresses and aprons and coats for the women and children.

My grandmother read the Bible daily and it was said that if all the Bibles in the village were burned, Mrs Thomas, Tŷ mawr, would probably be able to write out the whole of the Old Testament. ALL of it? I wondered some years later. Not allowed to read the *Sunday Despatch* while it was running excepts from *Forever Amber*, I spent many Sundays reading 'improving' books and, in an excess of zeal and virtue, decided to read the whole of the Old Testament. I struggled to keep my face impassive as, delighted and astonished, I plunged ever deeper into the scarcely credible accounts of sex and violence among the tribes of Israel. Occasionally my mother would look up from her knitting and I could feel her mild surprise at my good behaviour. (There was always something grudging in her approval of me, as though she sensed I was less biddable than appearances would suggest and even when I *was* up to no good I resented her sceptical look and tone of voice.)

Now, making rapid strides in my sex education, I wondered if this kind of carrying on was limited to times past and life in a different climate? It seemed improbable that there could be quite so much smiting, cleaving unto, lying with and begatting by the wrong people in the non-conformist villages of the Swansea Valley. Was it possible that my grandmother had memorised *these* bits? Was it possible that she'd even *read* them? These pages were never opened in Sunday School where we laboured over such subjects as 'Everyday Life in the Time of Jesus, with Special Reference to Cooking and Hygiene' and yet, there they were. Such was my regard for my grandmother's lofty cast of mind and my awe of the gloomy parlour where the family Bible lay on a table in the window that it seemed to me quite possible that by some Methodist alchemy these pages became temporarily invisible when Elizabeth Thomas, née George, opened the great cover and turned past the pages of our less exuberant, rather puny begats. For one thing, what could she have made of Onan? I had to go and look it up in the dictionary and she didn't even *have* a dictionary. Her poise and serenity were legendary and I wondered if a calm conviction such as hers could only be achieved and maintained by not reading all the pages of anything – ever.

My mother told me that even she, *quite* calm and serene, would go to any lengths not to be present on the day the slaughterer came to the farm. Only my grandmother kept her composure. After a strenuous bout of killing the slaughterer would emerge, blood-stained and call my grandmother and any others in the vicinity to view his work then, taking his knife, he would cut a thin slice of raw meat and, holding it up to the light, say, 'Sweet as a nut, Mrs Thomas, sweet as a nut.' 'And then,' said my mother, lowering her voice a tone, 'he *ate* the meat.' She left a pause so that I could fully dwell on the horror and then, almost in a whisper, continued, 'And then, asking to be excused, he would climb on to the pile of warm, bloody skins and, drawing a hide over himself, *go to sleep.*'

Severely shaken, everyone beat a retreat. My mother – no cissy – went for a wash and a lie down. My grandmother merely inclined her head to acknowledge the compliment to the quality of her beasts, said that supper would be ready in an hour, also hot water for his toilette and he would be welcome in the house and walked sedately back to her kitchen, pausing only to shake her head in mild reproof at two farm hands engaged in a violent pantomime of stabbing and eating and thowing up. One shake of the head from her was enough to stop what she called 'nonsens' (much crisper sounding than the English 'nonsense'), by which she meant exaggeration and excess of any sort. Much as I admired her for her stamina and her complexion, her frugal eating habits and her slim figure (her children were all inclined to run to fat) I thought that I'd like to have more fun than she did.

I never know precisely what my grandmother thinks about anything. I know her views of right and wrong are identical with God's and that, if anything, she admits fewer shades of grey than He does so it isn't necessary for her to go into detail; the white and black are simple and plain for all to see. I am always surprised by her silent tenderness with small animals and surprised by my earliest recollection of her; I must have been a baby when she held my outstretched hands and I sat facing her, sitting astride her raised ankle, bouncing into the air as she chanted 'Pedoli, pedoli, peDINK!' and made as if to drop me. 'Cheboli, cheboli, CHUBUT!' (What did it mean?) Now at the age of six, regarding her across the dark kitchen from my corner near the clock, I could hardly credit that she had every been so playful.

John, the living-in help, looks lovely as he eats silently. I have never seen a film but I imagine that film stars look like him. And only the other day he spent ages trying to catch me a mole as it rose in his little mole-hill. And he did it! (That's another one of the Impossibles like eggs and skylarks and fairies.) I think Meriel likes him a lot. Auntie Meriel has fun. More than most grown-ups. Her face is large and shiny and bright pink. It might sometimes look irritated but I can't imagine it looking frightened. She spends most of the day working out of doors and she drives the milk float down the hill and through the village in her khaki milk delivering coat and wellingtons, looking like a warrior queen standing on the springy back step where I am not allowed to stand. She calls 'Milk – o' in a special tune and measures out the milk, collecting all the village news, then 'Gee-up!', expertly negotiating the level-crossing and the sharp turn over the little bridge and back up the rough, stony path to Tŷ mawr. Riding with Meriel is my favourite thing.

At last I'm allowed to get down from the table and now I'm told that my mother is coming for me tomorrow and I'm well enough to go home and maybe go to school. I quite like the school. I go there so seldom I feel like a visitor. But now I shall have to rush around, visiting the animals and saying goodbye and checking up on things. I have so much to do every day on the farm.

Why do grown-ups have to do everything so suddenly?

Chapter Two

T his time, when I got home from Tŷ mawr I began to feel
really unwell. The doctor was called and he arrived, in a
hurry as usual, swearing under his breath, banging down his
bag and demanding what had I been up to now. He was the
only person who addressed me familiarly in the second person
singular, as '*ti*'. It was customary for parents to call their
children '*ti*' but for some reason mine used the more formal
'*chi*' and I was never wholly comfortable with this implied
closeness between the doctor and myself. I felt he was no
friend of mine.

When he left, instead of being put to bed with a fire in the
bedroom grate and all my treasures ranged around me (I
knew and appreciated the advantages of being slightly ill) I
was wrapped, still dressed, in a shawl and my father carried
me from room to room, glancing out of the front windows
each time he passed them. Then, horror of horrors, the
ambulance drew up outside our house.

Now, tuberculosis, 'the lung', was rife in the neighbourhood. People were taken away for long periods and sometimes they didn't return. Miners sufficiently ill with silicosis,
('the dust') were taken away and when they came back, *if*
they came back, they never got better. The ambulance was a
chariot of doom and death and when it passed by we would
stop, look away, hold our collars and chant 'Never swal-
low, touch your collar, never catch a fever'. Now it had

come for me. I couldn't believe it. What was worse, it was taking me away – on my own. In an instant, a panic-stricken instant, my universe lost its foundation, its wall against the world, its sheltering roof. This was as bad as my dog dying. My bones turned to water. It was as though I had nothing inside me except my pounding heart. My mother half extended her arms towards me but what could she do? Other arms were taking me and laying me on a bunk. The ambulance door closed on my father's handsome, anguished face and I felt that the Worst Thing had happened to me.

It was dark when we arrived at a big house surrounded on three sides by black, dripping trees with open country stretching away on the fourth side. I was undressed and put into bed in a large, dimly lit, high ceilinged room. Where was I? No one had told me anything, I suppose they'd thought that I was too ill to hear or understand. I did feel terrible. I lay there, afraid to move. There were the shadowy outlines of other beds and there was silence except for the sound of rain and something that tapped the window behind my head. When dawn broke I recognised the room; I had seen it with its high, dirty, damp-spotted ceiling in almost every drawing by Phiz in my mother's set of books by Charles Dickens. I hadn't thought such a room could exist in real life and now I was in one. Later I learned that the house was an isolation hospital. I spelt 'isolation' in my head.

There were thirteen of us in the room, boys and girls together; some much bigger than me. We all had scarlet fever. Humiliation was heaped on misery. I had to pee in a chamber pot in full view of everyone. Worse was to follow. As I grew more and more ill and couldn't get out of bed, the bedpan appeared and the boys on either side of me made my life hideous with their jokes about it. My squeamishness was against me and in a single day I was defeated and at their mercy. Even my imagination was against me. Peter Rice and Peter Boiling, the boys on either side, convinced me that unspeakable horrors lay under my bed, waiting for me to go to sleep before they heaved themselves up, and slithered towards my face . . .

I believed them. I believed everything they said. I would never be allowed home. I might die. I grew thinner and paler, grubbier, more anxious. But I didn't die. 'Oh, she's turned the corner,' someone said.

One day they told me to stand on my bed and look out, and there in the distance were my parents. They were holding up my colouring pencils and a doll and some books. I hadn't expected ever to see them again and for a moment I felt a rage as all-consuming as the misery I had felt at losing them. I had been gone six long weeks and I knew now that everything I possessed in the isolation hospital would be burned when I left. Didn't *they* know this? They were dismayed to be confronted with a pinched little creature with unkempt hair and a dirty nightgown, gesticulating wildly and crying tears of anger and frustration. My precious things were delivered to me. No one had understood my sign language or my distress. I looked at the pile on my bed and couldn't bring myself to touch anything. My beautiful long pencils had been snapped in half so that I should have something to draw with when I went home. They were ruined. 'She's an only child. A bit spoiled,' said one of the nurses. I glowered at them, hating them all. They weren't like the nurses in any of the books I'd read and I thought they were hopeless.

'Now you're getting better you can have a bath,' one of them said brightly and on Friday night a large zinc bath was pulled into the room and thirteen of us were bathed in it, one after the other. I came after one of the Peters and didn't need him to tell me as he climbed, grinning into his bed that he had pee'd in the bath. 'Thank God I don't have brothers and sisters,' I thought as I stepped into the dirty water.

Now I have something called eczema. There's a nasty crack outside each ear where my ear lobe joins my face. They say they'll cure it before I go home and they're painting my ears purple with 'permanganate of potash' – which I can spell. I've got over my anger and I'm happy. The Peters have gone home and I shall go soon; I don't care if I look strange.

Going home was an anti-climax. I've grown taller and none of my clothes fit. My possessions are sadly depleted and that makes me cross all over again. No school for a while. My mother is making a big effort to do something about my eczema which is much worse now. The hospital didn't make it better. We visit doctors and specialists and hospitals and herbalists. All the 'cures' are time-consuming and useless. There are long walks to the nearest bus stop, long journeys, then more waiting in ante-rooms. I'm learning a lot of poetry by heart. Chunks of the New Testament as well. Some of the cures make me look peculiar. For a while I'm covered in grease and wrapped in bandages with holes for my eyes, nose and mouth. When that doesn't work I'm unwrapped and a sharpened matchstick, dipped in white liquid, is drawn through the cracks in my skin. It turns brown and it burns me. The eczema has spread everywhere. Permanganate of potash is tried again at intervals so I have weeks when I'm purple all over. I'm not really bothered. I'm reciting a lot in chapel and Sunday School and my eczema goes away from my face just before I make a public appearance. At home my hands are bandaged so that I don't scratch myself, but I manage perfectly with my grubby, bound paws and I've learned to sleep on the flat of my back. Soon I'm returned to Tŷ mawr, to Mamgu.

I might be here for a long time and I don't mind that. School is very nice but not being at school is also very nice. I like my friends but I don't mind not seeing them for a while – there are plenty of animals to play with and it doesn't really matter if I don't do lessons either. I like learning songs and listening to stories and writing compositions, but I have plenty of books to read and I can write my own stories. I couldn't understand the sums or the clock and I don't think I ever will but I don't really need to; I don't have any money so I don't need to add and subtract, and I always know when it's time to get up or stop playing and go home.

I go down to Uncle Davy's house and walk along the white front behind the pillars and pretend it's mine. He has thousands of books and lets me read them. Sometimes he and Auntie Maya, his wife, make me spell words and I write things for them. Maybe they don't know it but every teacher I ever met has asked me to write 'A day in the life of a penny' and 'Callers at my door'. It doesn't take me a minute to write a composition. I learn English grammar from one of Auntie Maya's old books and I like that but when they get out the paper, ruled into little squares, I know what's coming and I say I'm not feeling very well and run up the Betws to the farm where no one makes me do arithmetic. My mother gives me poems to learn from *Palgrave's Golden Treasury* but mostly I just wander about and have a really lovely time.

My eczema is a bit of a nuisance and sometimes visitors stare at me if the cracks are bleeding. My mother and father have explained that only rude or inconsiderate people will stare at me and I am not to feel upset or shy. I should feel sorry for the people who can't help gawping. And that's what I do.

Chapter Three

Alltwen, Gwaun-Cae-Gurwen, Cwmllynfell, Bryn Amman. The ring of villages gave me a different perspective on the same familiar landscape of mountains and valleys where my grandparents and *their* grandparents had worked, farmed, ridden and walked over. My grandmother had travelled weekly from Tŷ mawr in G.C.G., over the mountains through Alltwen to Neath to sell her butter, carried in panniers on either side of her pony. One of my great-grandmothers had ridden from her farm near Carreg Cennen Castle, over the Brecon Beacons to be married, carrying her dowry of gold coins in her apron. My grandmother's mother, Elizabeth George, had climbed the Betws Mountain from Cwmamman with her husband to build the first little farm in what was now the orchard of Tŷ mawr.

I was aware of being at home everywhere. And I was especially aware of the line of women stretching back behind me. Men were deferred to, made much of, 'tended' to, even referred to sometimes as 'The Boss' but I was aware that I lived in a matriarchy. Women balanced the books, paid the bills, made the decisions and when necessary ran their own small farms and businesses alone. My parents came into focus for me as people now as I continued to spend time at home instead of going to school. I adored my father but realised that the force I had to reckon with was my mother, Sally Fâch Tŷ mawr, Little Sally Tŷ mawr.

My mother lived austerely so that the few pieces of frippery that remained from her past life, a life I knew little about, were so strange and so uncharacteristic that they assumed for me the quality of magical relics and when I was allowed, I lifted them carefully from the drawer in the bedroom, handling them, smelling them and laying them out before returning them carefully. I don't think they were ever looked at or touched except by me. There was a box of unused pink powder labelled 'Coty', dotted all over with drawings of swansdown powder puffs with ebony handles on an orange background. It made no sense to me; the unbroken seal, the colour called 'Rachelle' (what kind of colour was 'Rachelle'?). Then there was a little mirror with a coloured silk tassel attached that pulled it out of its black grosgrain silk case. I thought it was the prettiest thing I'd ever seen. (My mother never looked at herself in a mirror.) The silk handkerchief had a black paisley pattern on white and was only used for chapel-going. There was a bottle – an empty bottle – of 'Evening in Paris' scent, dark blue with a silver moon and the Eiffel Tower on the label, and an almost empty bottle of 'Californian Poppy'. (My mother never smelled of anything but soap.) As for powder, what sort of person wore powder? But oh, the smell of that box of Coty!

When I was seven and old enough to respect books and papers as a special treat I was allowed to look at my mother's photograph album. Slowly I lifted the interleaves of tissue-paper, never tearing or creasing them. She was barely recognisable and I found it hard to credit the reality of her life before my advent but there she was – the schoolteacher, dark and slim and intense, wearing the fashionably flat-chested dresses of the day, waists low on the hips, bodices cut in a low 'vee' and filled in with silk 'modesty vests' decorated with drawn threadwork and French knots. Her legs, crossed neatly at the ankles, were shiny in pale stockings, her feet encased in immaculate, fine leather louis-heeled shoes. She described each outfit in the photographs and eventually I knew them all by heart; even the price of the 'fur' tippet (10/6), the bottle-green coat (two guineas) – 'Very daring to wear that colour to school; green was safer if it was moss or leaf'. What colours there were: blue could be marina, saxe, misty, French navy or powder; pink was at its most ladylike (and therefore desirable) when it was 'dusty'. I was too young to appreciate the subtleties of grey; dove, pearl, charcoal and clerical. Hard to imagine a black so much blacker than every day black that it became 'jet' black. Dark brown was innocently called 'nigger'. Light brown was called fawn or donkey and didn't show the dirt.

She was at her most vivid and tender when she spoke of her time at Cwmamman School in the Amman valley which led west from G.C.G.. She and her brother, Davy the bed-burner, both taught in this valley but it had only been possible for Davy to go to the university. My mother's pupil-teacher salary paid for his digs and every Friday she would post a parcel of fresh food to him so that their mother could rest easy in the knowledge that he ate properly once a week at least. My mother shrugged aside my suggestion that it seemed unfair that she hadn't been allowed to go to university. 'That's how it was. Boys came first.' Then, meaningfully to me, 'But I wouldn't like to think it could happen today.' When they were both teaching they rose early – in summer John Dineen, the Irish labourer, would take a pitchfork and tap on Davy's window at 4.15 a.m., Davy would wake his sister and they would work in the fields or with the animals until it was time to breakfast and wash and change into teaching clothes then, still wearing boots, their shoes tied around their necks, they ran over the fields (never time to take the dirt track) the mile or so down the hillside and, leaving their boots at a neighbour's house, they boarded the little bus for school, decently shod, breathing hard but ready for the classes of some seventy pupils that awaited them.

Before she married, while she still lived in Tŷ mawr, my mother's week was long and hard because at night and at the weekend there was household work awaiting her after the day's teaching. Once a week, with her younger sister, Meriel, who was still a schoolgirl, she emptied and black-leaded the big range and polished the brass fender and fire-irons and the brass door knobs and handles and the twenty candlesticks that stood on the big oak dresser. The dresser was, she said, like an altar and she knelt before it cleaning the willow-patterned plates and the fifty lustre jugs. She wasn't put upon; everyone worked long hard days. 'Hard work harms no one,' she would say at this point, looking at me over her glasses for extra emphasis. Nothing however dampened her enthusiasm for her 'real' work at school. Married women were not allowed to continue teaching so she'd been obliged to retire before I was born but she still kept all her notebooks and teaching schemes for the year; beautiful, copper-plate labelling; pressed flowers and leaves, ways of coaxing 'slow' children to read. She especially loved the not-so-bright and explained how she kept them in a special, unthreatening corner of the big classroom until they knew enough to join another group.

'Were there any children who couldn't learn?' I asked, thinking of my hopelessness at arithmetic and hoping that there had been many like me, as bad, maybe worse. 'Not one,' she said firmly. This was the moment to ask about Billy. 'Tell me about Billy.' 'Oh well,' she would say as though I'd surprised her with the request, '*Billy* . . . well now . . . Billy *was* – *slow* – no use denying that, well the whole *family* was slow, so what do you expect? Lovely people, mind – children beautifully clean and tidy. Billy learned to read and write and count a bit in the end – and he got a nice little job when he left school, though he could hardly talk – cleft palate – poor dab.

'One year, on April the first, we all did April Fools in the morning. The headmaster didn't join in, of course, but he turned a blind eye. Billy couldn't do an April Fool. We explained it to him but it was no good. He laughed and nodded his head but he didn't understand. And the term went by and one afternoon before the summer holidays the class-rooms were nice and quiet, everyone working and suddenly there was all this shouting in the yard. I told the children to sit still and went to see what was wrong.

'The headmaster had come out of his study and was standing in the yard looking at Billy who was pointing at the roof and saying something that sounded like ball – 'all-all,' he cried. He was so distressed that Mr Williams went for a ladder and climbed on to the roof – it was quite low over the entrance, but when he couldn't find anything he called down, 'I'm sorry, Billy. Are you sure it's up here?' Billy's face opened into a huge smile and he doubled over clutching himself in an ecstasy of laughing. 'Bill-foo!' he gasped. 'Bill-foo!' April Fool, of course! It had taken him from April to June to work it out but he'd DONE it. Mr Williams came down and picked him up and hugged him and said, 'Well done, Billy bach.' Well, all the teachers had tears in their eyes. 'Oh yes, *everybody* can learn if you give them time.' We both looked at the album and she had a sad look on her face. I wondered gloomily if Billy had mastered long division.

It was a former colleague of hers who told me what a wonderful teacher she was. 'You're a very lucky young lady, especially since your school attendance is so poor. Not that that's your fault, I suppose. Your mother can teach *anyone anything.*' I didn't reveal that for some reason I wasn't being taught at all at home. My mother had said I could read anything I wanted, so I did but I still couldn't add, subtract or multiply, and as for decimals . . . Grateful to be left alone, I kept out of the way. 'You might very well never have been born,' continued the same teacher. 'Your mother was spreading her wings. She had her passage booked and a teaching post waiting for her in Edmonton, in Canada. Then something happened and she couldn't go. Tragic waste. Coaching is all very well, but it's not the same.' Canada! I could see that any impediment to such an adventure, myself included, could be classed 'Tragic waste'.

My mother looked startled when I asked her about it. 'Oh, old history,' she said briskly, not even looking at me and she wouldn't be drawn. Her brother told me that something happened on the farm and his salary and my mother's were both needed to ride out the crisis. Meriel had to leave school to come home and work with their mother. I never found out what it was that happened or what my mother felt about it, but I guessed that since she wouldn't talk about it it was something important to her. There were so many things that remained secret. I was insatiably curious and I watched the grown-ups and listened as still and quiet as a little animal, but they were too clever for me as a rule. There were secrets I never learned.

When I was seven and eight I rarely had to be up early to go to school so I was allowed to stay up later than my friends. Together my mother and I would begin an evening by listening to Children's Hour which was at once so foreign and so much a part of my life. We spoke Welsh at all times but I could say 'Goodbye, children, goodbye' just like Uncle Mac with his lovely English voice. We were alone; the fire glowed in the clean fireplace, supper had been prepared so my mother was free to sit and knit, her glasses perched on the end of her nose. There would be no more radio for ages (programmes were chosen ahead of time and we all sat down to listen properly). As a special treat, if my mother was in a good mood I was allowed to play hairdressers and 'do' her hair. Her own style was exasperatingly plain; hair drawn back and clamped in a kind of doubled over pipe-cleaner, then rolled up and secured at the nape of her neck in what was practically a bun. I gave her rolls piled high on either side of a side parting and I reversed the pipe-cleaner and bun part into a page-boy. Without the drama of lipstick the effect was never quite what I hoped for, but it made her look different and less like a mother. She looked at herself in the mirror and considered before shaking her head at our foolishness and telling me to put it all back as it was before.

She was beginning to put on weight and I couldn't understand why since food was rationed and she'd given up sugar during the war and often went without so that my father and I should have more (we accepted this without comment as something that mothers did). She was clever with food and clever with money and clever with books and poetry and maths but there her energy and inventiveness seemed to give out. Gone was the elegant schoolteacher of not so long ago and her thickening figure was dressed in the same four-square, dun-coloured costume and brown riding hat year in, year out. At home she wore a shapeless brown skirt and hand-knitted jumpers under a cotton overall. Undoubtedly she used her clothing coupons for my school uniforms and concert dresses and my father's immaculate three-piece 'best' suit. I didn't think to ask and disloyally wished she wore prettier clothes and lost weight.

She spent most of our time together 'improving' my mind and making sure I knew the difference between Right and Wrong, never missing a chance to point up a moral. Stories of children who Went to the Bad were recounted with gruesome relish.

Our conversations were hardly ever exchanges. I was kept in my place. I answered questions, I was lectured to, I listened. Sometimes I absorbed, sometimes my mind wandered. Now, as I asked a question, for once, my mother looked surprised, almost taken aback. Then she looked shy and there was silence as she considered this new departure in our relationship. Maybe she was nervous of advancing me to a position of equality as a confidante. If so, the temptation to speak was too strong and there in the warm, bright livingroom she told me the story of her other daughter, my sister whom I had never known, someone I had only heard mentioned on the edges of conversations that faded as I approached.

The Perfect Baby was called Gwenith Mai (born, like me, in May, I supposed). My mother described her clothes, who gave them to her and which ones my mother knitted for her and in what colour. Her complexion, her hair, her sleeping and eating habits were described. Nothing, no detail however small was forgotten or considered too trivial to be laid out between us now; laid out and considered and added to. 'And then, one day when she was nine months old I fed her and changed her and put her in her new nightie, the flannelette

31

with the pin-tucks above the waist and small appliqué daisies round the hem, and I wrapped her in the shawl that Mary-Annie had crocheted for her and she was beautiful and clean and going to sleep – and she went still. Too still. I put her on my shoulder and patted her and I looked at her again but now she was stiff and I called out, loud and Mrs Fred Phillips next door came running in and she took her from me and rocked her. Then she lowered her head as though she was listening and then she looked up at me and shook her head.' My mother's hand lifted from her lap in a small gesture. 'She was gone.' There was old surprise in her face. She shook her head, tears gathered in her eyes and rolled down her face. She didn't make a sound. The fire crackled and the clock ticked and the silence thickened in the bright room shiny with polished wood and old brass and new chromium. It smelled good and ordinary and safe but as we sat, each in her own little circle, I could see that nothing was safe at all. I walked over to her and put my arm around her shoulders. She didn't move and I don't know how long it was before she raised and dropped her hands again in the same small gesture of not under-standing and, wiping her eyes on the corner of her overall, she rose and walked into the kitchen.

There was the clattering sound of pots and dishes. I thought maybe I would like to cry but decided to save it until later, in bed. I laid the table without being asked and my mother and I were very nice to each other for the rest of the evening. Until I went to the Grammar School I was called by my third name, Ailwên. It was a made-up name and meant 'Second smile' and now I knew why I'd been given it.

Soon after the end of my mother's dream of emigrating she was standing in Prince's shop (it was called that because Mr Jenkins who ran it used to be the landlord of the Prince Albert pub, down the valley). Prince's sold *everything*; groceries on one side, hardware on the other and little metal boxes with bills and change whizzed about overhead between the coun-ters and the cashier's raised boxed-in desk. Across the busy room, she told me, she saw a stranger in police uniform towering over everyone in the shop. Times were hard for everyone in the Twenties; most of the local lads were out of work and depressed (and Welshmen on the whole are on the short side). The newcomer, wonderfully good-looking, looked very different from everyone around. 'Who is that?' she whispered to Mrs Jenkins. 'Well now,' beamed Mrs Jenkins, sensing a likely match, 'that's young Phillips from Llanelli. Just arrived and I'll introduce you.' He had a beautiful voice. He sang. He played the piano. He played cricket. He was a useful all-round athlete. So much she told me – once. This was not one of the told and re-told stories and I think she felt that for me to be told about the courtship and the marriage would have been completely inappropriate. She married this handsome, sweet-natured man whose grave smile could not have given her a clue to the sadness he carried inside him. Or maybe it did. She was no one's fool.

Chapter Four

He was the handsomest man I knew and he could do everything. He didn't like too much talk so from infancy I followed him around, keeping a still tongue in my head and hoping to be given little jobs. I held hammers and measuring tapes, shone torches, dug the garden. As I grew up I filled his fountain-pen, changed the blotter and tidied the pigeon-holes of his desk, turned the pages of his music scores, learned bass-baritone solos with him and, to my mother's despair, clad in wellingtons and gloves on the hottest day, helped him dispose of the night soil when we lived in a house that had an outside privy – squeamish right through, I didn't flinch when I worked alongside my father. When I was small I could see that I slowed him down but when we walked together he never lost patience with me. Not once.

Even I could see that he was in the wrong job and as I grew older, at eight or nine years, I could see that he had somehow withdrawn himself from a major part of his existence. The Welsh word for police force is 'Heddlu', peace-force. So, in a way I thought, he did his job very well because in our village peace reigned. When, on the pay day, there was a brawl outside one of the two pubs at closing time, my father would contrive to be strolling past, looking the other way and, in appreciation of the policy of non-interference, there would be a jumble of 'All right now, boss', 'No trouble now, boys', 'Good man, boss'. My father's expression remained fixed and inscrutable and maybe his reticence was misinterpreted as a grand aloofness or possibly even menace. He and the post-mistress and the chapel minister were great friends and held the secrets of the village and served as marriage-guidance counsellors, therapists and occasionally judge and jury. It was understood that nothing heard between the walls of the police station was ever to be revealed to anyone outside.

I would sit at the top of the darkened staircase at night while people poured out their hearts to my father, who would have paid good money, if he'd had any, to be spared the intimate confidences. I, on the other hand, was delighted. Grave and shy and beautiful, he sat and listened, seldom speaking and one night, one of his 'regulars', a miserable wife who gave her husband as good as she got – (even I knew that) – sensing that she wasn't arousing enough feeling in my father cried, 'And another thing! Do you know what he called you? Do you?' No response, of course. 'I'll tell you then! "Bloody waster!" You!' Dramatic pause, then in a crescendo, 'You! A man who carries *the weight of British justice on his shoulders*.' 'Mmm,' said my father while, upstairs, my toes curled with delight. 'Mmm. Look, I'll have a little word with him.' Realising that she would have to content herself with this, she allowed herself to be ushered out and as he closed the door he dropped his head for a moment, shutting his eyes, shoulders shaking slightly with laughter. Looking up he caught sight of me on the stairs. Taken aback, he shook his head and turned into the middle room. I understood that it was all right to enjoy the joke, but not all right to acknowl-edge it. I scurried back to bed, still laughing.

After an illegal pig-slaughtering during rationing he re-quired everyone to be extra discreet when contraband sau-sages and faggots and brawn were handed round the village. Baskets had to have a decent layer of blameless apples or cakes on top. To my mother's unspoken but evident displea-sure, he refused our share of the feast. When Jones the Post, who was a talented poet writing in the old metre, turned to drink while wrestling with an ode and collapsed, surrounded by undelivered mail in a place where it was impossible not to notice him, my father expected to be notified as soon as possible so that he could get him out of sight and finish the mail round himself.

There were darker events. Once a little girl was found dead on the mountainside and my father sat all night next to her body until the doctor could come in the morning. He didn't speak for almost a week after that. Every so often there would be an outbreak of poison-pen letters in the village. They were handed to my father who was only too aware of the author's identity. I knew where to look for the things I was not supposed to see and was enthralled by the letters, the blackmail threats and the blurry 'Peeping Tom' photographs of adulterous couplings. There was nothing there to upset or surprise me at the age of eight, nothing I hadn't read about in the Old Testament or my mother's French novels. 'A little word' was delivered and the letters would stop for a while. And people seemed plagued by what they referred to as 'nerves'. Occasionally I would be moved to the couch downstairs and my room given over to someone 'suffering from the nerves' who needed looking after for a while. I understood that I was never to reveal anything I saw or heard. I learned discretion and duplicity became second nature.

My father was accountable to his superiors in the nearest small town, Pontardawe. They were a rough lot, I privately thought. One of them with a passable singing voice was about to be received into my father's choir and as I passed him a cup of tea he remarked, '*The Messiah* – great! I don't think that I know it, though. How does it go? Could you hum it?' I was transfixed by such ignorance. I gathered that my father's position was uneasy and made even more precarious by the way he did his job and by the way we lived our life. His interpretation of his work was to keep everything ticking over as quietly as possible and to 'have a quiet word' rather than to make an arrest. Quite rightly, the lack of arrests was viewed with disapproval as it was considered unlikely that our village should be peopled only by the innocent. I dimly understood that our way of life was disapproved of as unsuitable. My mother directed children's plays and coached me as I began to make a name for myself locally and then nationally. My father accompanied singers, sang himself, trained a choir and organised 'Celebrity Concerts', raising money for charity. In the police force this was considered to be inappropriate behaviour leading to undesirable familiarity and from time to time I sensed that warnings were issued from above. An uneasy compromise would follow. My father made sure that his paperwork was impeccable, he took course after course, stepped up his night school activities, passed exam after exam up to Inspectorate level and, having become over-qualified, proceeded to run the tiny fiefdom in his unorthodox and to official eyes, hopeless, manner. Selfishly, I was grateful that my activities were never curtailed. We were very much at the centre of village life, yet slightly apart, keeping other people's secrets, never taking sides.

Once, during the war my father went away on a course and returned as a Bomb Disposal Officer for the neighbourhood. While Swansea, nine miles away, was pounded by bombs for three days and my mother carried me, wrapped in a blanket, into the garden and told me to remember that she was reading the paper at night by the light of Swansea burning, we experienced only one bomb which fell silently into a bog and disappeared. The yellow poisonous gas detector rusted on the lawn – was it green or red for danger? We forgot. I sat, enthralled, hidden among the piled-up gas masks while the Home Guard met in the parlour for tea and Welsh cakes. The meekest, most God-fearing chapel deacon was all for sharpening the pitchforks against the marauding Germans.

My father went on another course and returned with a rifle and a gun licence. When an envelope arrived addressed to the Home Guard, 'To be opened in the event of an invasion', a meeting was held where it was naturally decided to open the envelope there and then since the day of invasion might be a very busy and confusing one with no opportunity to be reading letters. The letter read, in effect, 'If you see one or

two Germans, shoot them. If there are more, bury the rifle.'
There was an un-heroic rumble of approval at this piece of
good sense. The more excitable members of the Special Police
and Home Guard were convinced that there were spy rings to
be uncovered in every chapel and one of the most dramatic
events that occurred during the war was Mr Evans' wild
midnight ride. He thought he'd seen a parachute and,
mounted on a white shire-horse, he galloped from village
to village armed with a wooden klaxon, crying in Welsh,
'Arise, arise! Invasion! Invasion!' After a cursory peep
through the window at the empty countryside, the village
turned over and went to sleep. There were sharp words in the
big police station in Pontardawe. My father shrugged.

Meanwhile, music was my father's 'real' life in the same
way that teaching was my mother's. I could see that both of
them were obliged to live once removed from the things that
mattered to them. However happy she was with my father
and however pleased she was to have a child, marriage and
motherhood had spoiled my mother's life. My father's joy in
life had been destroyed by circumstance. As a child, the oldest
of five miner's children, his facility at the piano had brought
him to the attention of a local music teacher who gave him
free lessons once a week. At the end of the hour he would run
home and immediately pass the lesson on to his brother,
Ronald, (like all families, however poor, they had a piano).
Together they played and sang and learned to play the violin
and the flute as well (and Ronald went on to be the organist at
the Baptist Chapel in Bynea).

My father never spoke of these days and it was his brother
who told me that when they formed a small glee-club and
began to give concerts, my father was one of the boys
'spotted' by a London talent scout who scoured the industrial
valleys of Wales looking for good voices. He was given free
voice training as a tenor (and then, interestingly, another
coach thought a mistake had been made and he was re-trained
as a bass-baritone). Several of his friends left for London,
most of them to the chorus of the Carl Rosa Opera Company,

but at this moment his father's health failed, he was silicotic and unable to work, and my father became the bread-winner of the family. The events of these years, the aborted musical career, the job in the steel works and then, thanks to his height and his talent for cricket, his seeming 'escape' to the comparative security of the Glamorgan Police Force at a time when unemployment was at its worst, were taboo subjects.

He never complained but I knew that he was 'making do'. When he organised concerts and artists from London came down, some of them friends of his, I wondered how he could bear to be reminded of how much better his life could have been. But he didn't display any regret or envy, he was simply happier than he was at any other time. Tom Williams, Dafen, a friend of his who had become a soloist in London, would stay with us and they would sing duets into the small hours. I loved seeing him in his element. And I loved running around, fetching and carrying for Eva Turner, Heddle Nash, Edith Coates, Vanessa Leigh, Olive Gilbert, Webster Booth and Anne Ziegler (her crinoline couldn't pass through our front door and she dressed in the back yard next to the coal house). The clothes, the jewels, the 'nerves', the rows were pure pleasure.

It never occurred to me to doubt that I was adored by my father. His undemonstrative manner, his formal, rather distant polite way of relating to me, did nothing to shake my conviction that I occupied a central place in his world. Although I never felt poor I assumed that like everyone else we had little money. One of my chief concerns was to make sure that my father was never saddened by his inability to give me something that I must have wanted. So I pretended that I didn't want anything because I didn't know what anything cost and if I did, I didn't know if that was expensive. My parents found this very difficult when it came to buying Christmas and birthday presents. I manged to cancel birthdays altogether, but Christmas was another matter and my parents made inspired guesses and bought me things I secretly longed for. I don't know how he came by it, but when my father gave me a beautiful old microscope I thought I would die of love and pleasure.

Some of the presents were a bit odd. One Christmas when I was eleven, we had a Christmas tree for the first and only time, and it snowed. I was going through an intensely religious phase and Christmas Eve was mysterious and romantic and my father gave me a very expensive book with a foreword by Julian Huxley which impressed me no end. It was called *Living Things and Their Evolution* and it suggested that maybe God *didn't* create the world, which was a notion I had never heard mentioned. 'Well,' he said, 'it's something for you to think about.' A year later he gave me the complete works of Oscar Wilde with no comment at all. That certainly gave me something to think about. I read 'One's real life is often the life one does not lead'.

Nothing could change my idea that something went badly wrong for him around this time. He gave away all his Caruso and Gigli records and stopped playing the gramophone. He stopped buying the Gollancz yellow-covered left-wing books. Doors closed with quiet finality. He began to read 'escape' literature, Zane Grey Westerns, one after the other. He played Beethoven hour after hour and every day I would see him reading a book in a plain, brown, loose cover. I couldn't see where he kept it until one day I saw him reach up and drop it behind a set of Galsworthy novels. Hating myself, but needing to know, I climbed on to the arm of a chair and fished out the book and saw that it was a well-thumbed New Testament.

There were times when he seemed to occupy a barely defined position in a family No Man's Land.

One day when I was little – about seven – I'd been sent by my mother up to my room and told to stay there until further notice. I was in real trouble and I was going to be taught a Big Lesson. I had finished crying. I couldn't cry any more and I sat on my single bed with its huge mattress filled with down from Tŷ mawr geese, my legs dangling, not reaching the linoleum covered floor. I was looking through the window of my small, lovely bedroom with its painted furniture. Below, the sun shone on the meadows of the nearby farm in Alltwen, the lane leading to it was out of sight behind high hedges and so was the field where I had intended to play, near, but not too near, the witch's house (she had once tried to put buttermilk on my sunburned shoulders and ungratefully I'd roared with fright as she approached, bent almost double, toothless, wearing long, dark, cotton skirts). Out of sight I and my friends lit fires (which was strictly forbidden) and 'cooked' potatoes and ate them almost raw and we made 'lemonade' from dandelion flowers or daffodils; anything that would turn water yellow. It was probably a forbidden drink. We were lawless in a quiet way. Nothing but the bedroom for me today and probably tomorrow as well.

It had all started because of my habit of investing ordinary things with almost supernatural powers – I 'acquired' as talismans and charms things which to other eyes seemed common-place. When, as a four year old, I first saw scillas in the garden next door I couldn't rest until I had cut them all and 'planted' them in our garden. I *had* to have them by me. There had been a huge row and I had finally understood that other people's things must be left alone but now, three years later, it had happened again, but this time the property wasn't another *person's* and I hadn't seen the harm until it was too late.

I was in one of my periods of not being ill and I'd been to Rhos School, which I loved, and I'd learned a bit of sewing. The class had been set the task of sewing little 'worms' of coloured cotton, stuffed with cotton threads. There were dozens of these little coloured tubes, designed to be part of some great plan, unknown to me. I didn't know why it was but I desperately wanted to keep mine. They were lovely. They were magical – and I decided to take them home. No one would notice that three were missing. At the end of the day the teacher said, 'There are three of these missing. Where are they, please?' Horrified, I froze. My moment to own up passed. 'All right,' she said, 'all desks open.' Inspired, I, the 'good' girl, the

42

invalid what's more, raised a hand and asked to be excused. I had a brilliant idea. Racing down the yard, past the lavatories, I stood on tiptoe and hurled the treasures over the tile-capped wall. All right, I could never get them back from that nettle-filled ditch but at least I would never be found out.

The teacher who had watched all this from the classroom window was waiting when I returned. She was 'disappointed' (she was probably confused as well; the magic of these inanimate objects was not easily apparent to grown-ups). I knew what 'disappointed' meant. It meant coming to the house and telling all to her friend, my mother. It meant making trouble for me. Sure enough, she arrived for tea and a long chat where I couldn't eavesdrop. After she'd gone there was a long silence then my mother, calling me in, sat down and just looked at me. Finally she spoke. 'I'm going to give you a dressing down you'll never forget,' she said, 'and then we'll decide whether or not you'll have to be sent away to Reform School.'

Reform School? Reform School? I'd heard of them. They were for hopeless cases; really bad, bad children. That was like going to prison. I took in the point of the lecture that followed. Public property was like *private* property. Property was sacred even when there were no visible owners. Yes, yes, yes, I could observe the laws of property if they were that serious but now I was feverishly reviewing my behaviour over the past few months and trying to work out my chances of survival. There had been a lot of Badness, I knew that far better than she did. Maybe this was the end of the road. My mind raced ahead. I'd read enough Victorian stories to know that, often, Badness led to Death and that death-bed scenes with confessions and forgiveness before the darkness fell on the criminal were the best ending for everyone concerned. I could see myself lying there, surrounded by *disappointed* people, being forgiven before I drifted off to a dubious after-life. I howled and howled. My mother shook her head sorrowfully, reprised the lecture and asked me over and over again what I wanted the

43

sewing *for*. Sodden with tears, I was beyond speech but I couldn't have explained anyhow.

And there was the incident of the poem to consider. That had happened only last week. Mrs Rogers-up-the-road had come to the house (looking *very* disappointed) bearing a poem, a love poem I'd written to her son, my friend, Geoff, with whom I walked to school. I was very taken with him because I could tell he liked me as I was the one whose skirts he lifted up in the lane beside the school when the boys chased us, flicking up our skirts and running away crying 'Ach-y-fi – disgusting' before collapsing with laughter and re-grouping. We girls pretended to be scandalised and offended but it was a game we liked a lot for the few weeks we played it before tops or hoops took its place. My poem, inspired by this proof of affection, had rhymes and looked just like a poem should, but my mother was furious and I had cried and promised never to do it again, though I cried only because I'd been found out and I couldn't really see why Mrs Rogers and my mother were so very upset. That, I now thought gloomily, probably made me even more bad. It was a small mercy that she didn't know we had shown the boys our knickers. Anyway, I had, it seemed, 'done it' now and I resigned myself to my fate. My mother had gone out. Would I know what was to become of me when she returned? When would that be? I waited.

My bedroom door opened and my father looked in. Then, without saying anything he went downstairs. Why had he opened my door? Tentatively I crept out on to the landing and, having loitered awhile in the bathroom where I used to write my poetry on the marble wash-stand, I slowly descended the stairs and sat at the bottom. My father had been playing the piano as he did every day, repeating the tricky bits over and over again, but now he began to play 'my' pieces, pieces he played for me to dance to. And now it was 'In a Monastery Garden' by Mr Ketelby. This was music for one of my sad, wafty dances.

I entered the middle room and made a few moody movements round the table. Next he played 'In a Persian Market' by the same composer. This music was for foreign, sultry dancing and now, gaining confidence, I twirled round the entire room. There was so much furniture that 'dancing' was mostly a matter of keeping to the beat while not bumping into things or jumping over them. My father sat with his back to me and played and played, mazurkas and waltzes and polkas and Souza marches and folk tunes about leaving home that made me cry each time I heard them and today, especially, provoked a storm of grief.

Then my father stopped playing and gave a small final-sounding cough. I was glad he didn't say anything because I couldn't decide what was right to say. My father had done me a kindness and I was grateful but I knew and he must know that my mother was right to be punishing me. I didn't think that he would want to be disloyal to my mother either. It was confusing and sad and it was all my fault. I packed myself off upstairs and settled down again to wait, with an empty fearful place under my ribs. The shadows were lengthening along the hedges. I didn't want to be sent away – if it was decided that I had to go might my father be able to save me? I stifled that thought at birth. I worshipped my father but I didn't want to test him.

Life was difficult for my father, but I couldn't decide if something went wrong or whether he simply ran out of steam. He loved me and feared for me and didn't involve me in his problems, but I thought about them all the time until selfishly, in the way of teenagers, I stopped thinking about my parents as interesting, separate beings. Something of my preoccupation with their story remained, however, like an infection in the blood, a residual unease, a fear of being crushed by circumstance. The over-turning of a way of life. An expulsion from Eden.

My mother forgave me and I wasn't sent away.

Chapter Five

My first appearances on a stage had not left a deep mark
on me. When I was four my mother washed and
dressed me for my first recitation in chapel and left me to
wait for her in the back garden. I fancy I remember the
sunshine there and the colour of my dress – yellow – and
the warmth of the sun on my bare arms. I think I remember
being lifted up onto the Big Seat in chapel, where the sunlight
beamed in through the large, plain windows and the var-
nished pews shone the colour of dark honey, but smelled
strongly of chapel: mints, bleach and polish. What I recited I
don't remember, only that I felt happy and at home, as though
I'd done this lots of times before. I have no recollection of
taking off my knickers in the backyard and hiding them in a
privet hedge as I was told I'd done, but I do remember that in
chapel, when my mother lifted me down from the seat beside
her and felt my bottom bare, she gripped me by my shoulders
and hissed urgently, *'Don't bend over'*. That was the first
piece of direction that I received. Mine must have been a rain-
soaked childhood but my memories are delightfully Mediter-
ranean.

My first acting part in the same year was remarkable only
for the fact that at the end of it I needed stitches in my face.
The auntie of the famous writer and journalist, John Ormond-
Thomas, taught us village children to dance (for years after I
treasured my tiny bit of 'tap' as one of my chief skills) and I

was the smallest fairy – in what play I haven't the faintest idea. But those fairy *wings*! Wings with bunches of silver trim smelling of rusty tin cans and utterly beautiful in my eyes. The dress was adequate and the socks were a disaster but my silver shoes and my wings filled me with pride. I thought, if only my feet could stay the same size I would always have these silver shoes. It didn't occur to me that I could ever have another pair of silver shoes. Little threads became unpicked from the strange material from which they'd been made and they also smelled curiously of metal.

The performance passed off unremarkably until the exit of the fairies and as the smallest dancer I led off and was seized by a sudden notion that I could add lustre to my performance by showing the audience what beautiful manners I possessed. I would graciously *give way* to the bigger girl coming along behind. I made an elegant side step, improvising a few arm movements, and then another little hop – on to the masking 'blacks' down stage right and disappeared, chin first, into the front row of the stalls. Mercifully the wings, being at the back of my costume where wings belong, were safe from the blood pouring from my nose and chin. I don't know if the show went on. I went to the surgery and as they clamped my chin I managed to convey through gritted teeth what was uppermost in my mind. '*Mind my wings*,' I growled. And they did. Everything worked out quite well. I was told never to do anything on stage that hadn't been *practised* but almost in the same breath people were heard to say, 'Lovely manners she's got though.' Fifty per cent success and my wings survived intact.

Like most Welsh children I was expected to sing in public. My father taught me my first solo, 'You in your small corner and I in mine', learned phonetically in English which no one spoke and I sang it in the same chapel where I gave my first recitation when I was four. As usual, I was lifted on to the deacon's bench so that I could be seen. My father was to accompany me on the piano which had been brought in for the occasion, the pipe organ being considered too intimidating. My mother was completely unmusical and anxious I shouldn't make a fool of myself and neither was my father too sure that I could acquit myself well. They kept asking me, was I nervous? I was not. Not at all. My moment finally came and I waited for the usual buzz of conversation to die down, then turned slightly in my father's direction. He, waiting to give me an encouraging smile and a signal that he was going to start playing the introduction, was mortified to receive from me an imperceptible nod that he should begin playing *now*, please. As the years went by, my talent did not keep pace with my composure and in that intensely musical environment I was relegated to being a chorister.

During my scarlet fever convalescence, when I was six and she was in her mid-seventies, my grandmother and I made a momentous journey from G.C.G. to Swansea. Together, we made our first visit to a theatre and my life changed for ever. I decided to become an actress and never forgot that afterwards, not for a single day.

Except for visits to chapel in the village my grandmother never went anywhere, so her appearance on a *bus* – to *Swansea* – underlined for me the gravity of the excursion as we set off for the Swansea Empire. Swansea was large and dirty and dangerous. A 'Swansea wash' was a lick and a spit. Swansea people ate shop cake and tinned meat and they stole children who didn't stay close to their parents. This was a big journey. My mother and her sister, Meriel, had fretted over the wisdom of taking my grandmother to a theatre – a place where *her* mother had believed the devil lurked high up in the dark corners – and they were apprehensive as we sat down. I felt like a queen in my velvet seat, waiting for the pantomime to begin. What was a pantomime? What kind of place *was* this?

Suddenly there was loud music – where was it coming from? The lights dimmed and the huge red and gold curtain rose slowly. My lips parted in wonderment and my jaw dropped slightly. Occasionally I closed my mouth and swallowed, then my mouth would open again in silent wonder. I didn't understand the story but I was transported. When everything stopped I shook my head, silently refusing to leave my seat or eat a sweet. This was magic. I had never known anything so absorbing and I didn't want to speak or move in case I broke the spell. I wondered how it was that a place could be at the same time so dark, hugely dark and so brilliantly alight. There was more light here than I could have imagined possible.

I wasn't rendered stupid, however. There was a principal boy but she was a woman and her legs were too fat and I hated the way she boomed and scooped with her voice as she sang, 'I don't want to set the world on fi-ire but I do-o want to set a fla-ame in your heart'. No, it was the whole thing that captured me. That and the chorus girls! When they linked arms and kicked up their legs I smiled the serene smile of perfect certainty. I knew what I wanted to be, I would spend my whole life in the theatre and I would be a chorus girl.

When the curtain descended again and the pantomime was over I was speechless and remained so, hugging my moment of revelation to myself. My grandmother's reaction was nervously awaited. Solemnly she shook her head. Like me she had been entranced by the chorus girls and they were exempted from the disdain that would have been heaped on anyone else's unclothed lower limbs. Finally she spoke. 'Skin,' she said, 'perfect skin. Never, anywhere have I seen such perfect skin.' Faces, innocent of so much as a dab of powder on the nose, beamed at one another in happiness at an afternoon well spent.

After the pantomime my mother took me home to Alltwen. When I got home I took out one of my most treasured possessions: a large Boots diary, two years out of date. I opened it and wrote in English, 'I am now resolved to be an actress'. My mother, passing behind me, looked over my shoulder and tossed her head good-naturedly, giving a small 'what next' laugh. I was affronted and hardened my heart a little against her. What was there to laugh at?

Brimful of lofty purpose, I decided to start preparing for my vocation. The chorus girls had linked arms and – so it seemed to me – had kicked both legs in the air at once. Down in the backyard I stood on the stone flags, my back to the granite wall of the house and tried to pluck up courage to do the same. One, two, three – No! Too scary – one foot would descend to save me. For days, whenever my parents weren't looking, I stood out in the yard, fists clenched, willing the courage to come from somewhere. Finally it did. Up went *both* legs! And I don't remember a great deal more. My bottom landed on the flags and my head hit the granite wall and as I crawled into the house, feeling sick, I reflected that there must be a secret method. I would be taught it later, when I was a student chorine.

As soon as I could move about more easily, I thought I would see how well I could manage the Fairy Queen's pose when she stood on tiptoe on one leg and, leaning forward with her wand, held the other leg out behind her, waist high. I thought I'd got it right but I couldn't be sure so I climbed on to the chair in front of my mother's dressing table with its triple-mirror which began low down, near the floor. This was great, I would be able to see everything. Up on to the back of the chair, arms outstretched, leg up and crash! – down into the mirror – which didn't break. I was so grateful it remained in one piece that I ignored the pain in my ankle. My stripy socks gave me away; the sprained ankle swelled and swelled and the navy stripes became thinner as the sock stretched. 'What's that?' said my mother, accusingly. 'I don't know,' I said, looking at my foot as though I'd never seen it before. 'This ankle is sprained,' said my mother as she cut off the hand-knitted sock. 'You must know how you did it.' Wild horses wouldn't have dragged the truth from me. There is more to this pantomime business than meets the eye, I thought sadly.

Since the revelation of my future which had occurred at the pantomime I did not find a great deal to nourish my resolve to be an actress (preferably an actress in fishnet tights and six-inch heels). My own appearances in chapels and town halls up and down the valleys surrounding Alltwen were immensely interesting and enjoyable, but only so-so in my grand scheme. Wales was populated by amateur actors, and my mother took me to plays, mainly 'kitchen' comedies or melodramas about the demon drink. I remained hatchet-faced and unapprecia-tive. She bought hardback editions of the 'best' West End plays of the year for herself and these I read over and over again. They included a few photographs and I became fas-cinated by an actress with a very ordinary, Welsh name. Edith Evans's face became as familiar to me as my own as I drew her over and over again in my big sketch book. Even at eight I was good at drawing likenesses. Nothing going on around me could equal those plays which I had never seen.

Later at grammar school I played in one-act plays by Miles Malleson with the other Good Actor, John Lloyd, and then a full-length play by Bridie *Tobias and the Angel* with Dafydd Rowlands. I loved *that* play and, playing the Angel Raphael was almost as marvellous as singing and dancing in fishnet tights. I read my first 'rave' notices and felt pretty smug until I looked at the photograph in the paper and thought, 'Oh no' – I had thought that I looked better than that. The picture showed a schoolgirl with lank hair, dressed up in what looked like and (were old) curtains, whereas I'd *felt* like a Towering Angel with a flowing mane of hair, shimmering in my gold brocade tunic. Nothing was quite measuring up to my private notion of what I wanted to be and what I thought I should look like. Except . . . There was an evening that swept me off my feet and reminded me.

My father took me to the cinema: the Lyric in Pontardawe. This was a most unusual event. Everything about it was novel; the long walk in the dark down the steep hill to the little town, everything looking different at night, everyone's curtains tightly shut, the streets empty. The Lyric itself, wedged between two shops, seemed huge to me – what age could I have been? Probably eight years old. It was a double-feature programme with a news report as well. I liked the frantic music that accompanied the Pathé gazette news and the over-excited voice of the man, but the news held no interest for me and I looked about me in the darkness wondering, as usual, how grown up did I appear, sitting in my rather scratchy, balding seat. I hoped it would seem as though I was there alone, leaned away from my father, surreptitiously licking the index finger of my left hand in order to make a little kink in the hair that hung straight over my left ear. The hair on the right side of my face was firmly secured by a large, much detested, silk bow but I felt that the sophisticated twist on the left side negated the childish ribbon and gave me a touch of glamour. I licked my lips and sucked in my cheeks to make interesting hollows and hoped I was being SEEN.

The first film began. I was so overwhelmed that I didn't understand a word of it. Apart from the panto, it was the first entertainment I'd seen in English and for all I know this film may have been American. It didn't matter; it was the funniest thing I had ever seen. Men climbed in and out of outsized machinery and sat on things I couldn't identify. It seemed to be called *Helsappopin* but I wasn't sure of that. The cinema was not full. People chuckled a bit and so did I, then they laughed aloud a bit. I laughed aloud a lot, then more – and more. I rolled in my seat, I patted my chest, trying to catch my breath. It was no good, I was transported by sidesplitting, choking, ungovernable roars of laughter.

My easily embarrassed father was probably aghast by this unexpected turn – I was a quiet child. He gave me a nudge. There was a man standing over him in the dark. 'I'm very sorry,' he hissed, 'but she'll have to be taken out if she can't keep quiet.' I wasn't abashed, I thought the man was mad, but I didn't want to be taken out, oh gosh, I didn't. I smothered my laughter as best I could, exploding into the occasional whoop, never prolonged enough to justify my eviction.

The film ended and I leaned back, damp and exhausted and beaming with satisfaction. 'Do you want to Go?' 'Out?' said my father tentatively. I supposed he meant did I want to go to the lavatory. Not likely. I was in an enchanted place and I wasn't about to waste a minute of the evening in a lavatory. I shook my head and waited impatiently for the lights to go down again. I didn't understand much more of this second film's dialogue either, but it was sad. *Very* sad. By the time the hero was sitting with his little boy in a kind of workhouse? soup kitchen? – penniless certainly, hungry as well, and the unseen orchestra was playing something that I thought was 'Danny Boy', I was in paroxysms of grief. Tears poured unchecked down my face; my hankie was a sodden little ball, my nose ran and my frame was shaken by violent sobs that grew in volume. The man was there again. 'I'm very sorry but if she doesn't stop crying she'll really *have* to go out.'

My father half stood up to go. Mulishly I sank down in my seat, moaning as quietly as I could. My father sat down again and handed me his big handkerchief and I wiped my entire face with it as though it was a face flannel. Why, I thought, did they show such films if they wanted people to be quiet, for heaven's sake?

Somehow I got through to the end of the evening. My hair was damp, the curl hung straight, the ribbon had wilted; I was exhausted and purged and I felt wonderful. My father and I didn't speak at all as we climbed the hill back to Alltwen. I was hardly aware of getting home and when my mother opened the door to us, I scuttled off to bed silently, washing and cleaning my teeth and bushing my hair without being prompted, anxious to preserve this wonderful feeling and take it, intact, to my bed.

Between the ages of eight and twelve or thirteen my very best friend was Mair Rees. We lived near enough to each other to be playmates when I was too ill to go to school and after the scholarship exam we both went to Pontardawe Grammar School. She had curly blonde hair so I felt her to be by nature superior to me. We both took lessons from the same piano teacher and played duets together in chapel concerts until, by virtue of regular practice and attention to correct fingering, she became my superior in technical skill as well as hair and continued as a solo pianist while I went on strike and at ten stopped taking those awful music exams and those interminable lessons where my lack of practice was exposed as I threw myself at the North Face of a chromatic scale, only to end up time and time again in a mangled heap of wrong notes. After Mrs Williams Music had departed clutching her tiny fee, my mother would appear holding the implements of whatever cooking task she had interrupted and stand there, shaking her head. My father couldn't begin to understand what sort of person would not *want* to practise so he didn't know what to say to me. He still played scales for at least half an hour every day. 'You've got a nice touch,' he once said encouragingly but we both knew that I didn't 'have it'.

The private lessons were discontinued. I studied music at school and took cello lessons there because I liked the Augustus John portrait of Suggia. I was not a musical asset to the school orchestra but I looked very convincing. Mair and I were both in the school choir and the times spent learning Miss Caryl Williams's ambitious programmes of Purcell and Pergolesi were among the happiest of my school days. When I became house-captain I had my own, smaller house choir and I thought I'd died and gone to heaven the first time I conducted it.

I was a stranger to self-doubt at this time and thought that it would be a really good move to write just one 'pop' song and try a bit of what the wireless called 'Variety'. Can't be hard, I thought and found a venue where my forays into light entertainment could be tried out. Mair was a reluctant, long-suffering partner in this venture. She loathed performing and it took a lot of bullying on my part to get her singing and dancing (I had somehow acquired a dim perception of something called a jitterbug) and playing bad supporting roles in my comic sketches. She was necessary because she was my acknowledged 'official' best friend and our mothers allowed us to spend all our spare time together so we had ample rehearsal opportunities and also she was the daughter of Phil Rees – the Oil, who had a little shop alongside his house and the upper part of the shop was a garage with double doors that opened on to the small back road where theirs was the last house before the road narrowed to a track past the cemetery. With the double doors opened wide and a sheet hung inside the empty garage, hiding the supplies of paraffin at the back, this was a perfect little theatre with considerable passing trade among people going to tend graves or taking a short cut to the chapel vestry.

We could only perform when Mr Rees was out on his rounds in the van and when Mrs Rees was also out for the afternoon. We charged a half-penny, not for admission ex-actly because the auditorium was the road and the audience stood leaning on the hedge across the way or sat at our feet, which pleased us more because then no one could pass through to the cemetery and had to politely dawdle awhile, holding their buckets and trowels and other grave tending equipment until we came to a stop. My big finish was a dance number set to a song I'd heard on the radio. It was really up to the minute, I felt, and a nice contrast to my affecting rendition of 'Christopher Robin saying his prayers' that preceded it. I'd copied down the words; they didn't make much sense but never mind. 'Maisie Dotes and Dozey Dotes and little Amsie Tivey, a Kiddlee Tivy too, wouldn't you?' we bellowed and I was really pleased to see that it sent people on their way smiling. Some gave us more than a halfpenny.

Later, refining the jitterbug, I persuaded Mair to let me throw her over my shoulder but it didn't work out at all as I'd hoped. I heaved her over my head, singing the while and instead of landing on her feet and doing something interest-ing, she fell on to the stone floor and just lay there. When her mother arrived home she was still sitting on the floor holding her head and bawling. I was furious and scared in equal parts. Surely, at eight, she should know better than to just *fall* in the middle of a dance and she was making a terrible noise. But what if I'd hurt her really badly?

As Mrs Rees began to try to make sense of the state of the garage and the money on the table and the possibility that Mair was concussed, I sidled towards the door saying, 'I think my mother wants me home now.' Neither mother quite got to the bottom of things, but the Oil-Shop Theatre was closed and I gave up trying to be a songwriter and concert party producer. I never did manage to write more than four lines of a 'pop' song so I decided to stick to performing for a while.

I never saw a variety show but I did see an amazing entertainment at Pontardawe. Next to the steel works and the polluted, evil smelling river, there was a ratty bit of open ground. It wasn't a place where you'd care to walk, except for the one and only time that the circus came to town. It must have been after the war and I must have been ten, a bit old to have been so ignorant. 'A what?' 'A circus and we're going tonight.' 'What is it?' 'Oh, I can't describe it, you'll have to wait.' I forgot about it. I didn't know what I was waiting for.

As we walked in the dusk down towards Pontardawe there was an unaccustomed smell in the air above the bad smell of the steel works and there were lights where there had never before been lights, not even when all the lights went on when the war ended. There was a glow in the air and as we drew nearer, I saw that the glow came from ropes of small coloured lights strung between the biggest tent imaginable and little – what were they? They looked like small, brilliantly lit open-fronted shops and there was a merry-go-round and bumper cars and music everywhere, different tunes, clashing with each other, yielding one to the next as we walked on. The smell was over-powering; the damp downtrodden scrub underfoot mixed with the smell of cooking onions and animal droppings and some kind of scent.

Inside the big tent there were trapezes and a high wire, which didn't seem very high and clowns who didn't seem very funny, and everywhere girls in fishnet tights. They didn't seem to do much and I wished I was one of them until they jumped up on to the ponies and did things I knew I could never manage, not even on long-suffering Tŷ mawr Daisy, tired out after her milk round. But I *could* wear a top hat and, whip in hand, point at the entrance as the drum rolled. I wanted to do *something*. The performance wasn't very long but by the end I was drunk on the atmosphere and the noise and the smell.

57

We walked about among the carousels and the little booths and my father, who was a good shot, won me a pink toy that broke and a fish that died. Strolling in that unusual light was like being on stage and I stood up straighter and longed to belong to this strange, exotic and mysterious world. Curiously, I noticed that although the circus was all to do with fun and diversions and happiness, the people left a lot to be desired. Their eyes were distant and bored and they scarcely bothered to look pleasant, let alone smile. They were strangely bad at entertaining and I thought I could do much better. I had plenty to think about as we climbed home; I simply had to get into a world where I could feed my addiction to lights and music and noise, living and belonging on the other side of ordinary life.

On my way to school in the morning I made a detour down to the field. It was squalid and dirty, litter underfoot, a cold, grey Welsh light all around; no music, the people were shabby as they walked around with buckets and brushes, doing the housekeeping. But looking at it, I remembered what it was like disguised by lights, the people clothed in silk and spangles and I wanted to belong to a world like this one and I was jealous of its inhabitants, even in their shabby morning selves.

Chapter Six

After my first brush with death at the age of six, I had scarlet fever again, chicken-pox twice, measles and yellow jaundice once, a broken wrist, a sprained ankle, fainting fits, tonsillitis several times and chronic eczema, but my life as an invalid was packed with pleasure. My father did something called 'beating the bounds' which, I suppose, meant walking around the whole area he looked after; a couple of villages, a hamlet, a few mountains and lots of smallish farms. From the age of seven to ten, unless the weather was very bad, I would be allowed to accompany him. He didn't like idle chatter so we walked in companionable silence and I lengthened my stride more nearly to match his, only occasionally having to break into a little trot. From time to time he would motion me to stop and lift me up on to a five-barred gate to watch rabbits playing in a field and, once, hares boxing; we would stand still and watch a buzzard idling until it dived down to its prey, then resume our steady pace.

For much of this time I lived in anguish at the savagery that lay beneath the scents and winds and changing colours through which I moved, half-submerged and half-asleep. I realised as I rolled like a colt in the grass that I was destroying dozens, probably hundreds of small living things and that as I collected stones and fallen branches for my own amusement, I was obliterating domestic arrangements too small and too complex for me to understand. There were times, when I must have been eight years old, when I would tear out of the house in the early morning and then stand stock still, thinking how could I move without creating havoc and on our long walks I would sometimes step in my father's tracks and pay attention where I placed my feet in scuffed Clark's sandals in case I stepped on and killed some small insect. I just couldn't understand why God had organised things in such an impossibly difficult way. Time after time I abandoned the conundrum and, faced with a long, inviting slope of soft grass, I broke into a murderous, unheeding gallop.

It was during these years that I took it into my head to try to look at everything as though I would never see it again. 'Look thy last on all things lovely' lodged, misunderstood, in my mind, and I was like a tourist in an exotic country, and would jink home at dusk, eyes aching, having failed yet again, half-aware that I was setting myself impossible tasks and more than ready for a deserved Ovaltine and a re-read of something soothing – *What Katy Did* or something by Enid Blyton – to reduce the pressure. I was only too good at letting myself off the hooks I manufactured for myself and when my friends weren't at school we all rampaged together, interfering with nature without a qualm; we dammed streams, flooded meadows, climbed trees, lit fires, stole windfalls and one year collected scores of ladybirds day after day, keeping them cooped up in match boxes for hours and hours.

I do not know what my father thought as we walked and walked, but for much of the time I didn't think of anything at all, fully absorbed in the constantly changing surroundings, tasting unfamiliar leaves and berries, sucking minute traces of honey from flowers and touching – touching everything. I knew I had as much right to be in the landscape as the oldest oak tree. I felt as small as an ant and as fierce as a lion.

Once out of the village, the countryside was bare of people. The farms were isolated and built in such a way as to be invisible until you were almost upon them. Some were small enough to be worked by two people and more often than not we would be greeted by silence as we entered the farmyard.

Repeated hullo-ing from a bit of high ground eventually brought a faint reply and we would settle down to wait. The kitchen door was invariably open but it would have been unthinkable to enter even if the weather was bad. The bachelor farmers employed housekeepers and my mother, when she asked for news of our day, always over-stressed their respectability. (Had it not been for this it wouldn't have occurred to me to think that they might *not* be respectable). Then I noticed that they also over-stated their propriety in many ways, assuming a massive severity of dress and manner and when they offered food and drink as befitted a woman of the house (men were not expected to be able to make tea or lay a table) the feeling was nicely conveyed that the Welsh cakes they had baked were not actually *theirs* to offer, nor were the chairs they invited us to sit on. Nor did the farmer behave proprietorially. Each party deferred to the other and their behaviour was underpinned with formality. A chapel-going housekeeper would know that I was a Reciter and I would be invited to 'do' a piece and, that done, I could escape the horrible strong tea and cake and skip off to have a good nose around in their outhouses, highly critical of anything organised in a way that differed from my grandmother's.

Far more interesting to me than these good and ordinary people was the lady tramp whom we encountered once every six weeks as she walked in a great circle through the countryside. She was tall and strong and she strode out vigorously. My mother threatened the usual dire but un-specified consequences if we failed to treat her with respect, and suggested it would be even better to ignore her which is what she would like best. My mother said that she was from a 'good' family and had *decided* to live as a Traveller and who was to say that that was wrong? (I could imagine my mother's face if I told her that I had decided to take up Travelling . . .) My father was the only person who knew where she was on a given day or where she went and I wasn't to be nosey, but I occasionally followed her at a discreet distance and never saw her sit down or slacken her speed and always had to turn home before I saw her do anything that might tell me something about her.

Sometimes we would visit a tramp who had built himself a home deep in a wood on the land around the Big House belonging to the squire, Mr Lloyd. As we approached through the undergrowth my father would clear his throat a few times and stamp about a bit so as not to take the old man by surprise. Maybe he wasn't old at all; he was heavily bearded and his long reddish-brown hair protruded under his jaunty, greasy pork-pie hat and I may have mistaken his shabbiness for age. He wore a muffler and a shiny raincoat tied around the middle with twine. His shoes were past repair and he wore a sock *over* one shoe. Since I never saw him move from his house I supposed he didn't really need shoes.

His cabin was a makeshift affair, not much better than the kind of ramshackle 'houses' I would build with my friends, but unlike any man I knew he could cook and I was so intrigued by his domestic arrangements – this was 'playing house' in a big way – that I would make an exception and accept the hateful, inevitable tea. Sipping it, I wondered if my mother would be pleased at my good manners or furious that I should be drinking from a tin can. I knew enough to make myself scarce when it was time for my father to have private conversations with these people and knew better than to ask tactless questions so their stories remained a mystery. I was given *Wind in the Willows* for Christmas when I was eight and it occurred to me that the animals in the book behaved rather as I was expected to; in some circumstances certain things went unasked, many things were better left unsaid, in the same way that the Wild Wood wasn't talked about, though who devised this subtle code of behaviour and how I learned it was another mystery.

Old people fascinated me. Not just old to me, but truly old; over eighty years old. One of the deacons in Alltwen chapel was over ninety and he was my favourite of them all. On Sunday I would walk slowly behind him as he climbed the steep hill home. He was spotlessly clean (I had no fondness for grubby old people) with round pink cheeks and snow-white, fluffy hair, just as I imagined Mr Pickwick to be, but older. I only ever saw him formally dressed in a warm flannel shirt with a small, stiffened round white collar and a thin tie, a watch and chain hung across his waistcoat under a heavy tweed jacket. I longed to be his friend and occasionally crept up beside him and walked slowly alongside until he turned in at his gate before Bwlch y Gwynt in Alltwen. Concentrating on his climb, he never spoke to me but this did nothing to lessen my devotion and I plagued my mother to ask his family if they wouldn't like to hand him over to us so that I could fetch and carry for him and take him for walks and read to him. 'You are eight years of age and old enough to know that old people are a lot of work. They are not *pets*.' Since I never lifted a finger at home I knew no such thing and finally I took matters into my own hands and called on his family to explain how, because I was hardly ever at school, I could give their aged relative far more care and attention than they could.

The youngish woman I talked to was non-committal and I thought the talk had gone rather well and was genuinely surprised and disappointed to see her avoid my eye as she left our house later in the day when I came home for tea. My mother called me in and, wearing her only too familiar sorrowful face, she sighed heavily as she began: 'I don't know where to start.' She knew where to start all right. And how to go on – and on and on. I couldn't understand why she was so angry or why they were so upset. I was given orders to keep my distance so I admired him from afar and thought what a shame, what a waste.

Most old people welcomed my attention. The old lady who lived alone next door (she was an exception, most of my old friends were gentlemen) let me play in her back garden out of sight of our back garden. Together we soaped an old plank of wood and leaned it up against the garden wall (strictly forbidden by my mother) and I climbed the high wall and slid down to my heart's content until a huge splinter embedded itself in my bottom and the two of us silently struggled to get it out, fleeing indoors so I could sob without being overheard as we dabbed on the iodine. All illicit injuries were kept from my mother until they could no longer be hidden and then the scolding was far worse than a festering wound or sprain.

When the old lady died I loitered about in the back yard until one of the mourners asked if I would like to view the body. Would I just! I shot through to the parlour and there, in the room where I used to pretend to play the piano on the polished table while she played gramophone records for me to mime to, was the open coffin. I gazed with interest at my first dead person, feeling that I ought to be a great deal sadder. I tried to muster a little tender feeling and a few appropriate tears but it was no use. I knew what it was to feel grief and as I looked at my old friend's body I remembered the agony I felt the previous year when I saw my dog being run over. My stomach tightened at the recollection of the nights I had spent crying myself to sleep under the bedclothes. I didn't want to feel as bad as that again if I could help it and no, this was nothing like as bad, though I felt it ought to be. I accepted a welshcake and left.

My passion for old people, my fondness for wearing a hat at all times except at night in bed, my pastime of delivering long impassioned sermons from the top of the pig sty wall generated no more than a mild and amused shake of the head; the place was stiff with real eccentrics and there was a sprinkling of mad people who were referred to as 'simple' or 'innocent'. These *real* lunatics interested me but I couldn't achieve the sophistication of those who looked after them. Their families liked them, and found them amusing as well as occasionally infuriating.

The little old lady I saw most frequently was cherished at home by her family and also offered rather proudly as home entertainment. Her 'madness' took the form of behaving like a little girl and visitors were invited to marvel at her as she scampered about, saying mildly rude words and giggling behind her hands. I was astonished that someone so old could be so agile; she really did look as though she had become a little girl again. When she ran into the road and lifted her long skirts to show her bloomers to the headmaster as he drove past, I was scandalised but her daughter could hardly keep a straight face as she lifted her finger saying, 'Naughty girl. Naughty, naughty girl. What have I told you?' The old lady laughed while hanging her head and sucking her thumb. I didn't care for any of that. I was not so old that I couldn't remember behaving a bit like that and I didn't like to think that such behaviour and such scoldings couldn't be left behind and finished with for good after a certain age. I didn't care for her little head, with its clean cotton cap, the sly toothless face and demure dress and apron and those skipping feet. I couldn't manage the robust easy-going attitude which I admired and envied. But I had reason to be grateful for it.

During these years it seemed there was nothing that one could do that was so awful that people wouldn't find it amusing. Except for my mother, that is. I tried her patience sorely with my pretensions. My affected attempts at grandeur must have been very embarrassing to her. I have a recollection of sitting in a rather smart front room when I was very small and thought to know no English at all, so it must have been round about my fairy wings time when I would have been four. I had invited myself into the house of a newcomer to the village – an English woman, the first I'd been near and I couldn't wait to get closer. My mother arrived in pursuit, apologetic and flustered, to be told that my visit had been most entertaining. It seems I'd accepted the offer of tea in the front room and had asked if I might go upstairs to the bathroom. When I came down I settled in the parlour – *much* posher than anything I'd ever seen – and the conversation – my very first in English which I'd only heard spoken on the radio – went something like this.

Me: 'Well, I *love* your lav.'

'Oh, thank you.'

'Yes, I love it because it's got a chain' [pronounced the Welsh way to rhyme with 'mine'].

'Ah, yes.'

'Mind you, I think ours is *cleaner*.'

'Oh, yes?'

'That's because my mother has just *gwyngalched* it' [Welsh for 'white-washing'].

'Yes?'

'Yes, we *gwyngalch* all the time because we've got *môch-y-cod*' ['wood-lice'].

'I see.'

On the way home my mother shook me as we hurried along and said in Welsh, 'Did you *have* to tell her that our lavatory is outside and that we're plagued with wood-lice?'

Shortly after this I was a bridesmaid, dressed in blue, chiffon velvet with a white collar. My hair had been put in rags to curl it and when I looked in the mirror I thought I was the most beautiful, sophisticated sight I'd ever seen. As we drove along in convoy to the church in Pontardulais my mother, in the car behind mine, couldn't understand why the road was lined with laughing, pointing people. After the service, an embarrassed relative of the bride sought out my mother and said, 'Could you stop your little girl from doing that on the way to the reception?' 'Doing what?' 'She's making strange faces and she's lifting her arm up and down just like the Duchess of York in the pictures.' Well, I felt so *grand* in my blue frock and curls, it seemed appropriate to wave at the dear common folk.

'Look straight ahead and don't you *move* or you go straight home and this'll be the last wedding for *you* my girl.'

Chapter Seven

O nly a generation away from a time of large families, I had just four relatives close to my age – my first cousins, Auntie Meriel's children, born, like me, in the front bedroom in Tŷ mawr farm. Huw was the first child, born in 1940. I looked and didn't touch and more or less ignored him until, in what seemed a remarkably short time, he made his presence felt as a capable, gifted farmer even before he was packed off to boarding school at the age of ten. I was impressed – from afar.

Babies held no interest for me so I scarcely noticed the next child, Gethin (born a year after Huw) until at five or six, he was old enough to reveal a congenial aptitude for idling away the day while the rest of the family toiled. We would sit on a five-barred gate concealed by high hedges, companionably taking in the view across to the Black Mountains. We swung our legs and didn't even bother to exchange glances as, from time to time, we heard our names called in tones varying between mild exasperation and this-is-the-last-time-I'm-calling shrillness. Bonded by our uselessness, we were fond of each other and once I was even moved, in a brief moment of cousinly tenderness, to put on his shoes for him before we set off for the village. 'Oh, come ON! Faster! Run! – Run!' I cried and it must have been a sign of his fondness for me that he did his best to keep up, hampered though he was by shoes firmly laced on to the wrong feet. It was evident that he would never make a farmer, but as he grew up he made an effort to help while I resolutely maintained my 'totally *hopeless*' status.

Elizabeth, born six years later, was pretty and clever and – I could tell – capable. It seemed as if Gwyn, the last baby, born when I was in my teens, would never grow up to look like the rest of the family; white and sickly, he spent his time, summer and winter, wrapped in a shawl on my grandmother's knee as she coaxed him to eat a little egg yolk or a spoonful of creamy rice pudding.

So, there we were – five of us; four and a half, given Gwyn's fragile hold on life. My grandfather had five brothers and sisters and my grandmother was one of eight children. She was Elizabeth George, the daughter of Evan George, a shepherd from Rhiwe Farm in Llanddeusant and Elizabeth Colman who ran a dairy in Garnant. My grandmother Elizabeth George was their youngest daughter and it was her skill and good management that made the Tŷ mawr thrive. She was a true, intelligent farmer like her mother-in-law, Sali. This generation produced enlightened women who realised that education was the only hope towards a freedom from the harshness of much of their life. That is not to say that there weren't softnesses in their life.

The communities were warm and self-sufficient. We had relations in Gorslidarn Farm to the right (where Auntie Kate dressed like a man and tended the sheep up on the hills while her husband, Uncle Dafydd, looked after their daughters at home) and Llwyncelyn Farm to the left of Tŷ mawr. There was a local herbalist who took care of everyone and who would 'order' the harvesting of special leaves and roots. His skill as a healer was streets ahead of his talent as a soothsayer. *All* his predictions were wrong and the women shook their heads at such ungodly carryings-on while the credulous men could hardly wait for the next revelation. In time something was bound to come true, they said optimistically.

Farming skills were partly passed down and were partly the result of observation. There was a strong awareness that men were in partnership with nature. Even as a little girl I was aware that the margin between survival and catastrophic ruin was frighteningly small. Farmers seemed to harbour feelings of love and respect and fear and resentment in equal quantities towards the land, much as sailors must feel for the ocean, I thought. The softnesses and the grace of life were offset by harshness which still obtained when I was a child (for one thing, it isn't easy to farm land where there is not a single level field) but I gathered that this was nothing compared with the grimness of life a generation or two earlier. There was a strong sense of having lived through and survived not-to-be-forgotten hard times, which might very well return.

The background to life was poverty and insecurity; rural economy had gone through a long period of weakness with the price of dairy produce at rock bottom (three of my grandmother's brothers had left for America during one of the exceptionally bad periods). I came to see that nothing was forgotten. My parents were Liberals and when I heard them speak of the iniquitous Tory feudal system under which tenant farmers voting Liberal were evicted, I assumed that these awful events had probably occurred while I was in hospital having my appendix removed the previous year. It was some time before I realised that they were speaking with passion and resentment about something that had happened in 1859. My mother profoundly disapproved of anyone who did not respect the hard-won secret ballot.

The pace of life was determined by horse power and horses were a source of pride – not the crazed, failed racehorses favoured by my grandfather but the clever, enduring shire horses that pulled the plough and the small cobs who worked at harrowing and drilling. The horses would walk twenty miles in an eight-hour day and some man-and-horse teams were experts at the 'turns' where the chains could tangle in a second of inattention. There was no sense of rush. There was no point in rushing work. It took a week to plough and harrow a three-acre field and that was that.

There was, however, unspoken tension in the air at haymaking time. Six fine days were needed to cut, turn, rake and carry the hay home. Friends and neighbours in the village would stop work and arrive, unasked, to help once the hay was cut. The first sound in the morning was the chink-chink of knives being sharpened and the clop-clop as the big home-made rakes with their wooden teeth were knocked and tapped to check that they were in good repair. Women and children raked in the gleanings but I did next to nothing and contrived to ride to and fro on the 'gambo' (the hay-wain). Two men would pitchfork the hay up and a third would build up the load. I sat higher and higher until the load was completed, then rocked precariously back to the barn thinking this must be exactly like riding an elephant.

Rabbits, mice and voles ran for cover, buzzards hovered overhead. Meriel and my grandmother and mother brought out tea and food but there was very little talk. Even I appreciated it was desperately important to get the hay in before the capricious Welsh weather broke.

And meanwhile Meriel and my grandmother went on with the relentless business of milking. Meriel had married the glamorous John, and he, very advanced, had started making silage. I loathed the unbelievably horrible smell of the silo pit where the cut grass was packed and squeezed in with molasses added to it until the whole airless horrible mess fermented. The cows *adored* it, thrived and gave good, plentiful milk. The cows were all named and had distinctive characters, the natural leaders doing most of the herding on the way home from the fields. '*De – re, de – re, de – re*' (Come, come, come) was the human cry that encouraged them on their way, the dogs darted about on the periphery but it was the clever ones among the cows that nudged the convoy into the cow shed where each cow made for her own stall and filled the air with soft, fragrant, grassy belches.

Occasionally I would help in the dairy. The milk parlour was as up-to-the-minute as funds would allow but it was hard work straining and cooling the milk and everything had to be washed and washed and washed in cold water until one's hands and feet had no feeling even on the hottest day. And as for the butter churn . . . it seemed to take hours of churning before the slap-slap of milk turned into the clurp-clurp of butter almost ready. I didn't have what it took and I couldn't wait to get back to my books.

Before the Second World War, about six thousand women farmed alone in Wales and there must have been more by 1945. I daresay many of them shared my lack of enthusiasm for the work but, unlike me, they had to persevere.

Chapter Eight

Many of my recollections of childhood are probably not recollections at all but stories I was told about myself or which I heard told as I sat under a table or chair, half asleep in one of those small, clean, brightly-lit, over-heated village kitchens while my mother and three or four neighbours sat around the fire in the range knitting, sewing or crocheting and talking, talking, talking. 'I'm just going out for a little "*clec*",' my mother would say in Welsh as she put on her shapeless brown hat to go and visit a neighbour. I can't translate '*clec*'. What was it? More intense than mere chatting, not as high-flown as discussing, certainly not gossiping (although a great deal of gossip was exchanged, thinly disguised as cautionary tales: 'Let that be a lesson to us all, eh?').

Too young to be left at home alone, I used to have to accompany my mother and I dreaded those evenings, with the notable exception of the ones spent at my 'Auntie' Hilda's house after she took delivery of a washing machine! With a porthole in the door! The village divided itself into fours and sat, night after night, contentedly '*cleccan*', not in front of the fire but around the Bendix as the clothes whirled around inside. It was wonderfully entertaining. Normally, nothing so interesting took place and I would read my book, wishing we were at home, only occasionally moved to prick up my ears. I didn't bother trying to make sense of the conversation when the voices were lowered and long silences were punctured by gusty sighs (I had no interest in death and obstetrics). When the tone remained low but the pace returned to normal and they talked of 'her' and what 'she' had done, the chances were that I was the topic of conversation. The variety of illnesses I presented meant I was a problem that exerted considerable fascination, not least of all to me.

They all knew a great deal about each other (and in my privileged position as my father's daughter I knew that there was a great deal they *didn't* know about each other) and because a part of every day was spent exchanging information and discussing what had befallen people or conjecturing what might have happened, which was even more pleasurable, each person acquired a known history, a story that was added to at intervals, each addition modifying and enhancing the overall portrait. Highlights from people's stories were aired at regular intervals and, familiar though they were, I do not recall anyone being crass enough to interrupt the patterns of the story telling. Never did anyone say, 'Yes, yes, we know all that, get to the *point*'. The long process of telling shaped the point, when it eventually arrived.

When my mother talked of *her* childhood I always waited for the bit where she described how, not much older than I was now, maybe nine, and entrusted with cleaning the big fender, she split her finger in two, such was the zeal of her polishing, and as she fainted her father caught her and ran her down the mountainside to the herbalist who saved her finger, 'who knows how'.

When my father, as a young lad of fourteen, fainted in front of the big furnace in the Llanelly steelworks ('and he shouldn't have been there in the first place at that age. It's criminal'), his grandmother, who also worked there, came and dragged him out and revived him and took him home, forbidding his mother to send him back and *she* took his place in her clogs and long skirt, with a man's flat hat on her head. I would nod to myself at the chorus of 'Terrible times, they were'. This was always followed by a cheerful account of how he saved a life in the Llwchwr estuary 'and would you believe, they only found out by accident. Didn't tell a soul. Typical.'

Mrs Rogers, a youngish widow who kept house for her brothers who took care of her and her son, would describe how she knew her husband's time had come when he 'turned his face to the wall and wouldn't look back into the room'. This made me cry quietly, no matter how often I heard it. Turning one's face to the wall . . . it seemed the saddest thing imaginable.

The brilliance of people 'who came up from nothing' was a deep well, visited often. My favourite was the story of the young son of a neighbouring farm to Tŷ mawr on the Betws who, during my mother's youth, 'discovered and *proved* the existence of a star' ('pages and *pages* of workings out!'). As he passed through our farmyard at the start of his long, long journey to the Royal Society in London they concealed their dismay when they saw that he was wearing someone else's suit which his mother had altered for him and she'd made one leg shorter than the other. 'Imagine! One leg shorter than the other. To lecture! In London!' Another story told how Mrs Hopkins-the-Farm reached up for a loaf that was hanging in a basket and it fell on her head and the crumbs got into the cut and she was dead 'in a week!'. Dying 'in a week' was somehow worse than dying on the spot or after a decent illness.

There was very little in the way of gentry: one small family, the Lloyds, who made no impression on the surrounding villages and took no part in Welsh life. When the squire left his wife and daughter in the big house, never to return, it was un-Welsh enough and sufficiently typical of something alien to be worth a mention. My mother would fall silent. She knew and I knew that the Squire wrote to my father regularly, arranging to meet him in secret in the dingle. My father kept an eye on the estate and would tell him how things stood. He would write to my father telling him that he wanted to visit and my father would meet him and they would walk through the wood and then into the dingle and sit silently, looking at the house and stables in the distance.

After about an hour, the squire would get up and shake my father's hand and leave as silently as he'd arrived. And his beautiful daughter would ride her horse recklessly through our tiny gate, up the narrow steps round the lawn to the front door, dismount and fall into the house and I would be sent out to play and later told never to tell what I'd seen. I longed to grow up to be like her even if she was 'three sheets to the wind', whatever that meant. 'Her mouth was a red gash and she was a fearless horsewoman,' I described her to myself. Agony for my mother not to be able to share these stories. None of these things were ever to be revealed outside the house.

The mythology of the village reinforced its reality but as I grew older I could hardly relate to the 'child' of four and five and the stories they told of me seemed more remote and less meaningful than the stories they told of the childhood of my mother and her friends. Could I ever have been so small and stupid? Where I was concerned my mother was fairly loyal but although she would have given me the food from her plate (this, it seemed, was a standard requirement among good mothers) her allegiance at the first sign of conflict was with authority; the teachers, or nurses or doctors.

'Odd' was an adjective that recurred in describing me and, in all fairness, had to be allowed. I wasn't prepared to mend my ways but I could see that it *was* a bit odd to wear a hat indoors and out for over a year ('and the *same* one – oh, it looked terrible!') It was 'odd' to assemble all the dolls in the house (except Teddy), line them up on the stone slab outside where the washing was pounded on Mondays and then, having rehearsed and conducted them in the Allelujah Chorus from *The Messiah* for two whole weeks ('Oh we were fed up with Handel'), take them up the steps to the garden where my father was planting runner beans and bury the lot with three doleful hymns and a funeral oration. I didn't remember burying dolls but I had not long given up delivering long, emotional sermons, full of '*Hwyl*' from the high wall of the old pig sty and there hadn't been any dolls in the house for years so I supposed my mother was not exaggerating. In any case, I wasn't embarrassed; nothing I did would raise many eyebrows.

I half-remembered the Moonlight Sonata-on-the-Swansea-Bus story and that happened before I was five. Vivid in my mind was the longing I had to seem alone and independent and I always sat apart from my parents on public transport. One sunny afternoon on an excursion to Swansea I sat alone in the front seat of an almost empty bus and, as usual, began to sing – quietly at first. My repertoire of Welsh folk songs and Edwardian bass-baritone drawing room ballads was extensive but on this day I began humming the music my father had been practising on the piano for weeks and, getting into the swing of things, la-la-ed my way through the whole of the Moonlight Sonata. My mother said, 'People were laughing. It seemed to go on for ever and I had to let her go on. It would draw more attention to us if we had walked down the bus to stop her.'

When I finally came to an end a gentleman sitting alone rose and sat next to my parents and asked if I belonged to them. He handed my father his card saying that I had given him a most unusual experience and he hoped that they would provide me with the formal musical education I surely deserved and they could call on him for advice on the matter. My father's jaw dropped when he read the name Sir Walford Davies, Composer. 'Imagine,' said my mother. 'She's got no voice worth speaking of and her piano playing will never be more than fair. She's got a good memory, that's all. The talent for music has completely passed her by. All the same – Sir Walford Davies! Can you believe it?' I didn't mind that they thought little of my musical ability. What use was music to an actress, I thought when they told me the story.

My oddness was disconcerting but my piety, when it took hold a few years later, must have been even harder to bear. Everyone said a short grace before one meal a day, but now, in our house, grace spoken by me became longer and more detailed and had to be said before anything was eaten or drunk at any time. The minister, trying to down a quick cup of tea on his way through the parish, was startled to hear an admonishing cough and, looking over the cup, saw my up-raised finger and reproachful look before I bowed my head and offered lengthy thanks on his behalf. Useless for my mother to try to widen the concept of godliness to include good manners and tolerance. I was smugly impregnable on the moral high ground.

Searching around for my most precious possession to give away, I lighted on my new (my only) overcoat and took it along the road to a house where there were six children, always shabby. 'Are you sure this is all right?' asked the startled mother. I grandly assured her that it was *more* than all right and went home bathed in a golden glow of virtue. 'But the Bible says –' I began when my mother found out what I had done. 'That's it! Enough! Go down there and fetch it back!' 'Fetch it back? I can't do that.' 'Do you want a good shaking? Go!' It was agony. I went, I fetched it back, my humiliation great. 'Don't ask me what Jesus meant,' snapped my mother, hanging up the coat. 'He *didn't* mean that you could give away your coat, your HARRIS TWEED coat that I've been saving and saving for.' My mother was not one of those who kept their young in line with the – very often truthful – refrain, 'I've given you the food from my plate . . .' In fact she never even talked about money, so for her to mention saving money meant I'd done something seriously wrong in her eyes and I was silenced.

When I remembered to I did One Good Deed a Day and did Good by Stealth but I longed to advertise my holiness. Only once again did I try to apply the lessons of Sunday School to real life. Realising now that we were all fairly equally situated and that there weren't any Poor to give things to, nor did I have anything to give as a rule, I hit on the next best thing, which was to give to the Undeserving. They had no thought for the morrow and so on the eve of an examination week I gave my carefully compiled revision notes to a friend who hadn't done any preparation at all. If the incident of the coat had exasperated my mother it was as nothing to her reaction when she realised what I'd done with my schoolwork. 'I want those books back on your desk NOW!' 'But I've done most of my revision and Jesus says –' 'Stop, before I shake you!' 'Her need is greater than mine.' 'Right, that's it! Do you seriously think that Jesus Christ wants to see you working behind the counter of Woolworth's? Because that's what it'll come to if you're not in the top three in your class. GET THOSE BOOKS.'

Not longer after that I gave up wanting to be a nun, which involved practising mortifying the flesh by standing on the cold lino in front of an open window in my nightdress. (I knew my mother would kill me if she found out about that.) I became a Freethinker instead and gave my parents a whole new range of embarrassments.

By the time I was nine I was almost well after my long catalogue of illnesses and my years of running wild were coming to an end. I had a secure place in my world. By now every detail of my territory was familiar to me because I had covered it slowly on foot, in all weathers. I could see, with my eyes closed, the pale café-au-lait dust of the lane with living rock protruding in wonderful shapes, smooth and safe for the passage of horse-drawn carts, the hay-wain and the milk-float. The little trickle of water in the gully that quickly became a torrent when it rained was familiar and always astonishing. I knew where the birds nested year after year (never tell the boys, they took the eggs and 'blew' them). There was just one five-barred gate where lizards basked on hot days. I knew the best place for frogspawn and where to go for the one half-hour in the summer when you could see the sky full of flying ants. I collected the first mushrooms at five o'clock in the morning, I knew the secret damp patches where the biggest clumps of celandine grew and how to hop-skip across the treacherous boggy field, where it was safe to ford the stream, when to see baby spiders hatching out and tiny black toads flinging themselves out of the water. I could smell rain hours away but it never drove me indoors. There were areas of my life where I felt unsafe and times when I was wretchedly unhappy but my worst feeling could be transformed in an instant into radiant happiness by a change in the weather.

Everything was familiar and everything was marvellous. My feeling of security went hand in hand with a feeling of insignificance. The mountaintops were exhilarating and awe-inspiring with their great windy views of the valleys below and sometimes there was nothing to see but the big sky and more mountains beyond. Not a house in sight, no roads, no trees, and a huge silence. More than once that silence had driven me, frightened, running down the mountainside, filled with relief to see the first disused cart track or broken, dry stone wall; signs of human life. I knew exactly what Wordsworth meant when he wrote of 'low breathings' coming after him.

However dimly perceived, it was all these things that I fought for as a little girl of five when I flatly refused to stay at the primary school in which I had been placed; the nearest one to my home in Alltwen. It was a tall, ugly building, positioned under a frightening rock face in the little town of Pontardawe which looked to me like a vision of hell, with its steelworks and polluted river and evil-smelling smoke and trees black with greasy dust. Not a natural rebel, I don't know where at that age I found the strength to overcome the strict well-meaning, implacable adults who were ranged against me but after what seemed like an eternity of silent, dry-eyed misery when I stood day after day with my face pressed against the playground railings, neither speaking nor eating, nor moving, *willing* something or someone to save me, I was allowed, one morning, to go home and to make the long walk in the other direction, deeper into the countryside, to a beautiful little white, one-storey school, set in fields on the edge of the village of Rhos. I hadn't known of its existence but I wasn't surprised when we came to it. I recognised it as the place where I wanted to be.

As things turned out, my illnesses began almost at once and I didn't very often attend school, but when I did I loved it. Because I was left undisturbed for years during my illnesses, when the time came for primary schooling to end it wasn't at all clear how much I knew. It was assumed that my knowledge of arithmetic must be patchy but who knew what all that reading had done for me? My parents had decided on a policy of non-interference where my reading was concerned. They had never suggested that anything might be too difficult or unsuitable. Consequently I read Shakespeare and Enid Blyton and Louisa M. Alcott and the *Dandy* and the *Beano* alongside Zane Grey and Mrs Humphrey Ward and old *Magnets* and Dickens and A. A. Milne and Trollope and *Sunny Stories* and the *News Chronicle*. My mother's nerve did fail a few times. She absolutely forbade me to read *Forever Amber* (so I read it in secret) and there were bits of *Anthony and Cleopatra* that she wished she hadn't let me read. I wondered why she'd forgotten what a racy read the Old Testament was. The only publication against which my face was set was Arthur Mee's *Children's Newspaper*, which my parents had delivered for me and which I rightly suspected to be Good for me.

I was over-sensitive in some regards and given to storms of grief over sad-endings – fictional – or the death of pets – only too real and frequent – but (rightly, as it turned out) my parents thought I had a steely streak and was not given to undue 'nerves', so it was decided that, at the age of nine, I should be allowed to have an early 'go' at the Scholarship examination which determined one's future at the age of ten and eleven. This was just for practice, they said, and at least it would reveal what I needed to be taught. If there was pressure, I was blithely unaware of it and had a delightful day out, back at school.

I read the Arithmetic paper with mild interest; baths of water emptying faster than they could be filled, trains travelling at X miles per hour, arriving after trains travelling at Y miles per hour, men working all day, failing to accomplish what three men working half a day could – or was it the other way round? These riddles contained very little to interest me so I spent my time with my chin in my hand watching the clouds in the sky outside. This was not considered to be a good sign but there was always the English paper. Horror of horrors, halfway through the allotted time I laid down my pen and, chin in hand, resumed my study of the sky.

My teacher reported back to my mother that things didn't look too good. No one wanted to worry me so they left me alone except to ask, casually, how it went. 'Oh, fine, fine.' 'Arithmetic all right?' I laughed, shaking my head and tried to remember some of the sillier questions about taps and trains. 'How about the English?' 'Oh, easy-peasy.'

My mother hid her disappointment and resolved to start coaching me as soon as summer ended. She was bewildered and unbelieving when my name was posted alongside the older children who had made it over the all-important hurdle. Confusion deepened when someone called round to explain that, alone among the pupils of South Wales, I had been given nought in the Arithmetic paper but that for the first time in the history of the examination they had been moved to award me 100 per cent for my English paper.

'What did you do?' my mother asked. I tried to remember. 'Well, Grammar – easy.' 'What about the Composition?' 'Oh yes, Shakespeare.' 'What do you mean, ' "Shakespeare"?' '*The Merchant of Venice*.' 'What about *The Merchant of Venice*?' 'Usury.' 'Usury?' 'Yes. Can I go out now?' My mother nodded slowly. The postmortem on the hopeless Arithmetic paper was postponed.

I took a great deal more interest in the Scholarship when I realised there was a Uniform involved and Houses and Hockey and a Debating Society just like the schools in my mother's Angela Brazil books. I began to shape up for a new life.

Chapter Nine

T he new life, when it came, was wonderful and frightening and a bit beyond me. I was still only nine and a year or so younger than the other new pupils but in my naiveté I was five years behind them. But that uniform! My mother had sent for samples of tussore silk from somewhere called Devon. Blouse lengths were ordered, and navy gabardine from Swansea. Auntie Syrviah, the Tŷ mawr dressmaker, was alerted and I went back to G.C.G. time and again to fit my tunic with its deep box pleats and 'secret' pocket for a handkerchief and a fountain pen pocket and hems and turnings so generous that the same tunic lasted the whole of my seven years at Pontardawe Grammar School. However many times it was let out it always had to be the regulation two inches above the knee (hated by the big girls who wanted long skirts like their mothers). The dressmaker also made my pale green, Greek-style P.T. clothes and my silk blouses with deep cuffs and big collars with rows and rows of stitching (not strictly allowed but very smart).

My blazer had to be bought; cheap, navy-blue 'utility' material, made magnificent by the badge. I breathed over my mother as she sewed it on to the breast pocket, willing her (no seamstress) to get it straight. The motto read, '*Bid Ben Bid Bont*' – 'Who would be a leader let him be a bridge for others'. Would I ever be able to live up to this? Yes! I thought. I want to be *good*. I want to be the sort of person worthy of this magnificence. There was a blue and maroon tie and even more than the tie I loved the satchel and my pencil box and rubber and fountain pen and mysterious geometry set and my big ruler, but I *hated* my navy raincoat.

My mother's determination to make everything last had run riot in the rainwear department. The coat was *huge* and came down to my ankles with a turned-up hem a foot deep. It submerged the glory of the blazer and tunic and I looked as though I was wearing someone else's coat. My navy hat had also suffered under my mother's prudent hand and sported a wide, childish elastic band stretched under my chin. I wanted to cry when I looked at myself, fully dressed. The Mallory Towers/Angela Brazil look, racy, confident, needing only a hockey stick under the arm to complete the picture, was gone and I looked puny and worried – a pinched, white face half-hidden by the hat above and huge collar below and then a mass of navy blue bulking down to my socks and small, protruding lace-ups. The disappointment was crushing and I silently raged against my mother who stood back admiring her handiwork. When he was brought in to inspect me my father nodded his approval which was no consolation to me. Daddy would always think I looked perfect.

Every day when I started out for school, as soon as I was out of my mother's sight, off came the hated coat and I slung it over my shoulder, shivering in the cold and getting wet in the rain but feeling ever so smart. The walk to school was exciting, away from the beauty of Alltwen, from Llygad yr haul – the eye of the sun – round Bwlch y Gwynt – the windy gap – where the wind *did* always blow, down to Pontardawe, across the little town with its grimy buildings, then up another hill to the beautiful, big white school which rose in terraces towards the fields and trees above.

It was a place of enchantment to me. I loved the confusion, the complications; you may walk here, seniors only on the bridge, prefects only beyond this point, no talking to the boys, walk in twos here, single-file only here. I was in a perpetual state of pleasurable excitement. I loved the life but I couldn't live it. The playing fields, the cloakroom, the changing rooms, the miles of road leading from school to my home were littered with my books, pens, gym shoes, text books, hockey stick, gym tunic, all picked up and returned to my mother who didn't know what to do with me. I *was* very young. It would have taken a lady's maid to get me through the day and there were worried conferences about my chaotic behaviour.

Blissfully unaware of this, I became more and more enthusiastic about every aspect of school life. There were 'traditions', some of which were being invented as we went along and I embraced each one avidly and formed passionate attachments to the staff and the big girls and I adored my form mistress, Miss Inkin, who also taught Greek history and was in charge of physical training and games and reigned over the Gymnasium which was the strangest, most wonderful building I had ever seen. I would have done anything to please Miss Inkin and I quickly became a good, fearless gymnast (this was my one area of competence) and it was this devotion that brought about my last childhood brush with death and at the same time gave me a breathing space to catch up with myself.

I had read enough boarding-school story books to know that 'decent types', 'bricks', 'good sorts' didn't 'cry off' games and gym when they didn't feel well. They kept a stiff (English) upper lip and soldiered on. So when, during one of our beautifully organised, almost balletic gymnastic lessons, quietly shinning up ropes, threading through square ladders, vaulting over the horse and the buck, balancing on the high bars and making perfect 'landings', I began to feel slightly, then extremely ill, it did not occur to me to ask if I could be excused. By the end of the double period that finished the day I could hardly move for pain. I must have showered and dressed and set off for home carrying my satchel with its six text books and six exercise books and I must have got myself across Pontardawe, but I don't remember. Nor do I remember beginning the long steep climb to Alltwen. I *do* remember climbing slowly and more slowly towards Bwlch y Gwynt and thinking, 'I'll just lie down here for a while'.

And it was there, lying on the pavement, that the baker found me and took me home in his van, laid out among the crumbs. I was dimly aware of the ambulance and 'apperitonitis and pendicitis' or was it 'peritonitis and appendicitis' and nothing more until I woke up in Swansea Hospital with a huge plaster on my stomach, feeling not bad at all. Hospitals – even this big one – no longer held any terrors for me and, wonder of wonders! I wasn't homesick. This time I *understood* about temperatures and bedpans and screens and the importance of keeping the bed tidy and the supreme importance of seeming to stand to attention while lying down, cheerful and silent as Matron passed by. She was much grander than the Consultants to whom she displayed a wonderful condescension even as she deferred to them. She never smiled and I watched her with keen admiration as she progressed regally around the ward holding her huge, starched headdress high. It was grand not to be confused and afraid. I spared a pitying half contemptuous thought for my six-year-old self in the fever hospital and settled down to enjoy myself.

They kept me there for quite a long time and then, instead of sending me home, despatched me to a convalescent home in Cwmdonkin Park, where a little speck of coal dust drifted through the window and, landing on a stitch, gave me a blue mark, like a miner's scar on my stomach. I wasn't allowed home for weeks. Maybe I'd been more ill than I had thought. I read voraciously, as usual, but now I found myself sleeping with a similar hunger. I could feel something happening to me as I lay there. I was growing, although it was impossible to tell for sure because I wasn't allowed to get out of bed. And I was becoming stronger by the day. Each morning when I woke I lay still, assessing the new, different me. And it wasn't just that my body was changing; I was pretty sure that henceforward I would have an extra skin, be less prone to melancholia, find that I was more *able* for the world. I watched myself lying there, gathering strength, looking forward to something wonderful.

Sali 'Wernwgan', mother of my grandfather Daniel, holding the Bible she used for teaching.

Elizabeth George, my great grandmother, who built 'Tŷ Mawr' farm, where my grandmother, mother and myself were born.

A great aunt with Bible in Gwaun-Cae-Gurwen.

My great aunt Rosina Davies, evangelist, in old age.

Building the small hay rick at Tŷ Mawr. Daniel, my grandfather, holding the horse's bridle; his son Davy and my mother standing in the hay-wain; my grandmother, in a hat, carrying Meriel.

My grandmother Elizabeth and me at Tŷ Mawr farm; Gwaun-Cae-Gurwen and Black Mountain are in the background.

Llwynhendy 'Glee Club'. My father (singing tenor), second from right; his brother Ronald (baritone) third from left; Harding Jenkins (bass baritone) extreme left.

Staff of Glanamman Primary School. My mother, Sally Thomas, front row, third from left.

Opposite page

Above: My parents, David Phillips and Sally Tymawr.

Below left: David, my mother's brother, at Aberystwyth University.

Below right: Meriel, my mother's younger sister.

Right: John Lewis, Meriel's husband and my favourite uncle.

Below: Meriel and John's children; *left to right* Gethin, Elizabeth, Gwyn and Hugh.

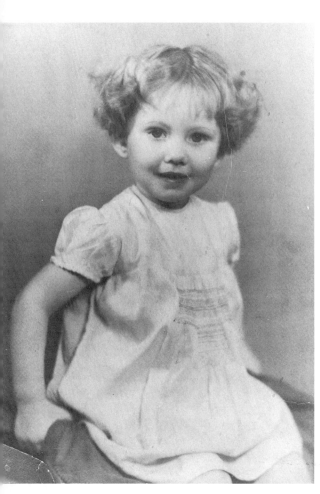

Above: My first performance in chapel, wearing Welsh costume, aged four.

Left: Hair crimped for my first portrait, aged three.

Below: Rhos Primary School. I am the one wearing a cardigan like a fur stole.

URDD (Welsh Youth Movement) Action-Song Troupe performing 'Hay Making'. I am third from right.

Below left: My best friend, Mair Rees (*left*), and me, aged eleven, playing two old men – a performance that won first prize at the National Eisteddfod and began my broadcasting career.

Below right: With Miss Inkin (*left*), my form mistress as a junior and my PT mistress throughout, and my mother (*centre*), 1947.

Above: A performance of *Tobias and the Angel* at Pontardawe Grammar School. I am on the right playing the angel.

Left: An early contract (fee in guineas), Ailwên mispelled, and before Jane reverted to Siân.

Below: Alltwen Chapel Dramatics (*The Light of the World*). My mother, the Director, is sixth from left on the back row; I am fourth from left on the front row.

READING (Live or Recorded)

THE BRITISH BROADCASTING CORPORATION
Head Office : BROADCASTING HOUSE, LONDON. W.1.
Broadcasting House, 38-40 Park Place, Cardiff
TELEPHONE AND TELEGRAMS : CARDIFF 3307

Our Reference : IK/03/CHO.

24th December, ... 194...

DEAR Madam,

We invite you to deliver a .... Reading .... as detailed below for broadcasting or for recording for subsequent broadcast reproduction, upon the conditions printed overleaf. If you accept, kindly sign and return the attached confirmation sheet, or reply otherwise, as soon as possible. (See condition 1 overleaf.)

Title .... Addunedau Ffl.
Date of Recording .... 22nd December, 1948.
Time of Recording .... 10.0 – 12.30 p.m.
Place .... Cardiff.
Date of First Broadcast .... 25th December, 1948.
Time of First Broadcast .... 5.30 – 5.55 p.m.
Transmission .... W.H.S.
Fee .... 10s. 6d. (Ten shillings & sixpence) + Rail Fare (Please Notify).

Letters addressed to speakers c/o the BBC will be forwarded, but for statistical purposes the letters may be opened before being forwarded unless we are notified of any objection. Letters marked "Personal" are forwarded unopened.

Miss Jane Eilwen Phillips,

Yours faithfully,
THE BRITISH BROADCASTING CORPORATION,

Welsh Programme Executive.

I didn't burst out of my chrysalis like a butterfly and the outside world had to wait for what seemed like a long time before I rejoined it, but when I took my first, wobbly steps I realised that I'd guessed right; I was becoming tall, in fact I was altogether bigger and I was bubbling with suppressed energy. Once home and 'downstairs' I organised and re-organised my desk, my father's desk. I catalogued all the books and, looking through the school work I'd done before I became ill, I realised that my head was now clear of muddle. The days of being swept along like a twig in a stream were over. I longed to return to school and still I was held in the doldrums of convalescence. Then, practising with my hockey stick on the sloping field behind the garden I ran into a rabbit hole and broke my ankle.

I could scarcely credit my bad luck and my mother was furious ('No one's going to test you in hockey, you know.'). At least I could lie on the couch downstairs, reading and looking out at March Hywel mountain. One day, I realised that I was seeing that precious landscape with different eyes. It had lost something for me. I couldn't explain it even to myself, but I knew that I had lost the key to some kind of magic that had been mine for ten years. It made me sad, but not very sad, to realise that I was ready to move on. And I was going to be able to leave this place I loved when I needed to go away to become an actress. Not once since I was six had I wavered in my determination to go into the theatre but I had wondered how I could live without the loveliness I was accustomed to. The relief at the realisation that I was going to be able to do so far outweighed my sense of loss and I lay on my couch reading and waiting and learning patience.

Chapter Ten

When I was a girl in the Forties, during and after the war, life was still chapel-driven. It was becoming fashionable in 'advanced' circles to sneer at non-conformism, with the inevitable hypocrisies that attended it. The University of Wales, 'our' university as it was thought of proudly even by people who would never see it, was described by George Bernard Shaw of all people as a 'non-conformist hole in Wales', but without religion it is quite conceivable that by the time I was a child Wales would have become a cultural annexe of England. In the second half of the nineteenth century the 1870 Education Act decreed that Wales should be anglicised. Westminster observed, 'The Welsh language is a vast drawback to Wales and a manifold barrier to the moral progress and commercial prosperity of the people.' Where I grew up people were still smarting over this insult. My mother, when she was little and was caught talking Welsh at school, had to stand out in the yard as a punishment with a board saying 'Welsh Not' hung around her neck.

It was chapel that kept the language alive and it remained the language of home, of literature and of entertainment. Hundreds of chapels were built in the nineteenth century; even when I was little there were three Sunday services and several meetings during the week. The chapel choir rehearsed all winter. Meriel remembers giving five spring performances of *The Creation* and *The Messiah* and I remember my father's never-ending rehearsals of *Judas Maccabeus*. All children learned bible verses and, like it or not, built up a good working acquaintance with the Old and New Testaments. When I made up and delivered my own sermons from the high wall behind the apple tree, even at the age of eight or nine, I was well able to keep going for a generous half hour, thundering against sin and lawlessness with threats of hell and damnation, making deadly eye contact guaranteed to chill the unfortunate singled out gooseberry bushes, before exhorting the entire congregation of runner beans, broad beans, peas, potatoes, lettuces, radishes, fruit bushes and solitary apple tree to rise up, joined in the glory of redemption. My mother and Meriel once or twice paused near the pulpit and nodded sagely. 'Well – Rosina,' they said. Grown-ups were given to gnomic utterances usually not worth pursuing, so it was some time before I bothered to ask my mother why 'Well, Rosina'? 'She would be your great-aunt and she was a bit – oh, I don't know, ask your Uncle Davy.' 'She was a bit what?' I asked him on my next visit to his house in the meadow below Tŷ mawr.

'Oh *jiw, jiw*,' he replied. 'She was a bit of a case, really. Anyway, you met her when you were – let's see, you'd have been five when she came to stay in Tŷ mawr when she last preached here in Carmel. You stared at her all afternoon.' 'Preached?' 'Oh yes, she was a *famous* evangelist. You'd have to turn up very early to get a seat when she was preaching and in fine weather they'd open all the windows and people would fill the graveyard, standing to listen to her. Sang too. People loved it. But we never knew where to look we were so embarrassed. Horrible voice like a hooter and it was *peculiar* to see a woman in the pulpit, say what you like. There's a book about her in the front room. And there's all that business about our land too.' 'What business?' I asked, scenting drama. 'I can't go into it and you'd better leave it alone too. She was – I don't know – very *extreme*.'

Davy was a busy councillor as well as an overworked

headmaster and I'd used up the time he could spare me in a day that began at 5.30 a.m. and rarely finished before midnight. I took myself off to look for the book about Rosina and stayed overnight in the spare room, reading about my unlikely ancestor who brought the first whiff of exoticism into my known background of strong, down-to-earth, deadly earnest realists. An exotic evangelist? That's what it seemed like and as I read the rather pedestrian book, little more than a detailed chronicle of her extraordinary day-to-day engagements, a picture emerged of a woman half in love with her own glamour and half determined to suppress it. When she was staying at a house in Lleyn, someone wrote of her, 'as she entered I thought Ellen Terry had walked into the room'. In one of her photographs the pose was similar to that of the actress on one of her postcards so Rosina ordered that all of hers should be destroyed. She was twenty at that time and leaving Wales to preach in London where she stayed at the Grange in Highbury with one of her many patrons, Mrs Jones (of Jones Brothers department store in the Holloway Road).

At Mrs Jones's house she sang, accompanying herself on the piano and wasn't averse to recording that a professor from the Royal Academy enthused over her 'contralto with pathos' and a retired diva hearing her said, 'The Lord Jesus Christ will lose her; Opera will snatch her up at once, the world will want her.' 'You will make a fortune as a tragedienne,' declared another after she had preached one of her hour and a half sermons ('sixty-four converts' she recorded). 'Oh no, that will never be,' she replied. 'There is nothing tragic in my nature and I know nothing of the stage. I have been saved from the love of earthly things. He gave me a voice to sing the Gospel . . . I am only a girl, the love song of the cross wins their hearts.'

Well. 'Did she really have a terrible voice?' I asked Davy. 'Oh Jiw, don't talk. It was awful. But she could hypnotise people – not the family, of course – but people really thought she was Madam Patti. She could preach though, fair do's.'

I returned to my reading. These women! As soon as I

thought my days were full and well accounted for, all my aims
and duties and ambitions neatly lined up and dealt with, I
would come across another extraordinary woman whose
energy and application made my efforts look feeble. Rosina,
I read with a mixture of admiration and dismay, had begun
preaching for the Salvation Army at the age of ten and against
her parents' wishes began to tour as 'The little Welsh Girl'
evangelist and singer. When I read that she left home saying. 'I
must be about my Father's business' I wondered whether I
would have liked her – evidently she wasn't bothered by self-
doubt. Still, when she was seventeen she sang and preached
every day for ten months. She read the Bible and she read
Shakespeare, then 'I communed with God and went straight
into the pulpit and the Lord filled my mouth'.

I wasn't interested in her godliness, it was her workload
that fascinated me. The endless travelling. She loved America
– preached to the Welsh surrounded by Indians in Mankato
on the Prairies, on to Minneapolis, Cambria (Wisconsin),
Columbus, Milwaukee, Racine, Chicago, then California
and Los Angeles which she thought 'quaint and delightful'.
She must have added to the quaintness when she gave a
concert, singing in Welsh costume before going to watch a
film being made. In Los Angeles she suffered one of her bouts
of total exhaustion and even, in true West Wales fashion,
'turned her face to the wall'. This meant that she lingered in
California and, having made the acquaintance of a Dr
Hubble, became a mature student at Los Angeles University.
'God bless the land of the free,' she wrote in Beverly Hills,
before tearing herself away to Coal Creek and Salt Lake City
where she preached to 25,000 people, then on to Denver,
Colorado. My eyes travelled down the list of 'engagements'.
I didn't know where these places were – Williamsburg,
Minneapolis, Gomer (Ohio, a North Welsh settlement),
Lima, Cincinatti, Toronto, Palmyra, Pittsburg, Ebensburgh,
West Bangor, Utica, New York – of course. She was 'well
guarded by the Ninety-First psalm'. And I was intrigued to
read that she preached to all denominations and refused a

salary. Money just came. 'A miracle,' she explained.

'Oh, she made *plenty* of money,' said Uncle Davy. 'Enough to try and re-claim our land – the huge Garreg Amman estate. She took the case right up to the House of Lords and then even she had to give up.' Land. Wrongfully appropriated estates. It was all like something in a book. It *was* something in a book. There was no getting round it, I was jealous. How could I possibly have a career like Rosina's when I had to go to school? I worked it out that Rosina was living by Faith, travelling and working non-stop, saving souls by the dozen every night and accompanying herself on the organ when she was thirteen, and that would have been in the late 1870s when it must have been a *lot* harder for a girl to strike out in the world. I could picture my mother's face if I left the house to go on the stage saying 'I must be about . . .' Well, no, I couldn't say anything like that because going on the stage wasn't anything like saving souls. All the same, the singing and preaching didn't seem very different from acting.

I went home on the bus from Uncle Davy's to Cwmllynfell feeling more than usually restless. I thought I remembered the tall woman in black with jet jewellery and a precious Gladstone bag, precious because her writing was in it and it had to be put in the parlour. I *thought* I remembered her in the pulpit in Carmel but I couldn't be too sure about that.

I was so busy thinking about Rosina and admiring my blurred reflection in the bus window that only gradually did I become aware that the man sitting next to me was fingering my leg just below the knee. We were in the third row, for heaven's sake. The conductor was standing a few feet away, facing us with his back to the driver. I couldn't think what to do. The man, whom I couldn't bring myself to look at, was fumbling away in a completely hopeless sort of way. I couldn't make a fuss and the fingering went on, so I sat very still for ten minutes until the bus drew into my village. I shot out of the bus, not a bit nervous once I was on the road. Even if he got out I was sure I could out-run him. He didn't get out so I stood and took a quick look at him sitting now in my window seat. Nobody I knew. An ordinary, small, middle-aged man. Shabby. It hadn't been very nice and I felt I should have reacted differently. Maybe pinched his hand. Or given him a Look. Well, I'd been too embarrassed for both of us to do anything.

I thought it best not to tell my mother and father and I took myself off to bed, washing extra thoroughly, brushing my hair a hundred times and scrupulously crabbing my way up and down my bedroom, doing the exercises Miss Inkin had recommended to strengthen the arches of my feet. Finished, I looked around. My bedroom looked lovely in the diffused light I'd arranged by draping the old runner from the piano top over my bedside lamp. Everything was in perfect order and I knew that the contents of each drawer and cupboard were in immaculate order. My books were arranged by subject and size. I got into bed, sinking into the feather mattress. What could I *do* to speed up the beginning of my REAL life in the Theatre? How would Rosina have dealt with my mother and the staff of Pontardawe Grammar School?

Chapter Eleven

It seemed to me unlikely that school days really would be my happiest days. It stood to reason that grown-up, vividly imagined, grown-up life was bound to be more fascinating, more thrilling. Meanwhile school was just fine; so fine that I scarcely bothered looking beyond the present. So, at ten, I said a cheerful goodbye to the only school I 'knew', the one in my imagining, with its tuck boxes and 'dorms' and '*caves*' and midnight feasts where I was a freckle-nosed, curly haired captain of games in the books of my mother's school days; a 'good egg' and just about the pluckiest girl at Status-quo Towers. Why did all that upper class bric-à-brac utterly beguile so many girls raised just this side of republicanism, exhorted to know their place and bend the knee to no man at one and the same moment? (I don't think boys were visited by a similar malaise.) Suddenly and overwhelmingly, reality in the shape of Pontardawe Grammar School loomed again, larger than fiction, fresher, brighter, absorbing and totally demanding.

My false start was over and done with and I was now back with pupils of my own age, though still the youngest in the class, a position I rather enjoyed. 'Now listen,' said my mother for the umpteenth time, 'this is your big chance. You've got to give it everything you've got. You've got to give MORE than you've got.' Well of course I had to. Without that last rider it wouldn't have been a true Sally Tŷ mawr-ism.

For once, she needn't have worried – I felt as if I'd been given the run of a huge adventure playground cum sweet-shop and I was going to explore and devour every bit of it. I wanted it all. It seemed that every small, bright kitchen rang with the same words: 'Education is your Passport, don't forget, and it's the only thing they can't take away from you.' We compared notes ruefully but with the minimum of disloyal complaint. We knew it was the truth. Surprisingly, it did nothing to dampen our spirits; the grim facts of life were acknowledged, understood and forgotten in the enjoyment of the newness of everything; new languages that we'd be speaking in no time, English emerging from between the covers of books and brown, fretwork-fronted radios as the language of new manners, new feelings even. Welsh assumed a new stature, something rather grander than my everyday, Swansea-Valley Welsh, the language of play; it was the language of poetry like Shakespeare's. I longed to take my hair out of plaits and speak French NOW. There was even a *dead* language. That was surely worth a full-page visa in the Passport to Life.

Pontardawe – the bridge on the river Tawe, 'Ponty' out of earshot of the staff – was a small school, though it seemed enormous to me. We were about three hundred and fifty pupils; equal numbers of boys and girls, looked after, chivvied, spied on, bullied, manipulated and cherished by a staff of twenty who did the work of forty. Schools were talked of in military terms; some were perceived as being better than others, super-charged launching pads of human missiles, and in a way this lessened some of the usual pressures of school life. Very occasionally there would be the whispered taunt of 'Swot!' if someone did spectacularly well at something but it was a half-hearted, feeble jibe. Brains were admired. Coming top was desirable. Our pin-ups were the barristers and scholars 'who'd come up from NOTHING, mind'. I don't think that the girls felt they were under pressure to prove themselves; it was assumed that we were equal with the boys and it was rather fun to put in a bit of extra effort and get ahead of them. The staff and Mr Rees, the headmaster, introduced a new element to add to the Passport concept of getting on in life; education, they conveyed to us, wasn't *for* anything, it was there, intrinsically good and ours for the taking. A posh job would be desirable but that wasn't the point. At home, this was thought about for a moment, then heartily embraced. Ethically sound personal advancement – what could more thoroughly fire up the Welsh parental heart?

The staff worked long hours for us. Every night, after school, they stayed on to supervise society meetings or take choir practice or dancing classes. I joined everything I could and found out in Mr Lines's art club that I could draw and then, because I desperately wanted to please Miss Agnes Thomas-Biology-Botany (who ran the Welsh Youth Movement at school and taught us traditional dancing and 'action songs', which were all the rage) I applied myself to botanical drawing and, showing promise, delivered myself, not for the last time, into my mother's hands. She embraced any enthusiasm I displayed that gave her the chance to divert my attention away from the theatre and all that 'nonsens'. Now, she supplied me with beautiful cartridge paper and Indian ink and mapping pens and I drew sections of all the vegetation I could lay my hands on, doing rather well it was thought, until I found myself making the long journey to Cardiff for a meeting with Dr Iorwerth Peate at the National Museum. Here my drawings were looked at and I felt a complete fraud to be treated with such encouragement and kindness and told to bring in more work if I was still serious about it in a few years' time. As for my mother, I felt sorry for her as she gradually realised that yet another of her stratagems was a failure.

It was an awkward situation for me. Provided that I did very well at school, I could go on performing. I actually enjoyed doing well at school and found no difficulty in combining the hours of homework each night with the long walks from Alltwen to Pontardawe and my involvement with the house choir, the gymnastic display group, the debating society, the Welsh society, the dramatic society, the French

97

society, the Youth Movement dance troupe. I had boundless energy and felt like a round peg in a round hole. Apart from my terror of arithmetic which become so acute that mathematics days were preceded by secret bouts of crying in bed, there was nothing but contentment in my life for the time being. I could however see that my problems would multiply. Then something happened that took me a significant step nearer what I wanted

My mother spent long hours practising for the Eisteddfodau – literally 'Sitting places' – where people gathered each week in different villages and towns to sing, compose music, write poetry and recite and to listen to long, detailed adjudications. They took place on Saturdays in chapels. The 'champion' Saturday reciters were as famous as the preachers who occupied the same spotlight in the pulpit on Sunday. The fashionable reciting style of the day was declamatory and dramatic, owing much to the fervent oratory and '*hwyl*' of the pulpit. My mother adopted a different approach for me; simpler, more colloquial. I was much too young to be competing at this level and she deployed the only weapons at her disposal: surprise and stillness and quiet. Initial reactions varied from amused tolerance to hostility but in a remarkably short space of time I began to be successful and in demand for concert work and it was because of my mother's strategy that at the age of eleven I became a broadcaster Greatly daring (and adding a year to our ages) she entered Mair Rees, my best friend, and myself in the big, annual National Eisteddfod in the category 'Dramatic Recitation for two, 12–16 years'. (This was after the closure of the Oil-Shed Theatre.) The 'National' was a very different proposition from the weekly Saturday Eisteddfodau I was used to. It attracted audiences of more than 15,000 people a day and lasted for an entire week. Unique in the whole of Europe as an Arts Festival, they said. I was impressed.

The set piece was difficult and unsuitable: a 'conversation' in the strict metre between a disconsolate man and his more cheerful self. The task she set herself was formidable. Not only did she teach us the meaning of words unused for hundreds of years, she made sure we faultlessly observed the internal and external rhyme schemes and the intricate vowel and consonant patterns (the rules for the twenty-four-beat metre used in Cynghanedd verse were laid down in 1450) and, having achieved that, she said, 'Now, I want it to sound like Mr Jones next door and Mr Morgan down the road having a bit of a chat.'

We practised all though the spring and on a summer morning made the long journey to Llandybie, then walked from the station looking for the hall where the eliminating contest was to be held. That found, we settled down to wait and Mammy found a place for us to have a nice damp tomato sandwich from the pile she made early that morning. We had a last practice in a field before going into the hall. I began to realise that this was a new experience for all three of us: these people were in deadly earnest, a lot of them knew each other, they were all older than we were and the hall was packed. No one gave us a second glance. An hour went by and we listened to the same piece over and over again. It sounded 'dramatic', all right. Loud too. My mother looked thoughtful and said nothing.

At last it was our turn. My mother's only nod in the direction of 'dramatic' had been to 'stage' the recitation. I was to ask for a table and a chair. 'Ask politely and wait without fidgeting until you get them. Look pleasant. Don't look worried.' When the furniture was brought Mair (the disheartened man) sat slumped in the chair (this was easy as she was by now very nervous) and I perched on the table looking perky as the more cheerful self (this was also easy, I was now very, very excited).

It was over quickly and I knew we'd remembered everything but my mother said nothing. Mair said she felt sick and my mother said it was her imagination. Then we walked round the town until we found the place where the results would be posted. When the man came with the paper that bore the names of the four finalists my mother walked up to the board quite slowly, then turned to us and nodded without smiling. We're through!

It was now the afternoon and time for more tomato sandwiches and a drink from the thermos flask. We had to find a lavatory and a tap so that we could be cleaned up. Then we walked towards the roar of the thousands of people on the Eisteddfod field where we could just make out the top of the huge marquee with the amplifiers relaying the contests and the adjudications to the people outside and red dragons flying everywhere. Mair said she really was going to be sick and she wasn't going to go on. I was so horrified that I had no words of sympathy for her. I could tell that my mother was furious and I prayed that she would find a way of getting Mair on stage. I walked away from them and thought about the piece. Our names were called and I looked round. My mother was smiling. Mair looked terrible but she was on her feet and heading in the right direction, up the steps and on to the enormous stage. There was a smell of damp, trodden-down grass and wood shavings and the murmur of more people than I had ever seen. 'Ask politely for a table and chair. Don't look worried,' and a new note, 'Wait, wait, *wait* until they are all quiet.'

The performance seemed to last longer this time and these people understood old Welsh because they laughed at the jokes that had until now felt embarrassing and less and less funny as the weeks of rehearsal went by. We were a riot! And we won! Hands down! My mother said, 'Well, there you are, you see.' Mair said she still felt sick. We were photographed by the press and went to the BBC mobile studio to repeat our triumph. We fell asleep on the train and then on the bus and I don't remember walking the last steep mile home to Alltwen.

None of this was meant to lead to show business; my mother still maintained that it was 'educational', 'to improve the memory'. 'And don't go thinking you're anything special just because you've got your picture in the paper,' she said, but I knew shortly after, when I started to work for the BBC on a regular basis, that I had made a significant step forward on my chosen path. Fortunately for me the BBC was, to my mother, as respectable as chapel.

I was now extra careful to do well at school. The better I did at school the stronger was my mother's determination that I should go to the university and take up a solid profession. My resolution to be an actress kept pace with my mother's determination but I had learned not to argue.

Then there was another obstacle to overcome. There must have been discussions about my future that included the possibility of my becoming an actress. After all, I was by now being written about in the press and offered more work than I could deal with, and I began to hear a new objection. 'She's got talent but she doesn't have the *steel*.' 'She's too sensitive.' 'She'll never be able to take the *knocks*.' 'She's the wrong *type*, altogether.' It was bad enough that they talked about me as though I wasn't there; how *dare* they presume to know what I was able for? And what did *they* know about the theatre? Or me? I was *sure* I knew what it would be like. And I was *sure* I could do it.

When I was younger, maybe eight or nine, after hearing my mother unsubtly holding forth about the rigours of the acting profession I myself had wondered about my ability to survive the 'dreadful hardships' whatever they might be and embarked on a toughening-up programme, getting out of bed after my parents were safely asleep and making my bed on a blanket on the cold, linoleum floor. It was a bit like training to be a nun, I thought. I had practised eating less than I would have liked and had finally decided that I *could* live a perfectly miserable life of privation if I had to. Now, three years on, I realised that I was going to have to learn something a great deal more difficult than patience and discretion if I was going to move forward. I was going to have to show my hand and force the issue. But how? Fortunately for me I acquired a few allies.

Chapter Twelve

When Eic Davies came to Pontardawe as Welsh master my life took an up-turn. I had been obliged to choose between Welsh and French as a matriculation subject and had chosen French partly because I wanted to be able to speak French and partly because Miss Vivienne Williams-French wore wonderfully tailored suits by Deréta and blouses with silk bows at the neck and suède shoes and came to work from Clydach, which was almost Swansea and it was rumoured with some awe that she'd been seen 'out' with a handsome American officer. I had hitherto thought that teachers stayed in all the time, marking homework after school, and I wanted to hang about near this dashing, daring woman so I tackled my irregular verbs with the extra energy due to such a sophisticate. I wasn't a student of Eic's but fortunately for me he became a friend of the family and volunteered to coach me in Welsh at weekends and after school.

By this time I was thirteen and we had moved from Alltwen to Cwmllynfell, a small village forty-five minutes by bus up the valley at the foot of the Black Mountain; Eic and his family settled in the village below our farm in G.C.G. Corpulent, with a noble head, a countryman's red complexion and huge mane of hair, he wore Welsh tweeds and knitted ties and walked the school corridors as though he was walking the deck of a ship, an evil smelling pipe clamped between his teeth. He was the Welshest person I'd ever met; not just Welsh

by accident of birth but passionately Welsh; Welsh Nationalist Welsh; cultured, educated Welsh. *He* told *me* about my
great-grandmother, 'Sali Wernwgan' and he knew about my
great-aunt, Rosina Davies, the evangelist. I began to consider
Wales and the Welsh afresh and thought that were it not for
the fact that I needed to get into the theatre, I would be very
happy to remain at home.

Our Swansea Valley Welsh was peppered with English
words for which there were no Welsh equivalents. Eic now
challenged us to invent new words to keep up with modern
life and to speak pure Welsh with no Englishisms. He himself
earned a place in Welsh history at this time by translating
rugby terms into Welsh – inventing a whole rugby vocabulary
– so that he could broadcast Welsh radio commentaries.
Under Eic, Welsh grammar became a game and thanks to
him I knew enough, in time, to sit and pass my university
entrance in Welsh. He also re-named me. At school I was
called by my first Christian name, 'Jane'. Out went the name
along with 'sitting room', 'centre-forward', 'telly'. In came
'Siân', '*blaenwr*', '*lolfa*', '*tele-wele*'.

Siân, which was Welsh for Jane, hadn't been used for
generations and it puzzled people even in Wales. When, a
few years later, I got into an Arts Council production of a new
Welsh play and, full of myself, took a bus to Aberdare to see
my first grown-up billing in a play, I stood across the road
from the theatre and, mortified, read very near the bottom
'with STAN PHILLIPS'. Stan . . . it was worse than all the
other names I'd become used to: Sean (a boy's name) Sy-an,
Shane, Cheyenne. I was too unimportant for anyone to bother
correcting the poster so I remained Stan wherever we played.
Eic laughed it off. 'Don't worry,' he said, eyes twinkling
through the smoke from his pipe, 'give it a year or two
and they'll know who you are, all right.' My heart skipped
a beat. What did he mean? Did he mean that he agreed I could
be an actress? Had he talked about it with my mother? I was
too afraid to ask in case he only meant that my name, like all
the other familiar Welsh words, would in time catch on.

I knew that he thought I was good. He wrote successful comedies for children and translated French and Spanish plays into Welsh which we performed in school under his direction. He'd listened to my first broadcasts and, very tactfully, he urged me towards better microphone technique ('more thinking, less acting') and he introduced me to his friends at the BBC and so I widened my circle of possible employers. For some reason, my mother never questioned the wisdom of my spending time at the BBC. Mr Rees, my headmaster, and she and my father all said, 'So long as she keeps up her school work.' I knew that one bad report would bring my career to a sudden end. My fellow pupils didn't find my unorthodox school life very remarkable. They were used to the fact that I led a public life. I wasn't secretive about my work but I kept it separate from my life at school. My pay cheques were modest and the money was put aside for books. Like everyone else, I received no pocket money.

I loved this budding career at the BBC but the early years were nerve-racking for all sorts of reasons. At thirteen, fourteen, fifteen, I was growing fast and outgrowing clothes faster than they could be replaced, but the school tunic had limitless turnings and the gabardine was standing up to the countless spongings and pressings, so there were periods when my school uniform was the smartest thing I could wear to work. I didn't mind this but it did emphasize my slightly awkward position, very much a junior and very much a beginner on the fringe of the resident repertory actors and the very experienced part-time actors who made up the large company that was needed for the big weekly output of plays, stories, drama documentaries ('features', as they were called), poetry programmes, schools' programmes and children's hour.

I had to struggle not to appear as gauche and panic-stricken as I felt while I gradually picked up the actors' and directors' shorthand. 'Wait for the flick then take a beat after the spot effect before you do a medium approach on page four.' Wha-at? Why didn't I ask? I was shy and everyone was always in a mad rush and simply forgot that I had no way of knowing the things that they took for granted.

The fact that everything was live intensified the pressure. It was *imperative* that no mistakes were made. This was before television had resumed properly after the war and Wales had very little professional theatre, so everyone listened to the radio and hung on each word, reacting sharply to faults. Many of the plays were fed into the network and my first Saturday Night Theatre (in which I played a large number of public school *boys*) was like going over Niagara in a barrel. Eic told me to imagine that I was playing to *one* family sitting together in one room and that did make the whole thing a little less intimidating. A little. It was bad enough, acting in Welsh but English . . . I agonised over every syllable. And regional accents . . . I wasn't to know that accents were never to come easily to me and I cursed myself for being so slow.

The actors in the company were wonderful. I never tired of watching them as they rehearsed, making it all seem so natural and easy. However, some of them were decidedly eccentric. When I had to give a full account of my experiences at home ('No, no, start from the beginning. You got off the bus . . .') I censored out some of the racier conversations. I didn't think my parents would approve of anything 'Bohemian'.

There were two actors who stood apart from the others: Norman Wynne and Ennis Tennusché. They were marked by an un-Welsh air. Norman drank, I thought, although here in the city it wasn't the crime it would have been in our almost teetotal circle. Still, it was better left out of my description of Norman. He looked grumpy and artistically dishevelled and not entirely happy with his lot. And he cooked! I had never met a man who could cook (not counting the tramp) but Norman would amble late into the studio, just in time to avert hysteria and disaster, and invariably carried a string bag bulging with groceries, some of them *very* strange; things that could *only be bought in Cardiff.*

One day as I stood at the microphone during transmission,

wondering what would happen if, for once, Norman didn't make it, the door opened gently and in he sidled. He crept up to the microphone and extracted from the string bag a rather grubby script which had been rolled around a bright red lobster. I had only ever read about lobsters. How wonderful, I thought, to be so insouciant and so sophisticated in one's eating habits – and so good at acting. He *was* good or his insubordination would have cost him his job. It did not escape me that the director, Elwyn Evans, who seemed to be seven feet tall, appeared even more inscrutable and frightening when, eyes narrowed, he looked through the glass window of the control cubicle at four actors stepping over Norman's lobster as they wove their way around the microphone.

Ennis Tennusché was beautiful. She looked like a model. As I stood beside her I felt over-athletic, over-fed, over healthy. She was thrillingly thin, her skin pale as ivory, her hair silvery blonde, pulled back into an immaculate chignon. It seemed to me that she only ever wore silvery colours; grey suits with long pencil-slim skirts, a little slit cut at the back so that she could walk in her incredibly high-heeled shoes. In the street she wore little jackets, nipped in at the waist, and carried a long, furled, black umbrella. Under her arm she held a large, flat, rectangular handbag and on her head she wore a small, flat, pancake of a hat. The only colour was the dark red of her lips which I never saw unpainted. She was the only person I'd ever seen who looked like an actress. It goes without saying that she had a lovely voice and when she chatted during breaks I found it an effort to keep my countenance neutral, partly because of the beauty of the sound and partly because I was truly shocked by the way she spoke of private things in public. Once she referred to her 'ex-lover' and the things he did that infuriated her. I blinked a few times and focused on the ceiling. 'Ex-lover'? What kind of talk was that? Boy-friends, husbands and fiancés, fathers and brothers were the total of possible roles for the men in one's life – outside books, that is. Ennis's conversation *was* like something in a book.

The other ladies, mindful of my age, looked faintly disapproving. They were *very* Welsh. Rachel Howell-Thomas had been senior to my mother at Ystalfera Grammar School. Untrained, she was a remarkable, experienced actress, married to a doctor, quiet, discreet, successful, plain, her large Slavonic face (a bit like my mother's) completely bare of make-up, hair scraped back into plaits wound round into unbecoming, flat 'ear-phones'. She had thick ankles and wore sensible shoes and suits. She looked nothing like an actress but she made movies and Paul Robeson had said she was one of the best actresses he'd ever worked with. She was always cordial but when she looked at me I felt my mother's eyes on me, filled with faint suspicion. As the years went by I gave her no reason to revise her doubts about me as, increasingly restless and longing to be up and away, I looked for mischief and found it.

Rachel played good women. Dilys Davies, her contemporary, played shrews, gossips, nags and viragos, and she was first-rate. She had a voice like a corncrake that could be heard three blocks away. Also married to a doctor, she was rich and, if not exactly pretty, she was striking; slim and bold with an inexhaustible wardrobe of bright, new clothes. She took me under her wing in a kindly, impersonal way and was always ready with advice, usually preceded by, 'The doctor says'. I never did find out her husband's name, he was always referred to as 'The doctor' and I was given to understand that he was infallible. 'The doctor says never wear bedroom slippers in the home. It's slack' and 'Always have a wash and put some make-up on before transmission. And always put a drop of scent on. It makes all the difference.'

The fourth established actress was Olive Michael. She was a widow; young and pretty and *tiny*. If I felt hearty alongside Ennis, when I stood next to Olive I felt like a giant. She looked like a little French juvenile but she carried with her a faint air of tragedy, strangely at odds with her cheerful manner and her facility for playing children; little boys and girls, lots of them, all in the same play, all totally different.

My only contemporary was Gwenyth Petty: blonde, as

sunny as she was beautiful, immaculate with flawless skin and beautiful clothes. We worked together for years and I looked up to her, though I sensed that our ambitions would take us in very different directions.

Prysor Williams and Moses Jones ('Moss') were the character actors and, unlike Norman, *very* Welsh. Ex coal-miners, they were short, slightly stooped, blue scarred and 'chesty from the dust'. Prysor was sharp and quick and foxy. Moses had a softness and a simplicity that would break the heart. I watched them carefully and realised that I was learning more from them than I was from the actresses.

The leading man was *such* a leading man . . . John Darren was absurdly handsome with, of course, a heavenly voice and a great deal of what I had just learned to identify as sprezzatura. He was so poised, so cool, so unruffled, so effortless in all he did.

Everyone, no matter how experienced, suffered from nerves in the days of live broadcasting. As the seconds ticked away and the warning red light came on, the silence grew palpable and as the voice of the continuity announcer up on the first floor identified the station and began to introduce the programme, we waited like greyhounds for the green light to signal the cue to begin and in those seconds everyone prayed that he wouldn't be the one to stumble, make an unpardonable 'fluff', or turn over two pages by mistake, or fail to squeeze into the correct place on a crowded mic'. The studio floor would be littered with discarded pages cut at the last moment and my special prayer was always 'Please God, don't let me have thrown away the wrong pages'. Studio managers stood by with their strange assortment of tin cans, old nuts and bolts, maybe a washboard which were to be pressed into service for 'spot-effects' and one had to be very careful not to get in their way.

There were a thousand things that could go wrong and we all twitched and frowned and waved our arms about looking thoroughly unappealing – except for John who, if he was anxious, never betrayed it as he negotiated his way through the chaos like a man strolling in his own garden. Except – and again maybe it was hell for him but he gave no outward indication of discomfort – he walked with the most attractive Byronic limp; the legacy of a cricketing accident at Oxford. Sunshine, green grass, dreaming spires, a lock of hair on the forehead, tie knotted at the waist, the song of willow on leather, gilded youth, sudden calamity, English voices . . . it was too romantic and the girls mooned over him. I, from very far off. When he casually complimented me on some little piece of acting I was struck quite dumb and could only nod gracelessly. He made the boys at school seem very – boyish, and he made the 'old' men in their forties who bought me meals and paid me compliments seem very – well – old and heavy-handed. As the years went by and I got to know him a great deal better I never quite forgot that most delicious of states, the schoolgirl crush.

I think John was glad when a new actor of his own age was chosen to complete the company. Michael Aspel was the latest heart-throb and the two dashing young men played all the dashing young parts and seemed to be having a lovely time. They were so capable and remarkably nice – for God-like creatures.

The company was augmented by people like me who came and went. Well, hardly like me – Donald Houston and Clifford Evans and Huw Griffith occasionally descended. And Richard Burton whose adoptive father, Philip Burton, had been a BBC director. Richard was a really lovely 'boyo' of a man with a huge capacity for beer and singing; a typical South Walian, good humoured and quick to make friends. A real man's man, I thought approvingly, and I was still in my teens when I was moved to revise that judgment. What did I know about men? Then there were character actors who had 'proper' jobs as well. (An awful lot of Welsh solicitors had equity cards.) One of them would drive me home to the west, saving me an overnight stay and a series of bus journeys. I adored speed and he drove way over the legal limit and, on very late nights when the road was clear, he would let me take the wheel. It was bliss and my mother would have killed me but I thoroughly enjoyed being as bad as I knew how.

By the age of fifteen I had achieved my full height of five feet seven and three quarter inches and if Eic was in the show and if I wasn't in my school uniform, he would slip me into the BBC club or the upstairs bar of the Park Hotel which was an unofficial annexe of the BBC in Park Place. There, I would sit quietly in a corner, nursing my orangeade until it was time for me to be taken back to West Wales by Eic who wouldn't have dreamt of letting me drive but who rightly thought it worthwhile taking the chance of getting both of us into an awful lot of trouble in order to let me sit in the bar and listen to some of the remarkable characters who inhabited the BBC at that time as they relaxed after work.

My very first under-age escapade was wonderful and I forgot my apprehension as Dylan Thomas *and* Gwyn Thomas filled the room with the kind of conversation I could never have imagined possible. It wasn't like any exchange I'd ever heard. Neither inhibited the other and the words cascaded between them, flashing like water. Not for the first time I thought that only second-rate talkers resented other people's cleverness and couldn't wait to push in and claim the attention. The two Thomases were lordly and careless, profligate with their brilliance. I thought I would suffocate as I laughed and laughed, trying to be inconspicuous. I was taken home before too much drink was taken so my impression of Dylan Thomas on a night out was of a witty, brilliant gentleman.

We broadcast together a few times, reading poetry. There would be four or five readers and it was quite usual for people, as they finished their pieces, to tiptoe out of the studio. Once, I was on last – petrified, as usual – and not at all sure if I felt better or worse for having the great poet sitting with me in the big Studio 2, waiting politely for me to bring the programme to a close.

On the whole I was remarkably well looked after in this

adult environment which was my other life, running parallel with my school life. Naturally, as time went by, less care was taken to censor the conversation that went on around me and from time to time my view of the world was given a severe jolt and I would mentally re-shuffle the opinions I'd been fed at school and at home by my mother who had an exaggerated respect for authority, insisting that *all* figures of power and influence were people of irreproachable moral standards. In her book clever men and women merited respect by virtue of their cleverness. Whether she really believed all this I didn't know but she handed down the belief as if written on a stone tablet from on high and I went along with it without too much thought. When I did think about it I assumed that human nature in Wales was just different from human nature anywhere else, past or present. Only gradually did it dawn on me that a large proportion of the people my mother looked up to were just like the people in books; sometime liars, adulterers, drunks and philanderers and that, moreover, they were terribly nice and, more importantly, terribly nice to me. The heavy fog of non-conformism hid a multitude of sins from general view and I would not have dreamt of revealing my fragments of insight to anyone in my other life at home.

The only people I came to dislike were aggressively puritanical – very establishment Welsh – chapel-going, narrow and disapproving of anything outside their own culture. I found it hard to conceal my dislike and there were a few directors I didn't work for at all, once we got the measure of each other.

There were fascinating people at the BBC whom I never got to know well; they appeared briefly and were gone again. John Heath-Stubbs, the poet, was one of these. He had very poor eyesight so I took him to and from the canteen and picked up his things as he dropped them. I doubt that he registered my presence and I was more than content to watch him and listen to him.

Richard Hughes was the first important novelist I met and

worked with. He took me under his wing and escorted me to a café in a desolate, bombed-out area of Swansea, near the BBC in the Uplands. The desolate café had the desolate food of the time. He undertook to improve my education and said, 'Now, remember this.' I perked up, thinking I'd have something special to write in my diary. 'Remember,' he said, slowly, 'everything tastes better if you smother it in Worcester Sauce.' I'd never heard of Worcester Sauce; such a thing never featured on the shelves of our village shop but for years after that when eating out, very pleased to know how to pronounce it, I requested Worcester Sauce and poured it over most things, heedless of the raised eyebrows, confident that I was doing the right thing on the very best recommendation.

I was young when I sat my matriculation (university entrance) examination – fourteen – and such was my fear of being made to give up work (acting was already work and school was a delightful sideline) that I prepared ten subjects and passed them all well, with distinctions in three. I was pleased because I felt very much in charge of my life for a brief while. The examination fortnight, sunny and peaceful in the big, airy gymnasium, with no sound but that of paper rustling faintly, the click of pens put down, picked up, tapped gently, dropped, the occasional gusty sigh and the soft tread of the invigilator was restful after the frenzy of revision. When I found myself challenged to write about something which I hadn't revised it was rather exciting – a bit like the nervous excitement before a performance. My eleventh subject was arithmetic and, of course, I failed it. My maths teacher was delighted that I'd somehow managed to master geometry and trigonometry and we tacitly agreed to ignore arithmetic. When I turned up for the exam he said, 'Look, it's a nice day, why don't you just write your name, then go and read in the field.' I could have hugged him. Why had I been so frightened of him for so many years?

That summer the excitement of passing exams wore off

and now I was truly becalmed and more and more frustrated as the weeks went by and I drifted towards the sixth form to prepare my chosen three subjects which, in two years' time, I would begin reading at a second-year level at a university. This was not without charm – in fact it was immensely attractive – but in my heart I felt that it wasn't what I ought to be doing. My acting was getting no better. If anything, I felt that it was getting worse. I'd outgrown my mother, I'd won the National Eisteddfod four times and had stopped competing. I didn't want to recite any more, I wanted to act, but I'd outgrown school plays. The occasional Arts Council stage play never lasted long enough for me to be able to try out some of the acting methods I read about in books and in actors' autobiographies and, in any case, I felt I was no longer able to help myself. The people who could and did help me were all at the BBC but I was desperate to work in theatre.

I walked and walked on the Black Mountains and on the Gwrhyd Mountain as though I could somehow walk away my problems. I went round in circles, my mind went round in circles. How was I going to achieve a life where acting – on stage – every night, night after night, week after week, was my proper occupation, not something I was grudgingly allowed to squeeze in between other 'legitimate' activities. I was fifteen and no one understood my wretchedness. Well, Eic did but he was no longer talking about it. A few people at the BBC were 'interested' to see if I would find a solution and they were 'sure' I would.

Despite myself, I was consoled by books and by the loveliness of my surroundings and by my own physical well-being. That summer I read a huge amount of Wordsworth and happiness kept breaking through in spite of everything. I felt a traitor to my sense of purpose as I relished the swing in my stride and smiled at the sun transforming the wet mountains when the sky grew huge and clear all around me. I laughed aloud as I raced home, trying to out-strip the thunder storm I could smell in the air. During the long evenings at home I brooded in my room and wrote sad poems about hopelessness and indifference. Unknown to me, my headmaster, S. G. Rees, was not only thinking about me, he was taking steps to help me.

Chapter Thirteen

'Report to the Head's study at the end of the morning.'
The prefect looked around the door of the lower sixth
form common room. 'Uh-huh,' said Audrey Watkins, my best
friend at grammar school, but I wasn't apprehensive. I may
have been seen talking to a boy (still not allowed) on the
bridge to the refectory, the favoured place for assignations
and the passing of notes. I may have been spotted walking
with a boy outside the school gates and, much worse, been
seen not wearing my hat in the street, but I doubted it.
Deception was a large part of my life and I was good at it
and rarely brought to book.

Before he became headmaster at Pontardawe, S.G. Rees
had been a gifted English master and he still amused himself –
and us – by taking the occasional class. He flattered us in the
sixth form by telling us mildly risqué jokes, making us feel
very grown-up and sophisticated. His old school, Gowerton
Boys' Grammar School was about to present Shaw's *St Joan*
and when the leading 'lady' fell ill, Mr Rees came to their
rescue by lending me out to play Joan. 'Learn it this weekend,'
he said casually and I jumped at the chance and, not entertaining the possibility of failure, spent a very enjoyable
weekend getting to know the play. By Monday I knew my
part. It was really *my* part by Tuesday; I was sure I was going
to play it better than it had ever been played. On Wednesday
the young man recovered and I was told to stand down. I was

disappointed but looked on the bright side and went on thinking about 'my' part against the day when I would, *surely*, play it.

Mr Rees may have felt slightly in my debt because he'd decided that I should forego tennis lessons in order to work on a programme of drama study that he would oversee. Life was full of these conflicts, I thought miserably. I was still a fanatically keen and good gymnast, a useful all-round athlete and an enthusiastic, if not at all good, hockey player and, of course, I adored Miss Inkin, the PE and Games mistress who had by now become a friend of the family and had taken me to my first ballet and my first opera and had, without offending my mother, given me the length of navy-blue silk to make what she (and I) regarded as an appropriate concert dress.

Under her guidance I'd forsaken my longing for waves and curls. 'All that prettiness looks common on you,' she'd said ('common' was a term of opprobrium widely used in those days) and surveying the results of her handiwork in the big mirror in my parents' bedroom I had to admit that, got up like a modern Jane Eyre, I certainly looked different and quite fetching in an odd way. I longed now to be in her tennis class and become a brilliant player but it was plain to me that learning about plays was more to the point so I made my excuses and hoped I wouldn't lose her regard. She didn't say anything but a week later she gave me a history of drama by Allardyce Nichol and I breathed a sigh of relief and settled down to my private classes with Mr Rees. He was a wonderful teacher and loved theatre so the lessons were laced with accounts of productions and performances he had seen and admired – or not admired; he could be caustic.

Now, he looked quizzically over his glasses as I entered his study. 'I assume you're familiar with *Twelfth Night*?' I was. 'You know Viola's meeting with Olivia, leading up to the willow cabin speech?' I did. 'Here's my cut of the scene, learn it by the end of the week. I'm going to have you assessed.

118

Maybe you should move on. Hugh Griffith is coming to look you over.' Hugh Griffith! I was speechless. Emlyn Williams excepted, Hugh Griffith was our greatest actor. He'd played in America. *And* in the West End. *And* in movies. He'd played King Lear, in Welsh as well as in English. He rarely played in Wales and it was unbelievable that he was coming here – to Pontardawe – to see *me*! My lungs were over full of air. I needed to take a breath and I couldn't. I must have changed colour in the silence and Mr Rees said briskly, 'All right, all right! That's all. Off you go.'

Off I went. Out into the dark corridor with its wood-block floor and smell of polish. There was no one to tell. This was the most important thing that had ever happened to me and I had to keep it to myself. I had good friends at school but my life was increasingly different from theirs and I was reluctant to talk about anything that pointed up the difference. My priorities were crystal clear and my mother – confusingly – had always made sure that they never went out of focus. 'You can't do your school work *and* act *and* . . .' go dancing, go to the swimming baths, go to the youth club, join the Brownies. All that was acceptable. Well, it had to be acceptable. The only thing I wasn't prepared to forego was boys and some-how, in spite of my almost total lack of spare time, I managed to maintain a series of somewhat ritualistic 'courtships'. My mother sniffed dismissively but wisely left well alone. But where did the acting fit into her plans for me? We hadn't had an argument about it for years but that was because I never brought up the subject. Now what was going to happen? If Hugh Griffith said I was no good, I'd persevere anyway. If he said I *was* good, what would that mean for me? Would my parents feel obliged to treat me seriously? Would he suggest that I left school? If he did, what would I do? My mind raced ahead. The thought of London terrified me. I couldn't imagine how I would live in a city, speaking English all day. Would I be capable of it?

At home that night I merely said that Hugh Griffith was coming to school and I was going to play a scene for him. I

119

didn't say that he was coming specially to see me. I could tell that my mother wasn't sure how she should react. 'Oh, yes?' she said, evenly. In my room I began working on the scene, going over it again and again and again. In the morning I got up early and went through it over and over again before breakfast. On the bus I ran it silently in my head. After three days Mr Rees called me into his room and asked me did I know it? Know it? I felt as thought I'd *written* it. Friday came and I went to school as though it was just another day and not the day when my life might change utterly. During assembly and morning prayers I rehearsed in my head. In the corridor I passed Eic. 'Okay?' he mouthed. I nodded. So he knew. No one else seemed to know. Or maybe they didn't care. Somehow, I got through the morning, then rushed to the lavatory to go over the scene a few more times. When would he arrive? What if he didn't come?

At last, after lunch, I was sent for and told to go to the assembly hall and, heart pounding, I entered and shook hands with a real actor. Now that the longed-for moment had arrived I was barely conscious. Everything I did seemed unreal, as though it was happening to someone else. Climbing the steps to the stage, walking to the centre, looking down at Mr Rees and Eic and at Hugh Griffith who sat apart from them, I was losing all sense of myself. I suppose I was saved by the amount of work I'd done because I got to the end of the scene and no, I *hadn't* fainted and he hadn't stopped me and now he was asking Mr Rees and Eic if they would leave us alone.

As he began to talk about the scene my mind cleared for the first time and my perceptions returned, sharp and clear. He was *directing me*! This was what I'd been longing for. I was astonished and delighted that there was so much more work to be done on the scene. Hugh altered everything; I played it twice as fast, then faster again. How could I have been so slow? Now I was too fast. 'No, no 'merch I. Throw it away, girl, but don't lose it.' Oh God. How? Try again. Hugh's faced loomed larger and larger as he joined me on stage; all eyebrows and nose and sardonic mouth and the brightest, most piercing eyes. I don't know how long we worked and suddenly he was saying, 'All right, my girl, once more – last time.'

After all the work I'd done and all the work we'd done combined, I felt like a new person; lighter, more agile than I'd ever imagined being. I finished and turned to him, absolutely sure that I'd done what he'd asked for and laughed with pure pleasure. I'd never had such a good time. He smiled his inscrutable smile and said, 'There you are. Who'd have thought it, eh?' 'Well done' would have been nice to hear. He said nothing and my newfound confidence began to drain away. I didn't know what to say. 'I'm just going to have a word with Eic,' he said, speaking Welsh for the first time except for saying '*merch*' for 'girl'.

After he'd gone, I waited uncertainly on the stage. The hall looked like the ordinary, familiar hall of everyday life. The magic had evaporated as Hugh left. I descended the steps and opening the door looked out into the corridor. Hugh and Eic were standing outside Mr Rees's study, deep in conversation. They didn't look in my direction and I began walking away from them and turned into the empty common room to look at my timetable. My heart was pounding now. My tongue felt strange. I didn't know how long I'd been in the hall. There was nothing to do but to slip back into the afternoon's classes. 'Excuse me please, I've been with the headmaster.' I felt ill now and had to force myself to concentrate.

Before school ended I was sent for again. Mr Rees was alone in his study. Hugh had gone and Eic was teaching. Mr Rees said calmly, 'It seems you're on your way. Mr Griffith thinks you might well win a scholarship to the Royal Academy and he thinks you should try for one next year when you're sixteen. What do you think of that?' I couldn't tell him what I thought. I wasn't thinking. I was feeling relief so profound that I longed to drop to the floor and burst into tears. I didn't think that Mr Rees's study was the place for that so I managed a polite 'That would be wonderful. Thank you very much, sir.' I'd been right, all along, ever since I was six years old. I *was* meant to be an actress. I was going to *be* an actress. How could I have doubted that today everything would start going my way?

Chapter Fourteen

W hat followed was the happiest and then the most desolate part of my life. It seemed as though my dearest wish was about to come true. Now that Hugh had made it clear that he was impressed, someone would be bound to do something and my parents would be obliged to cave in. Hugh wrote to them; I knew the letter was on its way and I was beside myself with excitement. I don't think my mother even replied to the letter. The rejection was total. There was no discussion or if there was one I was not included in it. The decision was final and my mother was implacable. Provided of course that I passed my exams, there was no question of my not going to university.

There was a part of me that hated my mother that year as I resumed the routine of school life; more and more homework, long bus journeys to and from the BBC in Cardiff and in Swansea. The resentment never quite left me. And yet, I could see why she behaved as she did. And I could see that everything she said made perfect sense. But not to me. What I most fretted over was my feeling that she had no faith in my ability. She had seen everything I'd ever done, except my rehearsal with Hugh Griffith, and it must be that she found me wanting. I got on with my preparation for university, determined to get through everything in record time and determined to prove my mother wrong.

Had I possessed a greater dislike of my life or had my

resentment of my mother not been tempered by some understanding of her thought-process, then I suppose I would have rebelled more vigorously at this stage. Only once did I openly oppose my mother. When she forbade me to do something or other on a fine Saturday afternoon saying, yet again, 'You can't expect to be allowed to act if you don't give up your spare time to catching up on your school work', I heard myself protesting that I felt 'exploited' and that I wasn't living a 'normal life' and that it 'just wasn't FAIR' and as I spoke, felt deeply embarrassed to be saying anything so crass, uttering such clichés. Had my father been present I wouldn't have been so rude. My mother looked disdainful and said nothing. I muttered an apology and was safely inside my bedroom before I began to cry from confusion and shame. 'Take what you want and pay for it' I had written in my notebook. I knew what I wanted and most of the time I was happy to pay the price but there were moments when the dull, mundane payments – no heroic gestures required – alas, seemed to stretch ahead without end. I would be so *old* before I could be a proper actress. Maybe too old.

Meanwhile it was luxurious to have only three subjects to work on instead of ten. I read voraciously and now that I had evolved a rough form of rapid reading my appetite was increasing to match my capacity. I made sure that my eye made a diagonal from the end of one line to the beginning of the next (rather than running back horizontally before dropping down). And I tried to 'drink in' the whole page before I began reading and of course I practised 'skipping'. There was probably more to it but this makeshift method helped me considerably. Set books formed only a small proportion of my reading as my parents and Miss Inkin began to buy me modern novels. One by one my parents gave me Aldous Huxley's novels in a pretty Chatto & Windus edition and when the set was complete and sitting on my dressing table, between two rather nasty bookends in the shape of galleons, I enjoyed looking at them before I went to sleep as much as I had enjoyed reading them.

What I really wanted at this time was to understand Cyril Connolly's column in the *Observer* and to know what he was writing about in his review column on the Sunday, even more, I wanted to be able to walk into a room and *talk* to Cyril Connolly! (*The Unquiet Grave* was my favourite book.) The retired schoolmistress next door gave me her old Conrads and her brand new volumes of Osbert Sitwell's *Right Hand: Left Hand*. I couldn't believe people could live such a life. I thought, how wonderful to *be* a Sitwell, stepped up my output of inferior poetry and made myself a turban out of the pretend silk runner on the piano. Miss Inkin gave me French novels in a lovely edition. *Mademoiselle de Maupin* was what I thought of as a *real* French novel and I thought how lovely to behave so badly in such wonderful clothes. She also gave me big books about Russian and British ballet, full of photographs of dancers who became intimates as I drew them over and over again. There was very little I didn't know about the physiques of Anton Dolin, Sally Gilmour, John Gilpin and Ulanova after I'd sat night after night at the kitchen table with my back to the anthracite fire, copying their photographs in mid-leap and listening to the Third Programme of the BBC issuing from the wooden face of the Ferranti wireless on the windowsill.

Miss Williams-French, still perfectly coiffed and suited, was not only dragging us inexorably through the thickets of the subjunctive and requiring us to learn by heart long pieces of sad, romantic poetry and particularly gloomy bits of Victor Hugo (which rather suited my mood), she was also telling us about French *movies*, not that there was any chance of us seeing any, and bringing us photographs of actors and actresses, so completely un-English and giving us a whole new look to aspire to, not that there was the smallest chance of my achieving that, either. As I became confident enough to begin bandying about the names of Gide, Malraux, Claudel and Jean-Paul Sartre – Miss Williams's extra gift, nothing to do with our set work – I *felt* sophisticated and gorgeous as though I too possessed an eighteen-inch waist, bound in a huge black patent belt and wore a fringe over huge black eyes, with lots of dark, dark lipstick on my small mouth like those French ingénues in the photographs. I lived a life of fantasy much of the time, tried on new personas for size and had to admit to myself that in spite of everything I was, on the whole, happy. I got on well with my schoolfriends and the staff and always had a romance on the go to liven up the day.

I was distracted by an increasing and greatly frowned upon preoccupation with boys at school, young men outside school and, even more interesting to me, secret flirtations with totally unsuitable older men which would have completely 'cooked my goose' had they ever come to light. My mother looked askance when I went to the Miners' Welfare Hall to see a movie on Saturday night (and this could only happen when I wasn't working – I would never have dreamt of refusing work in order to keep a 'date'). She didn't actually say anything but I thought it wise to be very discreet about my 'steady' boyfriends from school.

One day Rhydwen Williams said something that really upset me. He was one of Wales's most brilliant preachers with the dark poetic good looks that matched his fame as a crowned poet. He was in huge demand as a guest preacher and some years before, when we lived in Alltwen, he had pressed me into service to help out during long exhausting Sundays when he would preach two major sermons. I would recite from the Gospel of St Luke – my mother's favourite – and he would take a little breather. He introduced me to the plays of Emlyn Williams and, back at the house after the evening service, performed his favourite scene from *The Corn is Green* (I had to give my twelve-year-old reading of Miss Moffat). Now he came back into our lives as a friend of Eic's in Cwmllynfell.

I think they were enjoying a kind of pub-crawl with a very august personage from the BBC in London. They must have run out of things to do one night because my mother woke me up and said that there was a car waiting to take me to the Boblen – a tiny, inaccessible pub on the Gwrhyd Mountain above the village, presided over by a mountainous, good-humoured woman called Bessie'r Rock who was a stranger to licensing hours and sleep alike. I scrambled into my clothes and into the cold Austin Seven which bumped up the dark mountain road and turned left into the yard in front of the tiny pub. Inside there was a coal-fire burning and it was stiflingly hot after the chill outside. There was a brilliant, central, overhead light. Bessie made a place for me while the ten or so men told stories, extemporised verse and drank steadily.

At last, they cleared a place for me to stand and I recited for them for about half an hour. Eic had said only that it was *quite* important for me to do my best as there were one or two people who wanted to see for themselves whether I was as good as I'd been cracked up to be. Not knowing my audience but enjoying the challenge I showed off, beginning with the St Luke version of the Prodigal Son in Welsh, then moving on to the Nightmare Song in English, then continuing with my edited version of the trial scene from *St Joan* and then a little Baudelaire in French. What they made of this indigestible programme, heaven knows, and I certainly didn't know because, as usual, I was packed off home as soon as I'd finished and was asleep the second I climbed into bed.

Rhydwen called on my parents the following day. 'You know she *is* going to be an actress,' he said in Welsh. They seemed gratified to hear me praised by someone they regarded so highly and when he sat down and wrote an ode to me there and then they were impressed. He took me for a turn around our garden. It was cold in the east wind that blew through the village, from Cefn Bryn Brain. 'Don't worry too much,' he said in Welsh, using the familiar '*ti*' form of the verb, something my parents never did. It gave me a jolt. 'It *is* going to happen but there's no hurry. You're not going to come into your own until you're forty.' Forty? What could he be talking about? All my pleasure evaporated and I felt deeply exasperated and actively disliked him as he stood in the winter-untidy vegetable patch, looking at me with an amused ex-

pression on his handsome face. What he'd said was completely absurd but how on earth was I going to be able to
prove him wrong, imprisoned as I was in school, 'Lulled in the
doldrums of immaturity' I'd copied into a notebook. That's
me, I thought, miserably.

I'll show you, I thought to myself. After he'd gone I looked
at his poem to me written in small, neat handwriting. It was
very flattering and I especially liked the bit where he wrote
that the curtain call was the one moment when *I* would bow.
At all other times I would shine like Orion and *they* would
bow before me. Well! My mother reached over my shoulder.
'I'll take this,' she said and it disappeared along with my prizes
and newspaper cuttings and silver cups and I never saw it
again. Rhydwen's words had no practical effect on my mother
and father.

For the rest of my time at school there was nothing but
disappointment and frustration. Jill Craigie came to our
village to make *The Blue Scar*, a film about coal-miners.
Everyone auditioned for it in the Miners' Welfare Hall.
Everyone except me. It was summer and I longed to join
the queue. 'Revise,' said my mother tersely and I sat in the
garden reading and thinking that nothing would ever go my
way.

At school Eic began to direct *Blodeuwedd*, a play by
Saunders Lewis in which I played the enormous, wonderful,
title role of Blodeuwedd, the girl created from flowers. It was
the best part I'd ever worked on and Saunders was the most
controversial, glamorous figure on the literary and political
scene. He sent me a signed copy of the play and then, halfway
through rehearsals, the play was abandoned. We were censored and banned. I was stunned. The play *was* very un-
Welsh, full of illicit, joyful sex and violent death. There was an
outcry in the press against faint-hearted bigotry but the school
governors held firm. I was beside myself. It was so unfair! The
play was no more unsuitable than a great deal of Shakespeare
but no, what was acceptable in English iambic pentameters
from the seventeenth century was beyond the pale in modern

Welsh. The disappointment made me ill and, to my surprise, my mother was sympathetic. She was busy directing operettas in the Miners' Welfare Hall but she made sure that there was a supply of delicious titbits to get me through the evenings when I was at home writing essays instead of playing Blodeuwedd. Was nothing *ever* to go right?

The kitchen was a no-go area for me. My mother was a wonderful cook but she taught me nothing. I made a few half-hearted attempts to learn something from her. 'How much flour, then?' 'Oh, just a handful.' 'How long do you stir it?' 'Till it's done.' I knew a great deal about cleaning, however, having learned 'Housewifery' in the Junior School where we were taught to make soap, if you please, and learned how to whiten stone steps with bricks of something called 'Monkey Brand'. Modern methods were frowned upon. I loved cleaning and had a great sense of order, so my room was always spotless and as neat as something in a magazine. I arranged and rearranged the furniture, banished the overhead lamp and rigged up the only indirect light in the house, in all probability the only indirect light for miles around. At night, having completed my exercises to improve and strengthen the arches of my feet (Miss Inkin's suggestion, turned into an iron rule by me) I would lie in bed, reading and admiring the perfect order all around me. I exercised control where I could.

It had seemed as though my two years in the sixth form would never come to an end. I liked school, I had once loved it, but now at sixteen I longed for examination time and an end to it all. Mr Rees entered me for an exhibition to London University and made arrangements for me to sit the exam in his study. Eic thought I should go to Bristol which was the only university offering a drama course under Professor Tommy Taigh. I didn't really care where I went. As usual, I rather enjoyed the exams and I got through everything with no trouble at all. It was expected that I should do well in English and French but I had done so little work in History that failure was almost a certainty. When I saw the paper I realised that it was one of those question papers that cause short-lived academic scandals; completely 'off' the subject. I dredged around in my mind and came up with enough material from historical novels and plays to keep me writing busily, vaguely but entertainingly. When his better students failed or did badly and I passed, my History master made no secret of his displeasure. 'The knack of passing exams,' he implied, was something *girls* had and it was a bit cheap and quite without merit.

I was unrepentant and glad to be finished with his subject but I wasn't as pleased with myself as I had been when I matriculated. It was good to have cleared another hurdle but now I had another three or four years to get through before my real life could begin and I didn't know if I would be able to manage it. My attention had moved dangerously far away from the academic and it might be difficult for me to keep my two worlds from cancelling each other out.

While I was brooding over my general problem, a specific difficulty arose that woke me up and threw me into a frenzy. London University could not take students under the age of eighteen years. I was just seventeen. Mr Rees said that an extra year at school was not really such a long time to wait. I couldn't even consider it and only now realised how very desperate I was to get out. Representations were made to Bristol and I was accepted there instead. Carter Patterson the Carriers, the Pickfords of university trunks, picked up and took away my baggage containing all the required clothes for undergraduate life. In fact it contained everything I possessed. Then it was discovered that Bristol also had an age limit. My parents made frantic phone calls. My uncle did the same and the University of Wales agreed to squash me in at the last minute. They had no objection to an undergraduate aged seventeen.

Thoroughly unsettled, I took the bus to Cardiff, to Aberdare Hall, where first-year female students were obliged to live. My trunk was careering around the West Country and no one could find it. I had no clothes except the ones I stood up in. I looked around the college; endless queues everywhere, dim lights, confusion, the hateful city outside. However bad things had been, I realised that they were about to get a lot worse.

Chapter Fifteen

From the Mond Nickel Works onwards down the valley, Swansea had always presented to me a vision of hell. Acrid smells penetrated the red, single-decker Western Welsh bus. The black and grey smoke was shot through with sulphurous yellow, occasionally with a sinister little snake of green in the dark sky above some copper workings. The town itself in its blitzed, ruined state was warm and friendly and very Welsh and I always knew that at the end of the day I would be in another low, red bus climbing steadily past the dirt and stench of the Tawe Valley through the narrow Twrch (boar) Valley with space for nothing but a narrow road and a turbulent little river on the valley floor, until suddenly, as the bus pulled slowly up the steepest part of the road, Cwmllynfell presented itself in its full, top-of-the-world, Hollywood orchestrated glory. Violin music swelled in my head as the bus swung round towards the chapel. The landscape was limitless. That moment was like leaving a river for the ocean and it never failed to fill the air with exhilaration and grandeur. Every day I travelled up and away into a freedom that was as psychological as it was physical. It hadn't occurred to me that I was addicted to big landscapes and large skies.

Now I had to contend with Cardiff. Until now it had been a place that housed the BBC in Park Place, somewhere to leave as soon as work was done. I had been dimly aware of the Civic Centre – very white – and I remembered the Museum from my school days. I knew the route from the bus station to the Broadcasting House and I knew the little tobacconist where, greatly fearing, I had slid half-a-crown across the counter for ten Du-Maurier cigarettes. No bomb damage here. No slums as far as I could see. It was an eminently nice, clean, safe city and I hated it.

My father had left the police force and was now running a further education centre in the Vale of Glamorgan, outside Cardiff. My parents had arrived in the middle of a staffing crisis and my mother, who had never cooked for more than a small family, had stepped into the breach and was completely preoccupied running a large kitchen staff and cooking for hundreds of people. 'It's only arithmetic – multiplication,' she said breezily, composing menus and making dinky posies for the dining tables. They were meeting old friends from all over Wales and staying up late, entertaining in their flat. My mother had been bequeathed an ancient, fierce parrot who adored her, and my father was furiously painting landscapes in a small outhouse he'd turned into a studio. He was watched by an adoring dog who used to be mine and I was slightly put out to realise that I had moved far away from the centre of their attention; even the dog was perfunctory in his greeting. Of course, I had longed to be left alone and now suddenly I *was* – quite free and quite discomfited. It was as though, after all the years of fuss and struggle, they'd got me more or less where they thought I ought to be (not at all where *I* wanted to be) and, having done that, they'd rather run out of puff as far as I was concerned and discovered an interesting life of their own.

And my trunk was in Bristol! I pitched up in Corbett Road in Cardiff at an annexe of Aberdare Hall, The warden didn't really understand why I was late arriving or why I had no luggage but made it plain that I was a bit of a nuisance and I for my part struggled not to betray my dismay at my sur-roundings. For the first time I felt the impact of post-war austerity. Everything was brown and fawn. The furniture was cheap 'Utility' and seen at its worst in the common room which was arranged like a doctor's waiting room. The single, dim overhead light in its beige parchment shade with pretend leather stitching illuminated the upright chairs arranged around the room, the few bare 'occasional' tables and the grudging, unlined cotton curtains barely covering the frame of the bay-window that looked out on to the darkening topmost edges of the fabled Civic Centre.

We climbed to the top floor and I was shown into what had once been a box room; little brown wooden-framed bed, regulation desk, small wardrobe, chest of drawers, 'easy' chair, bare walls. 'Your bed must be made perfectly and everything that you have put away in the wardrobe or inside the drawers before my inspection at 7.45 a.m. or you will re-make your bed and miss breakfast in the Main Hall. As an Arts student you ought to be rooming with someone from a Science faculty but what can I do?' She shrugged. I couldn't really take her in. In fact, my mind wasn't really taking in anything much. I could hear her explaining the rules governing the kitchen (use of) and the penalties for staying out after 10 p.m. (dire but unspecified). Ten p.m.?! There was something about lights out and after that I decided not to listen at all. What had I let myself in for? I dumped a small bag with soap, towel and toothbrush and a hair brush, 'not on the bed, I think', 'Oh, so sorry', and followed her down the stairs, bidding her the briefest 'Good afternoon and thank you' as she made for her own study.

There was no one about and I walked into the fading autumn day. It was damp and it was to stay damp for months. I walked down Park Place towards the Students' Union. Beyond was the BBC; familiar, warm, brilliantly lit, with real carpets and 1930ish light fittings and furniture. I stood there feeling completely cut off from everything I cared for. Now that my parents had moved I had no way of going 'home' to the West. I was going to have to learn to abide by a myriad of childish rules and deal with people like the Warden. Who was she, the Warden? I didn't care.

I walked round to the front entrance of the University building and nervously inched my way into the crowded, none too brightly lit interior. Why was it so *dark* everywhere? My heart sank as I realised that I was going to have to spend hours queuing in order to register for my first year's studies. Now was my chance, however, to alter my programme slightly. Naturally, I would join the English and French Schools at a second-year level but I would drop History – I knew that although I'd done quite well in the exam I was way under the required standard. My matriculation result enabled me to read Welsh instead. Good old Eic. He'd given me another option. Obviously I was going to have to tackle all this in the morning.

What of the fourth subject which I was obliged to read and which would be started at a first-year level? Education seemed to be the favoured 'filler'. The queue was enormous. Well, I was *never* going to teach and the subject held no appeal for me. I drifted from notice board to notice board and came to rest in a deserted corner of the building. For the first time that day my interest awakened and it was with considerable if inexplicable excitement that I made my way to a desk with no queue at all. The man seated behind it looked discouraging. He seemed content not to be doing business. We went through the formalities and he said, 'Why do you want to join this School?' I replied that honestly I had no idea but I was quite sure that I *did* want to. So the first thing I did at the University was to enrol myself as an Intermediate student of a subject that I was to pursue with love and passion for the next three years and beyond. It was the only smart thing I did that term. Philosophy became my chief interest and my hobby. And quite unexpectedly, along with Latin and Physical Training, it turned out to be the only really useful subject I ever studied. English was pleasure and I was always grateful for the yards of poetry that I'd been made to learn parrot-fashion and which floated to the front of my mind, digested and compre-hended in their own good time, but Philosophy – ! It was philosophy and logic that held me together as I stumbled from

one confusion to the next. It also provided me with amusement – something which was sadly lacking in the life I was to
lead in this alien, un-Welsh city.

Back at the Aberdare Hall Annexe (I hated it even more on
second viewing) I heard the click-click of higher heels than
would have been considered 'proper' by our mothers and
nearly cried with relief as I saw the huge dark eyes, bright red
lipstick, upswept rolls of hair, pussy-cat bow and tailored
shoulders of my best friend at school. By all that was wonderful I'd wound up on the same floor as Audrey Watkins.
'Where are you?' 'Next room.' 'Soon change that.' 'We're
not allowed, we're both Arts and we know each other.'
'Rubbish. Leave it to me. Done your registering?' 'No.'
'Do it tomorrow. Where's your housecoat?' (Required pack-
ing. Not a dressing gown. A *housecoat*.) 'In my trunk. In
Bristol.' 'Soon get it back. Banked your grant?' 'No.' 'Never
mind. Do it tomorrow.' Sure. Thank you, God. Thank you,
Audrey. Everything would get done tomorrow. And maybe,
just maybe, life in the Ladies' Seminary mightn't be too bad,
after all. My mother would be furious. She thought Audrey
and I were bad for each other. Could be. I could feel a big
smile coming on.

Chapter Sixteen

I moved in with Audrey and the fearsome Warden looked confused but let it pass. My father drove into town in his new car, took me for a spin round the block and helped me open a bank account at Lloyd's in St Mary's Street. Sitting there, depositing the first part of my grant, I could scarcely credit my transformation at seventeen into a woman of substance, with responsibilities; bills to pay, books and food and clothes to buy. Hitherto it had never occurred to me to carry money other than the sums my mother doled out to me for my books, bus fares and meals. I knew that a hardback book cost 7/6 and that lunch could be bought for 3 shillings and that by eating a bit less I could buy cigarettes and no one would be any the wiser. My interest stopped there. Now all that would have to change.

From time to time I made an ineffectual dab at locating my trunk but Carter Patterson was a law unto itself and my trunk circled the south-west of England for weeks, returning to me in Wales just before the end of term. It didn't occur to me to buy more clothes so I was the girl in the brown-checked costume and made as if it was a deliberate fashion statement. Audrey got me registered and showed me around and I addressed my complete unpreparedness for normal, day-to-day living. I'd never made tea or boiled an egg or mended a seam or set an alarm clock or washed a pair of stockings. It seemed I'd done nothing with my life but read, learn lines, perform, do my homework, write poetry, draw, flirt with boys, and moon about. Especially moon about. I was too embarrassed to admit to my ignorance and pretended to take everything in my stride. I was exhausted and homesick for a house that no longer existed. Everyone had a home. So where was mine? Was Cardiff home now? No, not by a long chalk. I never became reconciled to the décor at Corbett Road and in fact everything all over the city seemed to be brown, damp and dim. The rain seemed wetter here, or maybe getting wet mattered more than it had in the country. I wore gloves and wrapped my college scarf round my head but I was cold, and whereas at home a bit of a run warmed me up in no time, here city pavements and too many people and city shoes slowed me down to a sedate, brisk walk.

Audrey and I made friends with the other girls at Corbett Road and we settled down to some sort of routine, the principal part of which consisted of wasting time, sitting in the only place that would allow us to make one cup of coffee last the entire morning. This was the foyer café of the Capital Cinema in Queen Street at the bottom of Park Place. I don't know what we talked about. Mostly, I just looked at people and listened. Looking at the Park Hotel across the way I could scarcely believe that I had had another, different life; one in which I actually sat composedly inside the building which was now far too grand and expensive a place for me to enter in my present life. Was I going backwards? I couldn't tell. There was one other café on Queen Street, a Kardomah where they served a more 'real' kind of coffee and where I was taken once or twice by older students (much, *much* older, those young men who had come to the University after doing their National Service) and where coffee was drunk at a more reasonable speed. There were two hotels, the Angel, opposite the Castle, and the BBC 'extension', the Park, and the only restaurant I was aware of was the Louis in St Mary's Street. Long and narrow and staffed by waitresses, it offered dull food; most things were arranged to be consumed on toast, tea was offered with food, coffee was thin and bitter, the china thick, good behaviour, while not specified, seemed to be expected. When my parents took me there for high tea we spoke very quietly and chewed long and decorously with a lot of napkin work.

There just wasn't much fun and I couldn't get accustomed to that. City life was constrained and muted and I didn't care for it. Now, more than ever, I worried about my future life in London, which must be a hundred times more of a city than Cardiff and would be a hundred times more difficult for me to live in. In my mother's absence I imagined what she would say. It would be something along the lines of 'You're not *in* London, yet and you're not in Cardiff to have fun.'

Months had gone by since I'd been offered a job at the BBC and this was the longest I'd ever gone without acting. Maybe no one would ask me to act again, I thought miserably, and since we were already halfway through the Michaelmas Term I decided that I'd better take a serious look at the academic work I might reasonably be expected to get through and also, with a faint sense that it was a mistaken move, I joined the University Dramatic Society.

English lectures were heavily subscribed and took place in the largest room in the building, Room 102. The Reverend Moelwyn Merchant swept on to the stage looking deceptively mild; bald head shining above a cherubic, rosy-cheeked face, black robed, grey suit underneath. Rather cheery, I thought. My pen was poised above my notepad and it stayed there and my jaw dropped slightly while Moelwyn, like a high-octane performer, got a few laughs, touched on the affairs of the day, gossiped aloud about people I'd barely heard of and then 'Gave his All' for ten to fifteen minutes. Hang on, I thought, desperately trying to keep up. If we were, as I'd supposed, looking at the Romantics, why was he talking about gardening? Any what was picturesque? Or was it The Picturesque? And what was that joke about his friend, John Piper and the Swan on Lake Windermere? I was still trying to get up to speed when, with a pleasant 'Good day', he was gone! I sat there for a moment, bruised but exhilarated and realised that I

141

was going to have to make a huge mental stretch if I was going to keep pace, let alone get into the Honours School at the end of the year. The room might be brown and cold, but Moelwyn was technicoloured and hot to boiling point.

At the other extreme there was *Beowulf* to contend with. Sweet's *Anglo-Saxon Reader* seemed manageable. The Norse sagas had a just-discernible appeal. But *Beowulf*! I held the big book in my hand and it felt like a ton weight. The possibility of my ever knowing what it meant seemed remote. I didn't think I had it in me to take on that kind of steady drudgery but I was going to have to try. Even literature students *had* to know their Anglo-Saxon.

A friend of my father's from Llwynhendy near Llanelli was Professor of French so I tried to bring my written French up to scratch but every time I delivered an essay I was confronted by my wretched carelessness. At my last oral I'd been given an unusual 100 per cent. *Talking* was fine, it was like giving a performance and now it cut no ice at all. I wasn't quite ready to accept the awful fact that for the first time in my life I was going to have to try really hard. My life of ease was over. Even Welsh had its equivalent of *Beowulf* with a twist to the torture in that whereas I *knew* I didn't understand any Anglo-Saxon I felt that I half-understood or at least could make a good guess at understanding old Welsh. No so. More real work stretched ahead.

Had it not been for Philosophy my spirits would have been lowered to a point of no return. There were very few of us in the School and Professor de Selincourt was my chief source of entertainment as he provoked his fluffy white hair into agitated spirals when threatened with insuperable problems concerning the day of the week (what could it be? – and in which term?) and where might his car be parked or should he go home in a bus (but whence might it depart?). Crouching under the desk out of sight, 'Am I here?' he intoned. Then leaping up with surprising agility, 'Or am I only here when you can see me?' Fun had returned to my working life. I'd read Plato's *Republic* at home so I half-knew what the year's work was about. A little unexplored corner of my mind clicked into action when we began the Logic course. It was heaven not having to struggle to understand. I had a bit of a knack for it. Doctor Evans had the shiniest, clearest mind I'd ever encountered and I finished each of his logic lectures wide-eyed, feeling as though I was stepping off an ice-rink. Not that Cymllynfell boasted an ice-rink and if it had, would Sally Tŷ mawr ever have let me go to it? But I had a sound imagination and following Doc through an argument was just like executing a 'triple lutz', I thought.

Occasionally, I allowed a worry to rise to the surface. There was probably a good reason why universities had an age limit for admission and was I too young for all this? I was old enough to see my limitations and to see that this place was rather above 'getting through'. I stifled the thought. I was committed to getting through as fast as possible and to getting *out* and *on* to London. It wasn't ideal but it was what I had to do. I don't know why, but it never occurred to me to drop out.

Chapter Seventeen

I got down to work and it paid off. I still didn't much *like* having to make such an effort but it was the way it had to be. I did get into the English Honours School and loved collecting the books for the two years that lay ahead. After a year of living at Aberdare Hall I was allowed to take lodgings in the town and perversely lead a less raffish life than I had when I wasn't allowed to. I had become adept at climbing silently through a bathroom window at the rear of the Annexe long after the prescribed curfew. My school romances, in spite of our protestations of fidelity, had withered on the vine and I'd acquired a succession of young men, all students, but all much older than myself, old in the way that people senior to one in any institution seem and remote as well. What could it *feel* like to have graduated and to be writing a thesis, I wondered to myself, as we queued for the 1/9 seats at the cinema or stepped out, dressed in unaccustomed finery to a student ball.

My affections were never much engaged. I realised that I was a bit of a sucker for brains and status. We were all, I suppose, preoccupied with sex in the formalised way of the Fifties, which didn't seem to have developed much beyond the formalised way of the Forties. Fear was at the root of our behaviour. I remember when I was a little girl, all the children in the congregation at Alltwen Chapel had been sent out into the front courtyard after the morning service and, only half interested, hung about playing and waiting for our parents to emerge. When the big doors opened, out ran a friend's big sister, crying as she rushed past us. We were completely riveted. She had been expelled from 'the body of the Chapel'. I could tell that my mother was torn between seizing the moment to preach a huge lesson and wishing to protect my young ears. When we compared notes afterwards, we realised that all the mothers had encountered the same problem and we had all been warned of the dreadful consequences of 'Getting into Trouble'; being driven out of the congregation was the least of them. Getting into Trouble meant the end of everything that made life worthwhile. Gradually we divined that Trouble was something to do with having babies. I noticed as well that when we walked home late at night after a concert in Pontardawe on the little dirt track leading to The Graig there were lights and noise in the houses where the Bad Women lived and that was something to do with Babies (and with Drink) and *those* women were never to *get on* in the world either.

By the time we'd got it all worked out we knew quite clearly that getting pregnant was the worst thing that could befall us. The girls were threatened with a lifetime behind the counter at Woolworth's and the young men knew that their contribution towards such a fate ensured that they would become providers, working at the most boring jobs imaginable while remaining chained in a dutiful and probably loveless marriage. Nothing much occurred to change this precautionary approach to life. Condoms were not a hundred per cent reliable, 'proper' contraception was available only to the legally married, so the Act was something that belonged only within marriage. In the horrible phrase of the day, 'anticipating marriage' was at best foolish and usually disastrous. Divorce was unheard of, so a marriage too hastily entered into for the sake of respectable regular sex could lead to a lifetime of duty and resentment unless there was a case of true love. What did we know of True Love at our age, we were asked with no pause for an answer.

146

So as undergraduates we all drove each other half-mad and a great deal of that was hugely enjoyable. Looks were analysed, the touch of a hand pondered over. Was that accidental or deliberate? Inflections and cadences of speech were examined. Advice was sought from the sisterhood. Excitements were curiously dated, almost like the thrilling glimpse of an ankle. When avowed lust had overtaken these protracted, complex manoeuvrings, foreplay was elevated to an exquisitely tortured art form. There was always great anguish – mostly feigned – and 'if only' figured largely in the late night, usually cold collisions in dark, discreet corners of the city. I seemed to spend an inordinate amount of time bruising my lips while freezing in the outdoor tennis courts in winter.

Morals didn't enter into it; I wanted to be as bad as possible but my conditioning held me in thrall; like all my friends and contemporaries Getting into Trouble was unthinkable, unwanted pregnancy was not an option. 'He married her to get rid of her' was the Irish saying I knew and recognised. Now I was beginning to get engaged in rather the same spirit. In the absence of a driving commitment on my part, young men grew testy and impatient. For me, given my ambitions, marriage, in any foreseeable future was out of the question and the next best thing was an engagement. I correctly assumed that even in her preoccupied, frantically busy state, my mother would raise the roof if I pitched up for the weekend, betrothed, so these short-lived liaisons were a closely guarded secret, not even shared with Audrey and the rest of the girls. Since they were so secret I couldn't quite see what purpose they served anyone, save to take the heat off me by putting a temporary stop to discussions about the future.

The future. I knew what I wanted it to be and that did not include being engaged, far less married, but faced with a general refusal on the part of my young men to take my plans seriously or, even worse, their confident belief that I would never make good my escape, I did what I'd been doing all my life, I stopped talking about things that mattered most to me. I could see that this effectively put paid to real friendships let alone love affairs but I felt that my hold on my own life was too flimsy for me to be in a position to sacrifice one ounce of the resolve I had first formulated so long ago. Frustration was making me more implacable. But I liked being pursued and I liked having dancing partners. Fuelled by irritation and anger at not being understood, I thought it a fine thing to be a Belle Dame. I could even see that this wasn't attractive behaviour but I was too unhappy to be kind. Round about this time I realised something which should have given me greater pause.

I was acting again. People had obviously been right when they'd said that I lacked 'push'. It hadn't occurred to me to go to the BBC to tell them where I was and ask for a job; I'd rather supposed *they* would find *me* and indeed I ran into a director on the street one day and he sent me a script and from that point on I was in constant employment and for the time being my anxieties were quietened. Since *I* thought that actors and actresses were the most interesting, admirable people imaginable, I assumed when I was acting and generally drawing attention to myself that this would make my admirers admire me even more. And I was genuinely surprised to realise that, on the contrary, the admiration of the many diminished the regard and goodwill of those who were, or ought to be, closest to me. Faced with reactions of hostility or displays of possessiveness and what I saw to be unreasonable demands, I thought merely 'how odd' and backed off. Love affairs foundered and engagements were broken and foolishly I never took the time to consider what had emerged as a pattern of behaviour.

Work – at this stage always for the BBC – took over all my time. My brief spell with the University Dramatic Society had not been a success. I played Desdemona for David Jones, a post-graduate student who went on to teach drama in America and my Othello was a mature student who was reading Philosophy with me after training at RADA and renouncing the theatre. Peter Gyngell was good but he was a mystery to me. How could anyone give up the theatre and go into – what was it? – something I'd never heard of (Computers, did he say?). Lyndon Harris, the President of the Students' Union – a very important and dashing figure – played Iago, very well, I thought. *They* were fine and I was ill at ease and tormented because I couldn't make anything work for me. My hair (dyed blonde – quite exciting) was wrong, my dress was wrong, rehearsals felt wrong, *I* felt wrong and didn't know enough to make myself right.

It was absurd but I had still not seen any theatre that I truly admired. When as a schoolgirl I won the National Eisteddfod in Colwyn Bay I had made my mother take me to a performance at the small seaside theatre. I *saw* the leading man and leading lady in the street, looking actorish – I envied the remnants of stage make-up still visible on their faces. His camel coat, casually draped over his shoulders may have been a bit of a cliché even then, but I loved the look. I tried to love the performance but I couldn't. The scenery was awful, the actors were far too actorish. I was embarrassed.

Worse, there had been a charabanc trip to Stratford-on-Avon to see *Hamlet* with a famous dancer in the leading part. I was beside myself with excitement and in the event sat there, pressing back into my seat, embarrassed again and unable to admire anything, especially not the famous dancer (this time the scenery seemed almost *too* good). The dancer leapt about a lot. Now, in Othello, I was embarrassing *myself* with my own inadequacy. I had a Platonic idea of 'Theatre' and so far hadn't seen or taken part in anything approaching it.

It was a puzzle and I was intent on solving it but obviously I needed help. I needed RADA, I thought longingly. Meanwhile, at the BBC, I was receiving lots of help from everyone. Well, almost everyone. I was slowly learning a little diplomacy and how to adapt to different directors but I was also learning that I had an uncontrollable resistance to being directed in what I considered the 'wrong' direction. A quiet, biddable girl, the last thing I wanted was to make trouble and I was only too aware that I was in no position to antagonise my employers. Also, my own lack of experience was perfectly clear to me so I was horrified by what occurred when I had a second opportunity to play *Blodeuwedd* for one of the radio directors who was mounting it in a theatre for a summer festival.

When I was offered the part I had an immense feeling of everything coming out right after all. Like all good things, it was meant. I *should* have played it for Eic when I was fifteen but maybe that had been too young and now, surely, I was the right age at eighteen and I'd had time to think about the part and Eic was pleased and Saunders Lewis himself sent me a message and planned to come and see me. The press was interested because of the scandal of the censorship when I was younger. This was important and I knew how to play the part. I was *sure* that although this hadn't been written for me I was a natural Saunders Lewis heroine.

The director and I locked horns almost at once. I hated his ideas for the play and especially for Blodeuwedd herself. I tried to compromise and failed. I could scarcely believe it was happening when I took the script, walked over to my director, put it in his hands and told him quietly to find someone else with whom to do the play and I quit. I think he was pleased to lose me and I was on the bus to my parents' place outside Cardiff before the tears came and kept coming after I'd descended from the bus and walked a mile down the deserted country road on the most beautiful sun-drenched afternoon. In the dining room I went to the huge armchair, curled up and wept and wept until I fell asleep.

I never explained what had happened to anyone, least of all the press. I was heartbroken, disappointed, but also a little unnerved by my own intransigence. This could have serious consequences for me in and outside the BBC but I consoled myself with the knowledge that I couldn't have done differently. '*Reculer pour mieux sauter*,' I repeated to myself. I had a genuine contempt for the director's ability and I resolved to ride out the débâcle and trust that the doors of the BBC wouldn't be closed against me. They weren't. I never worked for him again but when I joined the Repertory Company soon afterwards and anxiously scanned the board every Monday I saw that enough people had engaged me for their shows to ensure my continuing place in the Company. All the same, it had been an unsettling, worrying summer – and I still hadn't met the great Saunders Lewis, 'the Garbo of Wales' as the *Western Mail* rather inappropriately called him.

It should have worried me more, this lack of enthusiasm I felt for most of the acting I saw, but it didn't overly concern me. Somewhere, I felt sure, there were people doing what I would think of as wonderful things. (I wasn't at all supercilious in the manner of undergraduates.) I really wanted to like, to admire and it surprised me when, for example, I couldn't warm to D.W. Griffith's *Intolerance*, hailed as a masterpiece at the University Film Society and I was relieved beyond measure to encounter and love Ingmar Bergman in our one foreign movie house in Roath. The Hollywood of the Fifties dampened my spirits also and it was wonderful to discover that there was another world inhabited by foreign movie actors who looked just like people, only more so.

Smart West End actors (a specific genus in those days) passed through Cardiff on their way to London and I wasn't lucky enough to see anything inspiring until, one afternoon, an actor playing in Cardiff came to visit us at the University. The biggest lecture hall was crammed to bursting and it wasn't full of people who had come to cheer. The received wisdom of the day was that Donald Wolfit was a 'Ham' actor. Stories abounded about his self-centred productions where he hogged the centre of the stage while the rest of the company languished in the gloom on the sidelines. He was old-fashioned, said the Dramatic Society luminaries, his style of acting was passé. I didn't know what to expect as I sat there, waiting.

The door on to the bare dais opened and in walked a florid complexioned gentleman in a pin-striped business suit, followed by a brisk little lady with a somewhat fixed jolly smile on a face surmounted by a perky hat. She must be Rosalind Iden, his wife. They looked nothing *like* actors, I thought disappointedly. Then he began to speak; beautiful voice – easy to hear right at the back where I was perched. He talked about *Tamburlaine* briefly. The overhead light didn't do much to augment the fading winter light outside the big windows. I couldn't get over his ordinary appearance.

Then without any warning, he was acting Tamburlaine. Those that had come to mock began to pay attention. The silence was profound as he began to recite, 'Ah, fair Zenocrate, divine Zenocrate! Fair is too foul an epithet for thee', stocky in his business suit, Miss Iden standing by. Making no effort to charm, he took us all by the hand and gave us an unforgettable experience. 'Old fashioned', 'ham', 'modern', 'contemporary' were meaningless adjectives to apply to something that clearly was the Real Thing. At the end of the performance he acknowledged the tumultuous reception and was gone, striding out rapidly and nimbly, leaving his still-smiling wife to scurry after him as best she could. The artist wasn't much of a gent, I thought, even as I savoured the wonder of the afternoon. It was good to see the abashed faces in the auditorium which he had conquered.

A few months later I was made despondent by a conversation I overheard among those same bright, young men of the Dramatic Society who had been cowed and abashed that day by the quality of Wolfit's acting. 'Ah well,' said one, 'it's an old-fashioned style, of course.' Brutes, I thought, realising the fearful tyranny of fashion.

That was the best acting I saw while I was an undergraduate and for the rest of the time had to content myself with reading about actors whom I imagined to be wonderful. Edith Evans whom I'd never seen was still my favourite and I read and re-read her autobiography and her notices and the parts she played until I imagined I could hear her voice.

Chapter Eighteen

My workload at the BBC increased and it became apparent that some kind of plan had to be formulated. Moelwyn Merchant had been my first tutor when I entered the Honours School. He became an ally. He shared my opinion of myself in *Othello*. 'Oh, you poor dear,' he exclaimed the morning after the first performance, 'that hair! That pink dress! You looked like a meringue.' Pleased and maybe surprised that I took this in good part and agreed with him, he threw me a crumb. 'On the whole *not* good but that is exactly the way to play the willow scene.' He knew that I was wearing a track between the back door of the University and the front door of the BBC. He also knew and approved my intention of going into the theatre and understood that I really did need to graduate for my parents' sake. He drew up a plan for me and said, 'Now, this is the work you *must* do; these are the essays you *must* write and this is the minimum attendance below which you *cannot* fall. Let's see how you get on.'

Well, I got on. Just. There were some awful moments. By now I was working as a 'relief' announcer as well as acting and this meant that I opened the station very early in the morning and closed it late at night after the Epilogue and in between did a lot of the jobs that no one else wanted. I was never paid much for what was a prodigious amount of work. Iris Evans who wrote the cheques at the BBC used to say,

'Having your name in the *Radio Times* is worth £1,000 per year. No dear, I can't pay you more money.' It never bothered me. I always seemed to have enough money but I was never aware of having lots more than my fellow students. Some of my friends were rather wealthy. I bought books, as usual, and began to buy a few smart clothes as well.

I loved presentation work. When I began I was a well covered ten stone three, which was about right for my five foot, seven and three-quarter inches. Within months I was eight stone, the result of living in a permanent state of high anxiety (which I loved). I had always been dreamy – never wore a watch, never knew what day it was – and now I had to alter completely because from the moment I sat at my console in the tiny continuity suite, I was in control of everything that went out over the air, from my studio, and from all the other studios all over Wales and England. The least adept person imaginable, I had three turntables to operate; one on either side of my central control 'pot' (microphone control) and one large one on which I played daily 'soaps' or programmes lasting twenty minutes. Minutes and seconds had to be calculated precisely. I had to learn to write announcements that would last exactly the required number of seconds before I faded myself out and brought up another studio. It was a nightmare.

Morfydd Mason-Lewis, a wonderful broadcaster and a senior announcer, the best-known voice in Wales, was teaching me the ropes one day and I was thinking that this was a terrible venture, best forgotten, when she said, 'All right, I'm off. Take the next shift', and left the room. My thumping heart moved high into my chest and stayed there. My damp hands slipped on the controls as I frantically added and subtracted and scribbled. Occasionally through the glass panel on my right I saw my engineer, grinning broadly. I had no sense that anyone was listening to me but my mother had heard my voice and stopped in her tracks, horrified. 'Oh, it was terrible', she said. 'I kept expecting everything to go wrong.'

I would wake up at night convinced that I'd announced the wrong programme or allowed everything to over-run and had been late joining the Nine O'clock News – the worst crime imaginable. Becoming a radio actress had been a breeze compared with the rigours of being engaged as an announcer. It was assumed that one was fluently bi-lingual and decent at one other European language and canny with foreign words in general. Every broadcast sound passed through the little Continuity Studio so announcers were expected to be deft with the turntables and their controlling knobs, familiar with the pronunciation sheets that came in from London each day, careful at noting timing of programmes or the length of recordings and tactful with one's own announcements or one's filling in of unexpected gaps so that one programme seamlessly fed into the next. Technical mistakes were unacceptable. 'Kerfuffles', as the Head of Continuity called them – one's own, or hitches occurring in studios – were carefully logged and explanations and excuses noted. The Kerfuffle Column was amazingly empty considering that we were all on the air live most of the time.

The BBC was proud of its technical near-perfection and the rest of us were expected to keep up. Over-running was a cardinal sin. Having to fade out a programme in order to re-join the schedule on time or link up with London or Scotland was embarrassing in the extreme and somehow became a Continuity error. It was expected that we should exert a tight grip on everyone's activities. The tension was killing. I had to strain every nerve to exert more care than ever before in my slap-dash life.

And that was just the beginning; there was Attitude to cope with. One had to speak with authority tempered with a neutral friendliness – not *too* distant, be human; not too chummy, you're *not* anyone's friend, you're entering someone's home and you are expected to be one hundred per cent reliable, but remember always that you don't know what is *happening* in the home, don't impose a mood on them. You are speaking to millions and you are speaking to one or two people. Be natural. Being 'natural' wiped me out and I ached all over at the end of a shift.

Advancing to the status of news reader was even worse and my first time out – twenty-five minutes of terror in English and Welsh – half prepared and half unseen was listened to everywhere in the building. The ordeal was made worse by the sympathy and good wishes that came my way as I left Tom Richards, the editor, in the news room and raced back to my studio, clutching what there was of the news bulletin (extra bits arrived when we were on the air). Everyone knew that it was a major hurdle to get over. I was just eighteen and I had added two years to my age in order to be considered for the job. As I switched myself on to the air, identified the station and, taking a deep breath, forced a smile on to my face and said 'Here is the six o'clock news,' I'd wished I'd never been born. Twenty-four minutes and ten seconds later I was reading the last story – one I'd never seen – with one eye on the second hand and, coming into harbour at twenty-four minutes and fifty seconds, reached for my previously written announcement for the next programme, timed and checked before the News began. Then I switched through to another studio, waited for the programme to begin and laid my head on the desk among the mountain of discarded bits of papers. Looking up, I saw the engineer next door raise his fists in a victory salute. I felt as though I had climbed a mountain.

There had been no mistakes but that was taken for granted; there was more Attitude to absorb. Light hearted news stories were not to be presented as 'jokes', they were to be presented to the listener 'clean'. People weren't supposed to be *made* to laugh. Serious or tragic items were not to be dramatised or sentimentalised or sensationalised, the 'appropriate' tone had to be found. One had to get a move on without ever seeming to hurry, nor should it ever be apparent that one was stretching an item to fill in time. The list of do's and don't's was endless. At the post-mortem of my maiden voyage it was Attitude that took up most of the time. It was a bit like an acting job – trying to be the sort of person that people wanted in their homes. The chief note to me was 'No acting' and I thought it better not to reveal that I was going to have to act 'no acting' if I was going to make a go of this complicated job which I grew to love. I was very well taught by Morfydd Mason-Lewis and her deputy Harvard Gregory and I didn't ever make a mistake or 'fluff' during a news bulletin. My parents thought I'd had a personality change and for the first time I think my grandmother was impressed.

Of course I made some awful mistakes along the way, some so bad that they got me suspended. One of my nastiest moments in the studio occurred when, after having started the Epilogue disc in a tired state one night, I then had to lean over it to read the duration time. Revolving my head gently in time to its slow circling of the turntable, my chiffon scarf caught in the special rod that held the playing-arm steady. With one hand I flapped wildly at the window to the engineer's cubicle as my face was slowly and relentlessly drawn down towards the turntable. As I tried to hold steady, keeping disaster at bay until the last possible moment, I feverishly tried to compose in my head an announcement that would explain the horrible noise and the untimely end of the Epilogue that was about to occur at any moment. 'We must apologise to listeners but the Epilogue just ate my scarf.' Hardly. The engineer happened to look up and, seeing my unnaturally still head and an agitated arm, stampeded out of his little studio, through my ante-room, crashing into the studio just in time to cut me free and gently unpick the chiffon from the machine. 'Now, believe it or not, Siân,' he said, 'that's never happened before!' The engineers were my friends and saviours which was just as well.

I had by now joined an Arts Council Theatre Company, dedicated to establishing a Welsh speaking National Theatre. Raymond Edwards, who was later to become the first principal of the Welsh College of Music and Drama, was our young director of *Uncle Vanya* in which I played Elena. There weren't enough 'real' theatres in Wales so we toured for a year, all over the country, playing in buildings that were more or less the right size and more or less suitable.

Waking one morning in my flat in Roath Park, very tired after a one-night stand of *Uncle Vanya*, goodness knows where (I very rarely knew exactly *where* we were playing), I reached out an arm and turned on the radio in time to hear a London voice saying, '. . . and now we hand you over to Siân Phillips in Cardiff.' Nothing happened for a moment, then with one bound, collecting my mac and shoes on the way, I was in the street running towards the main road in my pyjamas. It was early and the roads were deserted; a solitary car happened along and the driver, seeing my desperate face, stopped and rushed me to the BBC, rather enjoying the drama (which I was not).

Fortunately, Cardiff is a compact city and, with no traffic on the road, I was in my chair within twelve minutes and switching off Bow Bells which had been playing over and over again since the London hand-over. Now, the Bow Bells record was used as a filler but *never* for more than twenty seconds. That was a Rule. The outbreak of World War III might just justify ten minutes of bells – might, but probably not. I switched on my microphone and announced, 'We must apologise to listeners for . . . [thinks] . . . a technical fault at the transmitter,' I lied. I maligned the engineering department. I was an outcast. The phone didn't stop for hours. By ten o'clock I was on the carpet in the Alun Oldfield Davies Suite where I had never before set foot and never would again. I think the august Reithian figure of the Head of Welsh Programmes may have wanted to see what sort of creature could commit such a crime. My suspension didn't last long and I was soon back in the bosom of a forgiving bunch of engineers.

I loved those days. The hours were long and the work was very demanding. I began to travel with the BBC Orchestra on outside broadcasts, writing their scripts and timing the programmes, and meeting the artists from London and taking care of them. Our orchestra did OBs of Concert Hour and

Music of the Masters from halls and chapels all over the valleys near Cardiff and artists were sometimes a little taken aback by the primitive conditions. I remember wondering whether one artist would be able to do the show as she lay on the floor of the shabby vestry in a none too glamorous concert frock while her worried husband poured warm oil into her ear (it seemed she was a martyr to pains in her cranial passages). When she struggled to her feet and began to sing I was stupefied. I was no expert but this was surely a *major* voice. Why wasn't she a star? I looked up her name again in order to give her a terrific back-announcement. 'You have been listening to . . .' – Joan Sutherland – surely she deserved better than a village chapel in the back of beyond.

Rae Jenkins, the conductor, was lovely and always impatient. 'Where's that bloody girl?' ringing round the corridors was my cue to appear with my clipboard and everything he might need to know at my fingertips. Only once did I let him down. The visiting soprano was about to reach for an inadvisable high note and Rae leaned forward over the podium and I – miles away in a reverie – was too slow to switch off the mic' as Rae hissed at the first violins urgently, and '*Drown 'er, boys*!' went out over the air. He didn't speak to me for a week.

I was engrossed in this world and I was finding enough time on the tour of *Uncle Vanya* to be able to put some of my notions about acting into practice. Sometimes I was, I thought, almost getting there. Mostly, not. In spite of this, I was coming in for a great deal of flattering attention.

I wrote my English essays in the Continuity Suite and it showed. My new tutor was S.L. Bethel. 'Pretty lousy,' he said, smiling sweetly as he returned to me the first of my 'BBC' essays for him. Oh help. My worst mark ever. What to do? Briefed by Moelwyn, he also became a friend. He and his wife invited me to tea and outlined a strategy for me. I was terminally tired and, to further complicate things, I had become 'properly', publicly, engaged. 'You're far too young,' said everyone. My fiancé, Don, was a post-graduate student whom I'd known off and on since I came up. I had also been on holiday with him. My mother had been thoroughly against my proposed trip to Sweden with two young men from the University, Don and his friend, Ray. I was nineteen and they were older. I'd first seen Don playing Troilus in *Troilus and Cressida* at College. He was a good actor, handsome, neat, incredibly well-organised, mad about cricket. I found him so – capable that I thought of him as belonging to an older generation altogether. He seemed to know what he was doing and for a brief while I enjoyed believing him when he said he knew what I should be doing. Ahead of him lay two years of National Service and another couple of years in Paris completing his doctorate. You must be *amazingly* clever, I thought, looking at him sideways as we walked along Queen Street.

My parents were guarded in their response when we returned from Sweden somewhat closer than we'd been when we departed. They liked and respected Don but they had Doubts. So did Don's parents. This was why they'd been reluctant to let us go off for a summer in Scandinavia. Although I'd asked permission I'd been determined to go. I could fund the journey myself and the young men were respectable and so were my prospective hosts, friends of Ray's. Their estate was beautiful and – well, there was nothing she could put her finger on but my mother felt it was Wrong and would lead to Trouble but she couldn't think of a way of forbidding the trip without saying something coarse and I enjoyed her discomfiture.

For the first time I was going to do something that had no obvious advantageous outcome. My mother was better off than she had ever been but holidays still didn't enter into her scheme of things. Of course, they didn't enter into mine either. When I said, 'I'm going to Sweden for the summer' I felt as though it was someone else talking and unreasonably I pretended to my mother that I thought taking the summer off was a perfectly natural thing for me to do. I blamed her for the fact that I was secretly appalled by the waste of working time and by the daring company I'd chosen. She brooded silently, spoke little, and glowered at me when our eyes met. I made as if I didn't notice and enjoyed infuriating her.

It was difficult for my parents. They had moved away from their families. Life near the big city was very different from life at 'Home'. There was no telephone on the farm. (Her brother's telephone was never used for chatting.) They were isolated; there were no neighbours. There was no village with its terms of reference and clear guidelines for behaviour. My parents didn't quite know what kind of life I was leading. They were adrift without a map and so was I to a certain extent, but I wanted to make a new map for myself. Defiantly I drew a line from Wales to Sweden.

Sweden was beautiful beyond my imagining and on one of the long summer nights I became engaged. Together with Ray, Don and I spent the idyllic summer walking and idling and dozing through the days, eating delicious food. We were there for the crayfish season and went to Kräftor parties that went on late into the night – huge trestle tables piled high with red crayfish set up under the trees and we were fed a sip of schnapps between each bite of crayfish. It never got really dark at night and we scarcely slept. The schnapps and the party atmosphere and the long lilac nights were a heady combination. Don and I grew closer and closer and what could be more delightful than to arrive at an understanding in such a romantic situation. He was not only attractive and charming, he took care of me when the idyll ended and I became ill on the long journey home. We were in love by the time we returned to Wales and had it not been for my ambition – conveniently forgotten during the romantic holiday – there was no reason why our proposed marriage shouldn't have turned out well. He was everything a normal woman could want in a husband.

After I returned I tried not to spoil our happiness with thoughts of how this marriage could accommodate my plans for myself, plans which hadn't changed at all but which appeared unrealistic to everyone except me. I hid my head in the sand. I hadn't told my mother anything much on my return but now, a few months later, I was about to become publicly, officially engaged, with a ring – and presents – my parents had to be told about it. I didn't want to tell them and was filled with apprehension.

Their reaction was everything I feared. They were taken aback. There was silence. Why, I thought, couldn't they just say 'How wonderful! Congratulations'? The fact that I myself was filled with anxiety was utterly beside the point. My fiancé-to-be was everything they could have wished – clever, brilliant, handsome, sober, reliable – and they didn't want it to happen. I could tell. I was furious. I knew from the way my mother's remarks were heading that she was trying to raise the question of my possible pregnancy. Did I *have* to get married was the question she couldn't bring herself to say and I wanted to smash crockery, I was so enraged. How dare she pry into my private life and how could she think I could be so *stupid*. Even as I sat looking at the floor or paced about looking everywhere except at them I understood that they were trying to articulate the fears that were running riot in me.

Understanding how unreasonably I was behaving did not prevent me from becoming even more contrary. I had tapped into a vein of resentment against my mother that threatened to engulf me. Engagements logically lead to weddings. Where did a wedding fit into my plans? It didn't. It couldn't. The moment my mother pointed out this problem, the engagement was determinedly *on*. The future might never arrive. My fiancé went to Paris to write his doctorate and I missed him and moped and worked and tried not to think of the problems I was laying up for myself.

After graduating I would need a miracle to get me out of Wales and headed for the Theatre and I didn't know anyone who had managed it. It hadn't come to my ears that a girl from Aberystwyth University had already done the seemingly impossible and was *in* the theatre in England. Rachel Roberts from Swansea was bold; she was a free spirit; she took all her clothes off in public – in *Aberystwyth*, such a stiflingly respectable non-conformist heap in those days that the odd swear word would have been enough to damn her as a loose woman. The enormity of Rachel's behaviour seemed to have paralysed the authorities. She wasn't sent down but she was talked about in hushed tones for years after in the Principality. But just when I needed her most, her fame had not spread south to Cardiff and when it did, it merely depressed me.

If that was *it*; if that was what it took then I was *never* going to be able to behave like an actress. I couldn't even *look* like one. The leading lights of the University Dramatic Society were outstandingly good-looking and very *noticeable*. They were English-speaking with voices that carried effortlessly across the Union dining room. They always seemed to be at the centre of a merry throng, they tossed their heads and laughed and were clever with clothes. My wardrobe was still full of mistakes which I had to live with. All the things I needed and wanted were hideously expensive and most of them were unavailable in Cardiff.

I tried not to think of Christian Dior and concentrated on my real problems which were multiplying as the weeks went by. I was approaching the end of my time at the University; one year to go and Moelwyn called me in for one of his infrequent but uncomfortably worrying chats. We sat in a garden, I on a swing, and I knew I wasn't going to enjoy the ensuing half-hour. 'Your life', he began. 'I don't think you've given enough thought to your engagement and what it is that will quite reasonably be required of you.' He was going to be the Reverend. He doubted whether I was going to be able to do the Right Thing. Had I considered my vocation? Better to stop now than create havoc later. Did I realise what a fine, sensitive person I'd become involved with?

I was accustomed to feeling like a victim and now he was making me feel like the Witch of Endor and I didn't like that at all. I couldn't tell him that I was feeble-minded enough to dread upsetting the apple cart almost more than I dreaded messing up two lives. And why me? Why wasn't he having this conversation with my fiancé? I looked glum and said nothing much.

'Please consider carefully,' he said pleasantly enough. 'Now – work,' he said, to my relief. 'I am assuming that you are not prepared to give up your position in the Arts Council Company. Nor, I take it, would you want to stop working at the BBC. Nor,' he went on as I made to speak, 'do I think you should.' That surprised me; I'd been expecting a sophisticated version of the Sally Tŷmawr lecture that I'd been hearing since I was ten. 'You now have to make a choice,' he went on. 'Having considered your work for me I think there is a chance that were you to concentrate on your work for the whole of next year, to the exclusion of everything else, you could – just could – do well enough to get a First. If you continue with your outside work then you will not. This is the moment to choose what you want.' It was horribly grown-up; actions to choose, consequences to accept.

Then he closed that conversation and we talked of other things and he shocked me into laughter as he spoke of a recent Shakespeare performance on film, almost universally praised, which he had found particularly brainless and appalling. We said goodbye and I went to visit my parents feeling more ill at ease than usual. Whatever my choice I doubted that it would please my mother; good work at the University and marriage. No marriage, possibly a bad result and a career. Career? That was completely unknown territory – every chance of total failure. As usual I dithered and confided in no one.

Chapter Nineteen

S o I embarked on what were to be my last few years in
Wales and the most difficult to account for. The sequence
of events had no logic, no shape, no meaning for me. Maybe I
had dug myself into a hole so deep that I stopped reviewing
my scanty escape routes and more than possibly, as I floundered mindlessly from one month to the next, I became
increasingly reluctant to confront my behaviour except in
isolated, appalled moments, quickly shaken off and put aside.
At nineteen I looked back at the child and the young girl who
had lain in bed and reviewed the contents of the day just past,
assessing and judging or approving and tidying up before
composedly going to sleep. I had cleaned my house each day
and now I was depressed to see how far I had fallen from
grace – grace gone for good, it seemed, as I flung myself into
an exhausted, comatose state or read until the book fell from
my fingers and woke in the bright lights of morning and my
bedside lamp.

It was as though, after years of focused behaviour, of
keeping true to my private resolves, of making sacrifices
where necessary and living a life the nature of which was
dictated by discipline and feeling the constant pleasure of
moving forward in the right direction – knowing I was doing
the right thing and *approving* of myself – now I became
childish and thoughtless and foolish and I *dis*approved of
myself and was miserable. So I slipped and floundered and

stumbled and kept my head above water – just. I didn't know and I didn't dare discover why I was so angry with my mother for example, but it was clear that relations between us took an ugly, inexplicably violent turn.

By this time, I had taken lodgings in Richmond Road with a Mrs Lewis. My home was a large front room in her house where she lived as a widow with her two grown-up sons who lived upstairs while she and I occupied the ground floor and shared her bathroom. She fed me in the cosy back living room next to the kitchen and I can't imagine that she profited at all during my two years with her because she overhauled my slapdash eating habits (mostly cigarettes with tiny amounts of food in between packets) and saw to it that I ate two huge 'proper' meals daily during the week and three meals a day at weekends, charging me £2.25 for board and lodging. She was white-haired and pink and white complexioned, inclined to stoutness and in manner the softest spoken, most gentle person I had ever been close to and we *were* close; she was happy to have a daughter-figure in whom to confide and to fuss over and I was delighted to find in myself a simple, uncomplicated, affectionate daughter.

We lived in perfect harmony in spite of the fact that she was a fervent spiritualist trying, and never succeeding, in her efforts to persuade me along to a 'meeting'. That is until, on a sunny, spring day in Cardiff, every garden over-stuffed with daffodils, I found myself in a little parlour where a cheerful little medium described in detail the layout and contents of the announcer's suite in the BBC in Cardiff. Then she seemed to be describing a much bigger broadcasting house, which was strange to me because at that time I had never worked at Bush House in London. I wish that I had known then that the doorway she described, flanked by two stone figures, was 62 Gower Street in London, the home of the Royal Academy of Dramatic Art. As it was, I wondered, after a moment's surprised pause, how she knew about the Continuity Suite, a place seldom visited even by the staff of the

BBC, and then dismissed her sympathetic warnings of a 'Bad Time' to come before the 'Good Time', when I would enter the building with the big stone figures at the door. 'Well, what did you think to her?' asked Mrs Lewis as we walked to the bus stop. 'Miss-us Lewis,' I said, giving her an affectionate squeeze. We each shook our heads smiling at the other's limited sensibilities.

On other matters we agreed and I, who had never confided anything in anyone, enjoyed our chats – heavily censored on my part – about Boys and Food and Frocks and she told me about her wonderfully happy marriage. 'He was such a good man – never –' whispering now, '*bothered* me too much. You know . . .' I was so enjoying my dear daughter role that I, who couldn't imagine anything better than to be constantly bothered, nodded enthusiastically. She made it easy for me to be thoroughly 'nice', I hoped that she would never know what a fiend I could be.

The academic year drew to a close and I stopped working in order to prepare for the Honours exam. Don came home for a holiday and there were rumblings of discontent on his part over my acting plans for the summer. These deepened into arguments about the future – our future; more specifically my future as a wife. Well, of course, I *had* no future as a wife on a campus – in Cardiff or anywhere. I began to inch the conversations around to this, making tentative noises about the possibility that a mistake had been made and that maybe we should call the whole thing off. (I had found that this was the usual progression of events and although it always made me sad for a while, well, it wasn't the end of the world) but events did not follow this course and I began to see that I was not going to be allowed off the hook with a few tears of regret. He was angry and hurt and terribly, terribly upset and intent on holding me to my side of the bargain.

I was alarmed. The situation had escalated in no time at all from a difficult one, fraught with future problems, into a compelling, very present crisis with no apparent solution.

Exams were looming. Even mild spoken Mrs Lewis (who had seen her own schoolteacher son through his exams) said, 'I hope you're not going to be seeing each other during the next few weeks.' My mother, with a flash of her old, confident conviction said, 'You stay at home, alone and SWOT for the next few weeks.' 'Few' weeks were negotiated down to two weeks and, feeling hard done by, I grimly settled down to a fortnight of cramming against the two weeks of exams which followed. Normally this would be something to be enjoyed but now, thoroughly un-nerved by the turn of events, I was rattled. However, I managed to pull myself together and my temperament came to the rescue and, at my best in a tight spot, I kept my head and organised myself back on track. Exams began well and I got into the swing of things and even coped well with the dreaded *Beowulf* and the other Language papers. My best paper was metaphysical poetry and the night before the exam I heaved a sigh of relief as I flicked through the texts with which I was truly familiar. Tomorrow was going to be a good day, my best, my easiest day. And we were almost at the end.

There was a tap at my window. It was Don. He'd not been able to keep to our arrangement that I should be left alone for the two weeks of exams. But he wouldn't stay long he said. There were just a few things bothering him. Before we knew it we were in the thick of a huge, emotional discussion about my intentions, my future, our future. Hours went by. Mrs Lewis tapped at the door. Normal bedtime had arrived. Then her son looked in to the room and retreated. It seemed that nothing could halt this awful circular argument. There was a big bag of cherries at my side which I mistook for an ashtray. I chain-smoked and ate dirty cherries covered in damp ash and cried and lost my temper and finally in the early hours of the morning we parted and I spent the few remaining hours throwing up in the bathroom.

In the morning I managed to make it to the examination

170

hall in time but, fighting waves of nausea, did very little writing. I kept thinking I would have to leave and be sick but that would mean I couldn't return and somehow I remained in the room hoping I would, miraculously, feel better. I didn't and I left the building hardly able to believe my ill fortune. And as I began to recover, misery and disappointment were replaced by outrage that he could have treated me so badly in a situation which he of all people should have understood.

The sense of outrage never went away but we never spoke of this awful night and its consequences for me. He must have felt guilty. It cost me dear, though, in the event it was one of those years which happen from time to time when the marking was so strict that people dropped a class below the one expected and there were a few Thirds and even Unclassifieds. There was a bit of a rumpus and complaints were made and then, as usual, the fuss died down. Moelwyn mourned my Lower Second (my mother couldn't bring herself to speak about it). I didn't tell him or my mother that I'd fatally missed out an entire paper.

It was the first time in my life that I'd not met or exceeded the expectations of those closest to me and while I did not enjoy the sensation of failure it was so much a part of the malaise within me that I experienced not a sharp regret at a moment of opportunity missed, but a resigned dull disappointment each time I thought about it. And every time I thought of my engagement I *did* think about it and of my weakness that night during exams. *Why* had I not been able to put my foot down and refuse to get drawn into a row? It should have been a simple matter to postpone the argument and let Mrs Lewis show him the door. I would have been within my rights at that moment, during the most testing week of any student's career. This was *my* time. *My* future.

What had happened was that for the first time I was being called to account. This relationship was not going to fade away gently and regretfully it was clear that I was going to have to answer for my behaviour. I had summoned up feelings I couldn't control in a person who was not inclined to be fobbed off by some vague expression of regret. And I felt guilty. It was my own lax behaviour, my sentimentality, my lack of responsibility which had led to a situation where I stood bereft of any sense of what was due to me; I felt as though through my bad behaviour I'd forfeited my own rights and everywhere I looked a door seemed to close. I was trapped and full of regret; mutinous and resentful at the same time.

Confiding in no one, I went back to work at the BBC and was actually happy while I was there. I couldn't accept the possibility that maybe this was the only way I could be happy – at work. It seemed so unwomanly to say outright that work was so much more significant than my emotional life. My mother seemed to be on the brink of saying something of the sort whenever the conversation came round to marriage, the position of women or my future. I headed her off. I didn't want that said aloud. What was it about me that made all those who cared most for me, who wanted to help me, shake their heads, smile ruefully and say, 'Sorry but it's not for you'? Childishly I wanted everything. 'I want. I want. I want. Why *not* me?' And to what end was I supposed to be renouncing my private life? I was marooned with no prospects of getting away, getting on.

In the middle of this confusion I decided to see through a project I'd undertaken earlier. Philosophy had become my favourite subject and I'd managed to get into the Honours School. There were only three of us and Professor de Selincourt really resisted taking on a woman, but I'd worn him down and now I wanted to complete a Philosophy degree. It seemed ludicrous to take on what was really another diversion but in fact it was the only sensible thing I did during this period and it afforded me endless solace and enjoyment. The patterns of logic were so beautifully inevitable and so *manageable*. While I tried to follow complex arguments, time stopped and life – horrible, messy life – was excluded for a while. In a year I was to marry – all discussion on this subject had been exhausted. My life seemed fixed, but I didn't really believe it.

Chapter Twenty

If I'd worked hard before it was as nothing compared to the regime I now set myself. *Uncle Vanya* was still touring. We travelled the Welsh countryside by special bus and it was evident that the Welsh appetite for drama was unquenchable. We were paid very little, were often cold and damp but Nesta Harris of the Welsh Arts Council did her level best to look after us and I felt very lucky to be experiencing a kind of theatre which I suspected had long died out elsewhere. Some weeks, we were literally barn-storming, arriving in a village in the late afternoon, unpacking our costumes, the actresses fitting up our, by now, ramshackle scenery and unloading furniture, the actors and stage manager running round the shops, the post office and the pub (men only here, of course) to remind people that we had arrived.

I loved being an Actress in Town. It felt great to be striding down the deserted main street of a village, knowing that in a few hours' time everyone would be crowding into the little hall to watch the play. Two muffled, capped, old men leaned on the windowsill of the village store smoking their pipes and one of them removed his pipe to say to his friend in Welsh as Maggie John and I passed by in the deserted street, 'Duw – there's a pair of high-steppers for you!' I glowed. It was true! In my yellow jersey and my red shoes, blue skirt swinging, I felt like a thoroughbred pony.

At 7.30 p.m. miraculously, as if from nowhere, there was

an audience which was augmented during Act I with people from outlying farms arriving after milking was done. Playing in the country was very different from playing in town. It was pretty certain that Chekhov had never been given in some of the halls and chapel vestries where we were touring and the play which had previously been respectfully received and well liked now provoked gales of laughter and loud comments which startled me at first, but which I quickly became used to and indeed grew to like. I hadn't known that Chekhov was supposed to be so funny but this felt all right. The response was artless and inhibited, never coarse or mindless. We were of course acting in Welsh and that Chekov world which all actors love to inhabit for the few hours allotted to them each night had never seemed so seductive, so convincing as it was then, played in my own language.

I was Elena and some nights I was good, I could tell I was good but I didn't know why and I couldn't reproduce my better performances. Some nights I was painfully aware that I was bad and I couldn't put things right. The harder I tried, the worse I became. These were awful nights and afterwards I lay awake feeling as if the whole point of my existence was disappearing. I did all the wrong things to try to remedy matters; I tried and tried and strained and struggled and read Stanislavsky and tried to implement his exercises and got everything wrong. I read books about actors long dead. I filled exercise books with notes, took advice from anyone, anywhere, kept a journal which mostly charted and analysed my failures. Praise was no help at all, I simply didn't believe it. I *knew* I was all over the place. I prayed for help to turn the corner into some kind of competence. I longed to be efficient. I longed to be *professional*. It was a sacred word. Once I was a professional most of my problems would solve themselves, I thought. Infrequently, but often enough to save me from going mad, I did what I knew to be a bit of good acting. On these occasions the relief was so great that afterwards I could not imagine feeling happier.

Towards the end of *Uncle Vanya* I became ill and played

through what was later diagnosed as pleurisy. I still didn't know how ill you were supposed to be before you stopped working. I had read that *real* actors worked no matter how ill they were and after the tour finished and I lay alone in my room in the flat I was now sharing with friends in Cardiff, I took my medicine and drifted in and out of a sick sleep and for the first time in ages I was pleased with myself.

I recovered and in no time was back at work, mainly at the BBC, taking care to keep well up to date with Philosophy, which wasn't difficult. The BBC was claiming more and more of my time and attention. I was deeply fond of the institution where I had, more or less, grown up. I loved the studios and the storerooms and the library and the staff, some of whom had been there since the early days of broadcasting. The Commissionaire had 'seen *everyone* come and go, Siân'. He told me that once, during a live drama performance many, many years ago, he'd brought a cart horse in through the big front door, turned left past the front desk, then right down a pair of steps to the wide corridor outside Studio 2 and, at the appropriate moment in the play, the studio manager had flung open the door and he'd walked the horse up and down on the hard floor while the actors played a rustic scene involving a cart horse on a microphone positioned inside the door and another assistant stage manager stood guard at the front door to make sure that no one came through making inappropriate noises. 'They were a bit short of effects disks in the beginning. Naturally we took the phone off the hook at the front desk for the duration of the scene.'

I leaned on his desk at night when the staff had gone home and we were almost the last people in the building and he talked on and I listened and I didn't bother to wonder if he was being strictly truthful. I wanted to be part of the fable of my favourite place. I never turned into the walkway between two converted houses in Park Place without feeling a kick of excitement in my middle. The Continuity Suite office was a former box-room on the first floor of one of the houses, not much wider than its window which overlooked the front entrance. Sitting there, writing scripts or making up the skeleton shape of pages for *Radio Times* with little descriptions of the programmes, I could keep an eye on everyone entering or leaving the building, and since I was there very early I was able to observe who came to work early and eagerly, and who came in late – hungover, blinking against the light as they hurried up the short drive.

One famous lady director always came late, making a star entrance, svelte in black, fur stole slung on one shoulder, an Osbert Lancaster figure in a big hat, accompanied by her small, less imposing husband (he was an engineer with a trembling hand - a bad combination). Once ensconced in her office she took off the trappings she showed the world as she retrieved her considerable mind from the fog induced by the excesses of the night before and vigorously laid about her. Running for cover, her secretary would come and sit in my office for brief respites from the mayhem upstairs. 'Oh Miss Phillips, can I sit for a minute? She's IN. Her feet are on the table and her teeth are in the in-tray. It's terrible this morning. We've got a day ahead of us.'

When I joined as a child, until I left at twenty-one, it was still very much an 'us' organisation. Live radio was exciting and in a crisis all hands went to the pump; cleaners and canteen staff chipped in unasked with praise and blame. Everyone in the building scrutinised everyone and everything.

The directors were almost without exception buccaneering types with a touch of the Red Queen about them. Working for drama director John Griffiths involved delicious terror. During transmission he would shake his fist at us from his directorial chair if he felt the performance was slipping a bit. We were on the air live so there wasn't much else he could do, but if goaded beyond endurance, he would leave the control cubicle and there would be muffled thuds as he made his way through a series of sound-proofed doors and into the studio. He was the only person I knew who could stamp on tiptoe. He would interpose his furious face between one's script and the microphone and semaphore violent instructions. And he did a lot of on-the-air editing (which is really living dangerously) and would dash around the studio tearing pages out of our scripts and throwing them on the floor. (This was in the days when the BBC could afford lovely thick paper that didn't rustle, though oddly enough the loo paper has always been hopeless – little leaves, stiff and shiny and quite horrible.) John turned out first class programmes but he was a law unto himself.

So was Lorraine Davies, a dark, gypsy beauty and one of the most brilliant directors at the BBC, with the temper and temperament of a Cecil B. De Mille. The control console table in the director's cubicle could only just withstand the pounding of her fists as she lashed the company on to greater efforts. I think the directors were so on the edge and so volatile because radio is a maximum effort medium. It demands huge amounts of physical energy. Lorraine gave me one of my first big star parts and it was to play a male cat called Ginger Tom in a children's hour serial and that was more draining than Saint Joan or Medea ever proved to be. Shortly after I began to present programmes on television, I was told that TV is a cool medium and demands a much more relaxed approach. Less, on camera, is invariably better than more. That may be. Radio is hot. *That* I know.

I was so beguiled by the BBC that, immensely flattered to be approached, I seriously considered an offer to join the staff and train as an 'anchor' on current affairs programmes, eventually to replace a famous woman broadcaster in London who was planning to retire. I'd begun interviewing and had even done a small outside broadcast commentary. All this was still frightening me to death but I did love it and my mother would have been *so* pleased with me. In her eyes, working for the BBC was as good as becoming a teacher. (And I was right – my grandmother *was* impressed.) At the last moment I drew back, remembering what I wanted to be. Politely it was pointed out to me that I had very little chance of success in the theatre, so why not pursue the attainable. I felt that maybe

I was making a ludicrous mistake. After all, I was as far away as ever from my dream of being a *real* actress.

All this while my personal life, patchy as it was, became more unruly than ever before. I smoked ferociously, and didn't drink to excess only because I was so naturally high the whole time that alcohol would have pitched me completely off kilter. Ignoring my engaged status, I scarcely slept and took up with a string of fascinating and unsuitable men, most of them middle-aged and well-off, with big cars and, in one instance, a trusty chauffeur-cum-valet who became my devoted slave and I doted on him rather more than I did on his master. I made up for those frightened, unhappy, chilled years in Cardiff by turning it into my nocturnal playground. A street where I'd once stood, looking west, pining for home, was transformed into the street where I'd watch the dawn come up sitting under a cashmere rug in the back of a Rolls-Royce. I drank champagne where I'd been fearful. I re-drew the map of the city where I'd been so frustrated and so cold. It couldn't ever again look the same; in the small hours I made it mine and in the daytime I faced it down and found that it had lost its power to intimidate me. I was much heartened by this piece of magic I'd wrought on my surroundings, only now that it was over, admitting to myself how deeply wretched a time I'd had, torn from my roots for what seemed an insufficient reason. Homesickness had completely over-powered me for three entire years and had been all the more severe a malady because I knew that there was no reclaiming my land of lost content. I was sure that it was gone for good. I knew it.

I began to write a novel. It was about loss and exile and loveliness and I wept gently as I wrote. There was a café I'd found, upstairs on Churchill Way on the corner of Queen Street and I installed myself there when I wasn't at the BBC and drank coffee and wrote and wrote for hours on end. I was a stranger to the writer's block. I think I was trying to write a solution to my life. One day, I thought, I would look down at the page and there it would be: the answer! Eureka! The end. Or rather the end of the beginning. The heroine was a musician but she looked remarkably like me. I tried to extricate her from the impossible chains of duty and obligation and liberate her into a world of happiness and music. But I couldn't. She became more and more enslaved. Dreadful things happened to her. I couldn't stop the torrent of misfortune and I wept. The pages were blotched with coffee and salt water.

At night, when I slept, I dreamed that I had done something so bad that it could never be forgiven. What was it that I'd done? On waking I half-thought that I'd killed someone and lay there, heart racing, feeling a bit sick. It was amazing to me how life, ordinary, rather cheerful life, could continue above such a layer of confusion and darkness. There was never any question that I couldn't get on with my work and though I had a sense that something bad was going to happen to me I also had a tiny, inexplicable feeling that something wonderful was just around the corner.

My relationships, all illicit since I was an engaged woman, were rather charming and I couldn't feel bad about them. They were desultory, which I liked, they were undemanding, which I loved, and they were at all times pleasant and pleasurable and civil. Maybe I took a little more than I gave but good manners prevailed throughout. I think I liked my diplomat best. He had low taste in food and we gorged ourselves on Kraft cheese slices on toast, served by a butler on the best Spode. We both had reason to be discreet and on the whole we were circumspect, but as I scandalously ran into my future father-in-law as I emerged from the Angel Hotel after an afternoon's dalliance. I realized that I truly wanted to be found out. As is the way of these things, I wasn't.

My marriage approached. I tidied up my personal life. That is, I said a fond farewell to my gentlemen. I passed my last exams. Now, if ever, was the time to get on with my life as I wished it to be. But how? There were rows and tears and scenes, endless scenes. No one seemed to notice. It was like living in a waking dream. I was making my fiancé so unhappy already. Part of me could remember why it was that we had fallen in love in the first place and I was so sorry that it had come to this; part of me however just wanted to survive and that part had teeth and claws and was cruel. In the end, the coward's part prevailed. I couldn't bear to be the cause of any more unhappiness and I chose a funereal wedding dress – grey. Grey shoes, grey gloves, NO flowers.

As I put on my silly pink hat in the bedroom, my father rocked me to my foundations by saying quietly, 'You don't *have* to do this you know.' He *knew*? I looked at him in silence. I had been feeling numb but now I experienced a surge of conflicting feelings and the chief one I recognised was anger. Anger at my beloved father standing before me, still the handsomest man I knew, not speaking and I knew he would say no more. I loved him at that moment and was also sorry for him but fair or unfair, reasonable or not, I was also full of animosity towards him. Why hadn't he spoken before? Why wouldn't he say more now? What pointless questions, I thought. Spiky and resentful and ungiving, I looked away and shook my head. 'I'll be all right,' I said briskly and walked out of the room.

The rest of the day was spent concealing what I could only identify as irritation; hardly a grand emotion but I was not in a grand story. My store of anguish was all used up and when I set up home in a rented flat I did so in a calm and methodical manner, feeling that my part in the affair was all over; I'd done as much as I could and now everything could unravel naturally in its own time. My husband deserved better than this, better than me, but I also deserved better than this; me. My husband was doing his National Service. I was a faithful wife – no more wild nights. I lived alone in Cardiff and waited for what was to happen next. Soon, I thought.

Chapter Twenty-one

W hen Herbert Davies walked into the room I nearly laughed aloud in recognition of the arrival of a kindred spirit. He was the rescuing cavalry in the form of one well-dressed, bohemian figure spreading chaos as he moved across the space between us, scattering papers, displacing furniture, his reporter's eyes darting everywhere, not dwelling on anything but, nonetheless, hoovering up every detail. I felt as though he'd seen everything he needed to know about me in the first minute. We shook hands and he moved away at once, restlessly picking up chairs, putting them down, sitting down, standing again, looking at the view through the window, darting the occasional quizzical glance in my direction. I stood still, hardly breathing, wanting to make sure that I absorbed and remembered everything that was happening. He was talking to me about plays, about acting and I listened with half my attention; I could afford to catch up later. For the moment the important thing was to allow this meeting to unfold uninterrupted. My fairy godmother had given me the talent of being aware of happiness as it occurred and I was happy now, more than completely, overflowingly happy. Something wonderful was happening.

I knew that Herbert was a director and a journalist on the *Western Mail*. He was soon to become the Head of the Central Office of Information in Wales and then a full-time director at the BBC in Wales before moving to Australia. At this moment he was offering me a part in a new play, maybe I was being asked to read for a part. It didn't matter. I was, I knew, going to play Iris in Saunders Lewis's new play – his first modern play. Herbert told me the plot and described the character. There'd be a bit of money. I wasn't interested in money. The Arts Council would produce. Saunders would emerge from his eyrie and attend rehearsals! I couldn't believe he would do that; he never went anywhere.

I left the large house in Llandaff with *Gymerwch chi Sigaret?* clutched in my arms and went home to my neat, cheerless flat and read the play twice. After the second reading I was beginning to know my lines. They really were *my* lines; this part could have been written for me. I couldn't go to bed and I read it again. Now I *did* know a good deal of it. In bed I lay and thought about the play. Had I been offered it? I hadn't been listening. I woke early, still thinking about the play and went to work for the repertory company and finding it hard to concentrate on the schools' programme I'd been assigned to. If I played *Gymerwch chi Sigaret?* my days of doing programmes like this would be numbered I realised, pleased. I'd paid my dues, meeting visiting artists from trains, fetching their cups of tea, smoothing their way and now *my* turn had come.

Herbert was in touch with me merely to tell me the time and date of the first rehearsal. So I *was* Iris. It was just as well. I would have died if I hadn't been given the part. The first reading was terrifying. Saunders was there and I found it very difficult not to stare at him the whole time. He was tiny *and* big, his slight, energetic figure supporting a large, noble head with a high forehead and fly-away hair and, most noticeable, huge, beautiful eyes and a sweet mouth. His voice was high and remote, and his accent, unexpectedly, northern Welsh. He was formidable and there was nothing he could have done to put me at my ease. I was keenly aware of being in the presence of our greatest living Welsh writer, one of our Great Thinkers, a Hero. I knew and loved yards of his verse, there was no possibility of my feeling at ease. But I did think that I understood the heroine he had written and my fears dropped away as we began to read the play.

Rehearsals were wonderful and went on for long hours – as long as they needed to. When the rehearsal rooms were closed for the night we went to Herbert's house and his wife fed us and gave us coffee and we went on working. The most thrilling part of rehearsing was showing work to Saunders and having him correct it or approve of it or decide that he needed to re-write. Working with Saunders as he worked on a play was the most exciting thing that had ever happened to me. And I was being helped. Herbert was able to teach me as we went along and I began to feel like the 'real' actress I was desperate to be as Herbert met my demands and gave me more time and attention than I had any right to expect. We lived, breathed, ate and slept the play and the opening night was like a dream unfolding.

Rehearsals had been dark; the winter nights had been dark, the rehearsal rooms had been dimly lit, so had Herbert's front room. Now there was colour everywhere; *real* light, *real* colour, the kind that I'd seen in the pantomime in Swansea. I waited alone on stage in my bright red skirt (my great-grandmother's long red Welsh flannel underskirt, her *pais*, cut down to something approaching a New Look, 'foreign' sort of skirt). There were lights on me as I stood there on tiptoe but as the curtain rose and I began to dance the opening scene to the music of *Rosenkavalier* I was dazzled as more and more light flooded on to the stage and it was the best I'd ever felt.

Herbert had rehearsed me to the point where I had no worries, no fears, no self-consciousness; the play, worked on now by the audience, entered a different dimension and altered and I altered with it, half guiding it, half swept along by it and not knowing which state was which or where the new path was leading but never in danger of missing my footing; the familiar and the unfamiliar existed side by side in the same moment.

Expectations had been high for a new play by Saunders Lewis; the audience was glittering, we were being covered by the English press (what could *they* make of it?), the response at the end was overwhelming. 'Remember tonight,' someone said afterwards. Saunders actually appeared and caused a sensation. Herbert looked as though he was relishing a private joke. He didn't say much but he had to be pleased. We were a hit, a huge hit.

The entire tour was as exciting to me as the opening night had been. Once again, we played what seemed, on the surface, improbable, unlikely places. It didn't make any difference; performing the play was like riding the big dipper; farm hands, sophisticates, townies, academics, all responded in the same way – rapturously – and I never wanted the ride to end.

Before it ended Herbert and Saunders summoned me to a meeting. They made an odd pair; Saunders was so small, so wispy, so unbendingly tough and Herbert so large, so physically present, so flexible and enquiring. Now he deferred to Saunders – the poet as the strategist. To my amazement Saunders, the Welsh Nationalist, opened the conversation by saying that it was time for me to leave Wales. 'You must train,' he said, 'and you must train in the best place, surrounded by the best theatre. So you must go to London as soon as possible.'

I looked at Herbert who remained expressionless. My heart was pounding and I couldn't respond. Did he know that I had just married? This was non-conformist Wales and at that moment I was all non-conformist girl. Didn't being married effectively preclude any chance I might have had of getting away? I didn't voice my question. I could feel Herbert regarding me quizzically. How much did he know? How much had he told Saunders about my situation? There wasn't much he could have said. No one except myself knew anything about the circumstances of my marriage, only that it had abruptly occurred. If I appeared to be uncertain they might both turn away from me.

Saunders was waiting for me to speak and the silence was lengthening. Making some huge omissions I said, speaking the literal truth, 'That is what I most want.' 'Very well,' said Saunders briskly. 'Understand that this is not going to be an easy road to travel. Examine your motives very carefully and be prepared for considerable hardship.'

I nodded and Herbert took over, saying that he would send for the application forms to the Academy and coach me for my audition. 'However,' he went on, 'in my opinion you won't get anywhere much until you are forty so I suggest that we make it clear that unless you're good enough for a scholarship you are not going to go to RADA at all.'

I was appalled. Forty? Again I remembered Rhydwen's words years ago. At twenty I couldn't even imagine being as old as forty. It was a lifetime of waiting. What did he mean? It wasn't the moment to start an argument and I stifled my protests. I did, however, question the wisdom of holding out for a scholarship. I had no idea how good I was, so surely getting into RADA would be difficult enough. It seemed insane to limit my chances by making clear this rather grand condition. Herbert was implacable. If no scholarship, then no training, no 'proper' career, no England.

'You'll have to get accustomed to being poor,' Saunders concluded, 'so I suggest that you make an appointment to see the Director of Education in the City Hall and ask him for a grant. I'll give you a letter of recommendation.' That seemed to be all so I left them and walked down to the Capitol Café for a cup of coffee, a packet of cigarettes to chain-smoke and to think.

Chapter Twenty-two

In my mind, RADA was a fabulous place peopled by gods and goddesses. My dream at fifteen years of age, of a place where nothing mattered except acting, where I would belong and be content and live the life I wished to live, had persisted into my grown-up twentieth year. I had never thought of the reality of it. Unattainable and wonderful, it had remained fixed and unchangeable like a fairytale. 'Once upon a time and far away, there was a wonderful place . . .' And I had also grown accustomed to not being allowed to go to the ball. Now, almost casually, RADA was being talked about as something reachable and possible in a knowable dimension but the years of vainly waiting had left me a legacy of inertia and I drew back from the ordinariness of writing a letter to the Academy and licking a stamp and walking to the postbox. Surely it couldn't be as simple as that? I couldn't allow that the business of making a dream into reality could be so easy.

Where *was* RADA? 'Oh, I've done all that,' said Herbert. 'We should get the prospectus any day.' And still we didn't talk of my changed circumstances, and the fact that I wasn't free to go anywhere. Just once Herbert said, 'So why *did* you get married? When I heard about it I assumed that you were pregnant and had to marry and that you'd subsequently lost the child.' 'No,' I replied, rather shocked by his matter-of-fact tone, 'it wasn't that at all,' but I couldn't bring myself to confide in him. Also, I didn't have a reasonable explanation.

He did not seem very interested and the subject was dropped but it had become my ceaseless internal monologue. What to do? And then, how to do it? I didn't know anyone who had ended a marriage, nor, I was sure, did anyone in my family; divorce was not an option in our lives. Confused, I went about my work and talked to no one. When I wrote to my husband I told him nothing of this.

The prospectus arrived! It lay on the table between us. Herbert and Joyce, his wife, were interested and pleased. I drew it towards myself and as I began to read my confusion vanished. The words before me were almost familiar, as though I'd read them before. Guilt and remorse might well remain but I knew what I was going to do, no matter what it cost. If it was within my power I was going to go to this place which I was recognising as though I'd been there in a dream. It seemed like home beckoning me. I would rather have died than voiced any of this and when Herbert began to consider audition pieces I shed my fancies and joined him in a practical and none too serious consideration of ways of displaying any strengths I possessed while conceal-ing my weaknesses – 'And there are plenty of those,' said Herbert.

There were set audition pieces, including a piece of scrip-ture – rather dull. 'We'll do that,' said Herbert. 'No,' I protested. It was completely undramatic and it was short – over in a flash – no chance to shine. 'Leave it to me,' said Herbert and he suggested I should offer as my own choice the Willow Song from *Othello*. A song? I was aghast. 'Trust me,' he said. The scholarship pieces were not, it seemed, so crucial. The important thing was to walk into the room on the first day and make an immediate, unassailable impact.

Yes, I could see that but I'd never done an audition. I'd never even had to do an interview and most of my energies in everyday life were bent towards being as self-effacing as possible. 'And keep your voice down, people don't like *loud* girls.'

'All right then,' Herbert was saying. 'Rehearse the pieces on

Wednesday and Friday next week?' 'Yes, I'll know them by then.'

I don't know what I was expecting him to do. I was accustomed to working things out for myself and having someone apply a little polish. Herbert was asking me to do things that sounded completely mad. The piece from the Bible was being taken very slowly with big pauses and impossible upward inflections. What did I sound like, I wondered, listening to my own alien delivery. A bit like Dylan Thomas maybe. A bit like a revivalist preacher, possibly. My accent was standard English but the effect was strangely Welsh. Was that good? He said I *had* to do it his way and I obeyed.

He re-directed the Willow scene, which he'd seen me play. 'Not good enough,' he said to my chagrin; I'd been rather pleased with that bit. We edited the scene with Emilia so that I could play it alone and I became acquainted with it as though for the first time. It was more interesting, more affecting, more frightening than I had appreciated. I went through a downcast period when I realised how much more work there was to do than I had hitherto appreciated. Then my high spirits revived as we rehearsed again and again, week after week and I could tell that I was improving and sounding less odd as the audition grew nearer. But still I had no idea if I was really bad or really good. Herbert said nothing. It was time to negotiate some leave from my jobs at the BBC and find somewhere to stay in London in the neighbourhood where all Welsh people stayed, in Paddington near the Great Western Railway Terminus, where as a nation we got off the train and seemingly too apprehensive or too tired to go further, set up as suppliers of milk or mistresses of respectable boarding houses with Welsh-language chapel timetables in the hall.

It was also time to tell my parents what I was about to do. Full of apprehension, I boarded a small red Western Welsh bus and made yet another miserable excursion to the Vale of Glamorgan. Very rarely had I been the bearer of good news recently, I reflected sadly. The journey passed far too quickly and I tried to make the mile-long walk to the house last longer

191

than it should. I was hoping for inspiration as I walked along but when I found my parents doing accounts in the office of the big house and went with them to their apartment for tea, my mind was still a muddle of discarded opening gambits.

No matter how I dressed it up or justified it I was going to have to tell them that I was going to run away and that, if I could help it, I wasn't coming back. I couldn't begin to calculate the strength of their reaction. How many levels of trouble was I dealing them? There was the scandal to contend with. Shame, loss of face, the collapse of appearances were powerful and important elements which I had inherited and was trying to dispense with. How much more potent they must be to my parents who, with *their* parents' example, before them, had in a seemingly unchangeable society not only been given a framework of rules and values, but had inflexibly lived by them. It was the fashion to deride the inevitable hypocrisies of the narrow code of conduct by which we lived in Welsh Wales but, although I was about to break new ground in bad behaviour, I believed that there was something heroic in the self-denial, the self-control, the strength required to live through days and weeks and years of duty rather than inclination. I looked at the two faces before me in the big airy sitting room, very un-Welsh with a formal English garden outside, and I saw the same serious, level expressions that looked out from those damp-spotted family portraits at 'home'. Home was far away and sorrow for my disenfranchised parents overtook my fears and nervousness for myself. It should have been so easy for me to make my parents happy and proud. It seemed so unfair to be bringing home more trouble.

And there was the less lofty question of security; mine and, in a way, theirs. Although I had chosen an unorthodox route, I had, surprisingly, arrived at a position that might be even more satisfactory than the future they had planned for me. How would they feel as I turned my back on that? My father's reaction was unfathomable. My mother? Hard to tell. The antagonism that had seethed beneath the surface of our relationship in the year that led to my marriage had subsided without erupting and there was an uneasy calm between us. It was as though we had finished a passage of arms and, whereas nothing was concluded, something was over and done with. Odd as it seemed, I considered now that the impetus behind the events of the past year had derived not from the relationship between myself and my lover, but rather from an imperative impulse to have some kind of contest with my mother; if not an actual contest, a dialogue all the more violent in that it was indirect, never spoken.

I told them what I was going to do, at least, I told them what I was going to try to do. It was understood that in the event of a success, there were to be consequences which would be dealt with later. Not for the first time, they astonished me. They cut straight to the end of a discussion they didn't bother having and, in effect, they simultaneously advised me to cut my losses and go. They finished each other's sentences. They were in perfect accord. 'And count on us,' they said, more than once. 'Anything we can do to help.' I was shamed by their generosity and sympathy. There was a rider. 'Let this be an end of marriages,' said my mother. It was easy to submit. After a period – years – of thoughtless childishness, I was at twenty beginning to recapture the sobriety and lightness of my childhood self. I could remember how happy I was when I was focused and unshakeable and it was as though my parents knew this. Everything is redeemable if I get my scholarship. I have a second chance.

Chapter Twenty-three

R ehearsals with Herbert went on. Work went on. For the
first time I was aware of the importance of having
money and anxiously I scanned the BBC Repertory Company
board to make sure that I had enough bookings to be kept on.
I did all the presentation work I could get. There was no stage
play to occupy me. Work on the novel was suspended. Life
was being lived, not written about.

As Saunders advised, I made an appointment at the City
Hall to talk to the Head of Education for Glamorgan County
about the possibility of obtaining a grant for an acting course.
The meeting was a disaster; I forgot Mr Haycock's name as I
walked down the corridor to his office and wasted the initial
five minutes mentally rifling through likely bucolic surnames:
Straw, no; *two* syllables, Thatcher, Fielding, Snodgrass, oh
give up. I hated asking for things and I especially hated asking
for money.

To make matters worse I didn't really see why the local
authority should give me another grant, but I could glimpse
on his desk a letter in Saunders's writing and Herbert had
doubtless called in a few favours, so Mr Haycock didn't reject
my application out of hand but he wanted me to explain how
he could be sure of getting a return for his money. This being
the first time he'd been asked to give money to a potential
drama student, he was at a loss to understand how to
calculate the end result. I told him that the outcome of an

actor's training is impossible to predict. 'You seem very highly thought of,' he ventured, cautiously, indicating the papers on his desk, 'and you will not be needing a grant unless the Academy gives you a scholarship which would indicate that it also thought highly of you.' 'There's still no certainty,' I replied and he seemed taken aback that I was not being more persuasive. When he pressed me to convince him that I had a good case I felt so intensely irritated that all I wanted to do was to end the meeting. I couldn't afford it but I knew that I was going to scupper my chances of a grant within the next few minutes.

Before I got around to this something occurred which did indeed bring the meeting to a close and not in a way I would have chosen. 'I see that you married recently,' he remarked. 'Yes,' I replied, 'but I'm afraid . . .' and to my horror I began to cry. This was unbearably embarrassing for both of us. Councillor Haycock looked down at his large desk and my stifled sobs grew until, choking and gasping for breath, shoulders heaving, I gave way to a terrible fit of weeping. Shaking my head and gesturing an apology, I gathered up my things and left as fast as I could, making for the little park across the road from the City Hall where I sat and snivelled for a bit, appalled by my precarious emotional state. I dried my eyes and thought I would deal with it later. Nothing to do at present but apply a plaster to the inconvenient wound.

I did not in the least blame the local authority when I was informed that training an actress was thought to be inappropriate expenditure. I don't know why but I really didn't want that money. Now I had to make and save as much money as I could and hope that later on I would think of another way of raising funds. Oddly, for me, I was not at all worried about the practicalities of the enterprise.

December 1955 and the week of the audition was upon me. On previous journeys I had been guided 'across' London by other people; it was a noisy jumble of impossible-to-follow signs. Would I ever reach a destination on my own? I seriously

196

doubted it, I had no sense of direction and was terrified of traffic, lacking the most basic of townee skills. Thinking back, I reflected that a trained dog would learn how to work the transport system with more ease than I had displayed, rooted to the spot like a rabbit, unable to distinguish words in the alien human roar that accompanied the terrifying sound of buses and cars and the distant under-the-ground trains. I had gone where I was told to go. Others had bought tickets, read signs, chosen escalators and platforms. 'How?' I marvelled, knowing that I was as spectacularly incompetent and vulnerably hopeless as a country bumpkin in Bartholomew Fair. 'Don't lose your money,' lectured my mother. 'Don't lose your ticket.' Every time she saw me she added another warning 'Don't'. She had no reason to have confidence in me when I had none. I thought I must compartmentalise my day; endure the trials and terrors of getting to Gower Street from Paddington, follow the map to the Academy, allow time for getting lost and probably robbed, then calm down, forget my surroundings and concentrate on the audition. Oh, please, let me concentrate as I never have before.

In the event, I concentrated so hard that London, the physical fact of the huge city, shrank to a room in a Paddington boarding house and a room in 62 Gower Street, the Royal Academy of Dramatic Art. When I went home I had nothing to tell of my journey except my recollection of the audition and my subsequent conversation with the secretary, Miss Brown, and even that had begun to assume a dream-like quality.

The Paddington bedroom had been as clean as a new penny and cold; multi-coloured, small, all-over patterned carpet (designed solely so as not to show dirt), fighting and defeating the refined, hardly-there-at-all wallpaper and the pink satin upholstered stool, a dare-devil piece of luxury in front of the walnut-type veneer of the low-fronted dressing table with its big triple mirror. I may have slept in it, but chiefly this served as my rehearsal room and I moved the furniture and stood and looked dispassionately at my reflection in the middle mirror on the dressing table which could be tilted slightly so that I could see almost all of myself.

I looked as Existentialist as it was possible to look without actually applying the correct Juliette Greco make-up. Tall, tiny waist, belted. Plain tight-fitting sweater; long, full woollen skirt, flat shoes. So far, so good. I didn't have a good coat in the appropriate style but I wouldn't be wearing a coat so that didn't matter. The face was almost right. On the credit side, a faultless complexion (eczema temporarily at bay), regular features, dark red mouth, actressy and interesting at the same time. But the hair and the eyes . . . totally unremarkable; the former falling straight to my shoulders, clean but ordinary, whereas I would have liked it to billow, darker and thicker and more aggressive. The eyes were no more than nice eyes. I wanted big, mysterious, dark pools and had no idea how to achieve this without making myself look silly. I smelled of 4711, a Christmas present (rather more worldly than Yardley's Lavender). It wasn't exactly how I wanted to look but it was going to have to do.

I went through my pieces several times (not too loud, just in case). I stood looking at myself. 'Are you any good at all?' I thought, quite calm now that the decisive moment had all but arrived. My reflection looked blank. I didn't have the remotest idea. I imagined the worst outcome. Someone – a man – would raise a hand and stop me and say something like, 'I'm sorry but you are not at all what we're looking for.' It wouldn't surprise me at all. I was shooting for the moon and prepared for the worst.

In the morning I went through my pieces again and then I was walking towards Gower Street, so contained in the little circle I'd manufactured around myself that I did no more than note in passing that the entrance was familiar; Mrs Lewis's medium had described it in detail three years ago. That didn't seem significant or even interesting, my attention was reserved for the interior: a smallish hallway, dark with a grand, wide staircase at the back. 'Not there, please,' said a tall, military-looking commissionaire figure in green livery indicating a

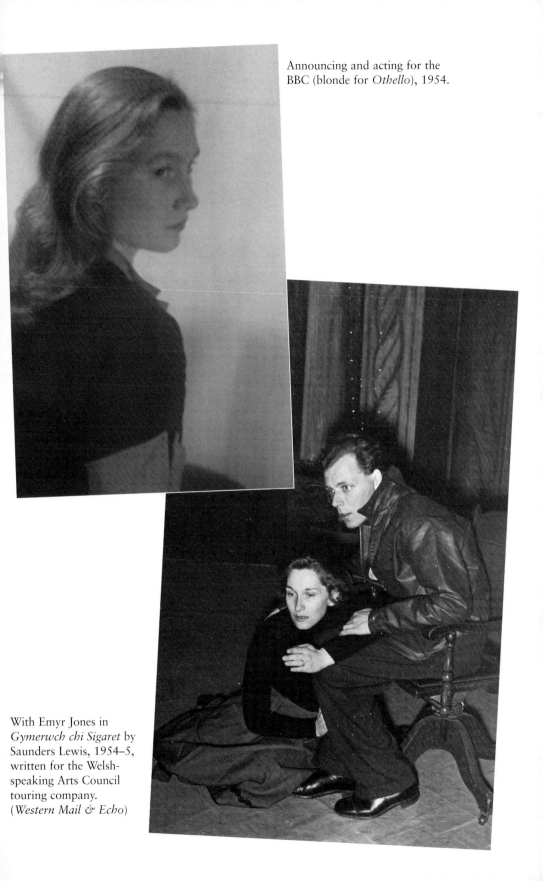

Announcing and acting for the
BBC (blonde for *Othello*), 1954.

With Emyr Jones in
Gymerwch chi Sigaret by
Saunders Lewis, 1954–5,
written for the Welsh-
speaking Arts Council
touring company.
(*Western Mail & Echo*)

An attempt to establish a Welsh-speaking National Theatre – the Welsh Arts Council touring company's *Uncle Vanya*, with me playing Elena.

My RADA friends: Hélène Van Moeurs,   Charles Kay,

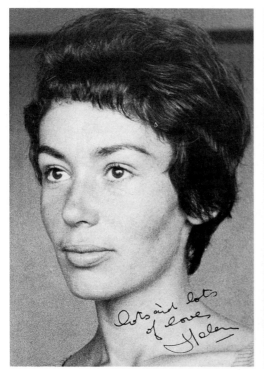

Above: Undergraduates at Cardiff; I am on the left (hair dyed blonde for Desdemona) with my best friend, Audrey Watkins.

Right: Sir Kenneth Barnes, one-time Principal of RADA.

Thelma Whiteley

and Edward de Souza.

Above left: John Fernald, Principal for most of my time at RADA. Hardest of task masters, best of teachers. (*Paul Tanqueray*)

Above: *Magda* at the Vanbrugh Theatre, 1957.

Left: *Les Justes* by Camus, directed by Guy Brenton, with the Tavistock Repertory Company (I was on loan from RADA).

Below: A gesture of friendship from Flora Robson to a troubled drama student.

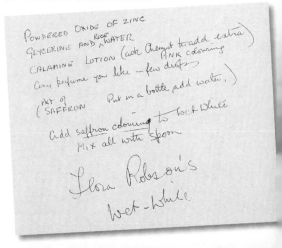

POWDERED OXIDE OF ZINC
GLYCERINE AND ROSE WATER
CALAMINE LOTION (ask Chemist to add extra PINK colouring)
Any perfume you like — few drops
PKT of SAFFRON   Put in a bottle add water.)

Add saffron colouring to look White
Mix all with spoon

Flora Robson's
Wet-White

Fredrik Ohlsson 'Tesman' in *Hedda*, 1957 (now a noted actor and writer in Sweden).

Dora Gordine's bronze portrait head of me, playing *Hedda Gabler*.

Sailing to play *Hedda* in Norway.

Playing *Hedda* at the National Theatre, Oslo.

Opening the first commercial TV station in Wales. *Land of Song* ran for three years, from 1956–9.

Rehearsing for *Brad* (*Treachery*), the Welsh play by Saunders Lewis, 1958. *From left to right:* Emyr Humphreys (producer), Emlyn Williams, me, Richard Burton, Hugh David, Gareth Jones, Meredith Edwards and (*foreground*) Clifford Evans. (*BBC*)

Right: Playing St Joan at the New Belgrade Theatre, Coventry, 1959, with Jack Rodney (pictured) as Dauphin, Alan Howard and Frank Finlay.

Below: Peter O'Toole in *The Long and the Short and the Tall* at the Royal Court Theatre, 1959. (*Zoë Dominic*)

Young TV star, late fifties.

Peter O'Toole.

much humbler little staircase round to the right. As I moved through the hall I saw things that set my pulses wildly racing. There was a bust of George Bernard Shaw who I knew had been involved in the creating of the Academy, a portrait of Violet Vanbrugh and on the walls great boards – they seemed huge – with names in gold letters. Those names! I was in a Holy of Holies. These were gold medallist actors and actresses who had trained here, in this very building where I was standing – Charles Laughton, Hugh Griffith, Barbara Jefford.

Then I was round the corner and ascending a poky dark staircase and being ushered towards a lecture-room?, a studio?, at present a waiting room and filled with people like me, hoping for a place. There didn't seem to be a 'type', I noticed gratefully. Some were very young, some were middle aged, some were *very* good looking, like people in a magazine, but others were plain and ordinary. I sat down and tried not to get distracted. I wanted to go through my pieces in my head but I couldn't help hearing the conversations around and behind me. Oh, mercy, they sounded so *English*. I was painfully aware suddenly that for all my (thanks to the BBC) faultless pronunciation and for all my 'good ear' for languages and notwithstanding the constant reading and writing in English, I was still thinking in Welsh. I felt like a foreigner and suddenly at the mercy of that wretched reflex common to my race which whispered 'English is superior'. It only took a second to re-adjust and say, 'No, it's not'; but the fear and shame of that second were debilitating. Someone said, 'What fool would do the *Bible*, I ask you.' There was laughter and I closed my eyes and silently began, 'And Jesus went thence, and departed into the shores of Tyre and Sidon.' Herbert, have you got this right?

There were a lot of us, maybe fifty, waiting that day. When my name was called I crossed the corridor and was shown into a very big room with three large windows looking on to Gower Street. Some of them were darkened with what looked like left-over blackout material. The room seemed empty. Where I entered there was a 'stage' area – not raised, a few chairs and small tables, haphazardly positioned against the walls. Then I saw that at the far end, almost out of sight, four or five people sat behind a table. Someone must have indicated that I should begin. 'And Jesus went thence . . .' oh God, I sounded too loud and these pauses were painful, I could only just hold them but they were in my blood and the piece came out exactly as Herbert had rehearsed it. It didn't sound smart. It didn't sound *English*.

I moved a table and a chair and began the Willow scene, miming the hair brush and table carefully and 'placing' Emilia in the scene. There was no possibility of going wrong but my singing voice was a bit wobbly to my ears. 'Mine eyes do itch, doth that bode weeping?' To my surprise I *was* in tears. I finished and went out and back to my seat in the waiting room. Nothing happened for a while, no one was called, until an elderly woman in a brown felt hat came in and called my name again. The next applicant was called at the same time and crossed the hall to the big room, while the woman in the brown hot took me round the corner and said, 'Oh my dear girl'. I looked at her, puzzled. 'Is it possible for you to come back to do your Scholarship pieces?' 'Yes, of course, but does that mean . . . ?' 'Oh, no, yes – no, you *have a scholarship*, no doubt of that, but it would be good to hear your pieces.' I leaned against the wall. 'I've passed, then?' 'Oh, my dear girl, they – we are so happy that you are coming to us.' Tears welled in my eyes and she put her arm around me and gave me her handkerchief. It was the happiest moment of my life.

My mind registered nothing of my return to Wales. The letter came confirming that I had won the Maggie Albanesi Scholarship and was expected at the Academy in January. My parents were pleased. They were, I think, impressed. What were they impressed by? As much, maybe, by my success in getting there and back in one piece without losing anything or getting myself run over, as they were by my admission to RADA. This was a relief. It was uncomplicated, as though we'd *all* been wanting this for me and here it was. I didn't tell anyone about Miss Brown and myself sharing a hankie. I was not planning on any more public displays of emotion and, anyhow, I wanted this to seem ordinary, normal, to reduce the temperature. Herbert smiled and nodded and said, 'Knew it.' Saunders counselled careful preparation before entering into a life I had longed for for so long. 'Think carefully what *sort* of actress you want to be. You might become an artist, who knows.' They both repeated that my troubles were not over by a long chalk. Saunders said and then wrote, 'You must learn to live on the knife-edge of insecurity.' I wasn't sure what he meant. I didn't think he was talking about financial insecurity. How could the insecurity he was meaning be a good thing? And why should I not become successful – soon? Herbert said, 'You have a long haul ahead of you,' and he grinned wolfishly as though it were a big joke to be relished. We'd see about that, I thought, and began my preparations for departure.

Chapter Twenty-four

Write a cheque for the remainder of the lease. Post it. Pack books. Divide china, ornaments, cutlery, linen. Pack, vacuum and dust. Arrange transport. Leave letter.

'Leave letter.' A shameful, cowardly item on the list. 'Divide china' – even worse. A scrupulous division of assets weighs little or not at all in the scales of fair dealing. Unwilling and unable to explain myself, tired of talking, I'd make my excuses by letter and quit the country, the marriage hardly begun, the obligations, the past.

I burn my unfinished novel, tear up my wedding photographs and, looking through my papers, keep only my exercise books with notes about acting; my attempt to understand Stanislavsky's 'Method', a précis of Michael Redgrave's lectures on acting, by far the most helpful to me of all actors' observations. 'To act well, and to act well repeatedly has become an obsession,' I see underlined. My book of childhood poems, mostly in Welsh, written for Eisteddfod competitions seems to have gone astray and it doesn't bother me. Even the ones that won prizes were vastly inferior to the poems written by Dafydd Rowlands, the head boy at Pontardawe School, and now a 'grown-up' poet. There's a slim file of late teenage poems in English and I open it cautiously. I must have been pretty unhappy at seventeen:

Consciousness of self returns
Limbs sprawled in still abandon
And a head that burns
And burning turns on the? [– I seem to have
    had trouble with the adjective] tormented pillow.

Pages later I seem to have reached for a watery oblivion:

A wreath of foam
A moment's peace
And then hear still the Life-yell underneath.

Oh, please. Obviously I'd decided that annihilation was pointless. There were *lots* of depressed poems and I made up a special bundle for the furnace, pleased that I was obliterating my younger, embarrassing self.

This time I was aware of the journey from Cardiff to Paddington. My mother insisted on accompanying me. She seemed different again, strangely sweet in her manner and part of me was glad she was with me. Two small suitcases – very little luggage with which to be starting a new life; one raincoat, two pairs of shoes: one flat and one cuban heeled, two skirts, two blouses, two sweaters, plus my requirements for the Academy: really horrible black cotton tights that wrinkle, ballet shoes, leotard, dance shoes. All my smart, 'bourgeois', BBC clothes – stiletto heels, pencil-slim skirts, outside-broadcast long frocks – have been dumped. I felt I had to pare down and rid myself of bric-à-brac. Simplicity was to be the keynote now, I decided. I had to forget that I had ever been a professional actress, forget that I had rarely been out of work, forget that I'd had a responsible BBC job, an office, a secretary, forget my respectable 'prospects', wipe the slate clean and become for the first time a true student. Maybe my mother sensed this and it made her warm towards me.

As we pulled into Paddington she indicated the grubby backs of the houses and said, 'Well, there it is, let's see what you make of that.' She delivered this in a mild voice, at odds

204

with the challenge of the remark. Her sense of occasion had led her to overplay the moment. She should have been high above Hampstead looking down at the dome of St Paul's, instead of sitting in a dingy train crawling along Westbourne Park Villas. I beamed reassuringly at her.

My carefully organised Welsh digs had fallen through; my prospective landlady fell downstairs and broke her leg. I was not displeased for myself. It was arranged that I should lodge temporarily in Earls Court – and curiously with a niece of Richard Burton's whom I did not yet know. I felt dangerously indifferent and quite unable to take an interest in the practical arrangements. My mother came with me to Goodge Street and I was seized with concern for her and made her promise to stay put in the little café near the Underground station while I went over to RADA on Gower Street. We were to meet later and I told her I would take her back to Paddington. All this to-ing and fro-ing seemed unnecessary but I was terrified that she would get lost – or run over. After I had registered and been shown around the building I hurtled back to the café to find my mother *returning* from Liberty's in Regent Street. How clever of her. London did not intimidate her in the least. To me it was as exciting and perilous as the Amazon Jungle and I could not wait to wave my mother off and negotiate the journey to Earls Court and sanctuary. Would they remember I was coming? Would they have changed their minds? Would they be out?

Earls Court *was* a sanctuary; the girls were in, they did remember I was coming. They showed me the kitchen and my room and I retreated there, too exhausted and apprehensive to speak. They were music students, I gathered. One of them practised the same phrase over and over again. The Underground moaned somewhere around or below us, my meagre possessions were quickly unpacked and I was washed and in bed – for the first time I could remember without a book to read – listening to the alien sounds of this city which I had been dreading for so many years:

Oh do not trust that wicked man,
Be careful what you do – oo
Tum tum tum *tum*
Tum tum, tum tum
He'll do the same to you

resounded over and over again through the small flat. I felt strange. What was it? The thought of RADA in the morning was exciting; would I get there in one piece – and on time? I'd get up very early. There was something else. I realised that I was smiling in the semi-darkness. (The streets of London could never be truly dark, I thought.) I was smiling because I had fallen in love and was deeply, unexpectedly in thrall to the city I had so dreaded. How could that have happened so quickly? Like all love affairs there was little explanation and no arguing. This was *it*, all right. What a bonus! I fell asleep thinking of the corridors and staircases of RADA. Having no sense of direction, I had not retained any notion where anything was, where anything led. I'd have to start again in the morning. Light-hearted as I hadn't been for years, I fell asleep.

Chapter Twenty-five

On my first day I was in WC1 long before RADA opened its doors and I took a cautious walk round the neighbourhood. There were small hotels on Gower Street and one of them had a Welsh name. I had to find somewhere permanent to stay; what a luxury it would be to have a room here. However, I had already adjusted my wishes to suit my pocket and I knew I could not afford a cupboard in this part of London. I shouldn't waste time wondering how I would live after my savings gave out and I surprised myself by the ease with which I accepted this careless attitude.

I'd never worked so hard in my life. There were seventy-three new students, divided into three groups. The Gower Street house rose five floors above the street and there was also a basement where our lockers were housed. During the day we ran and ran and ran; up and down the building and also across the roof and down into the building that fronted on to Malet Street, behind and parallel with Gower Street. Unpunctuality was a cardinal offence and it was a nightmare running down to the basement after each lesson to change into the appropriate dress and get back upstairs in time for the next lesson hundreds of stairs each day, taken two at a time, in terror of being late. Excuses were not accepted. At the BBC I had learned the hard way about time-keeping, but this was worse – there just *wasn't* time to get from A to B, change, and get back to C. In the theatre, they said, one would always be expected to be ready to rehearse at least ten minutes before time, so get used to moving fast. I would. I did.

The first week was especially fraught for me because I couldn't remember where anything was. I learned to identify a few people from my group and tried to keep them in my sights as I struggled in and out of tights and rummaged in my locker for books and shoes and tried not to give up on my appearance. Glamour was not required but I could see that an undergraduate's total disregard for appearance would not be acceptable.

Each night I went home and only just managed to prepare for the following day before falling into a deep, dreamless sleep. I was in awe of the staff; some of them were in plays, some were celebrated, some were alarming, others bore famous names. There were seventeen of them and each one knew something that I wanted to know and was determined to learn. I was equally in awe of my fellow students; they were so *English*. I remembered Gwyn Thomas's observation of his first days at Oxford. 'I had landed on another planet and I had never seen such large, confident Martians. Some of them might have been on horseback but I never really looked up to find out.'

These people all seemed to have more skills than I; they were quicker and funnier and better at accents and much more graceful, some of them were dancers and didn't have to endure the torment of beginning ballet lessons from scratch. I was the worst fencer by far. And my voice was all wrong! In the space of a few weeks I was reduced to rubble. I couldn't do *anything*. Astoundingly, I wasn't cast down. No reversal, no humiliation – and there were plenty – could extinguish my profound contentment. 'Keep up! Concentrate! Oh, for God's sake! The girl in the red shoes,' said Richard Ainley brutally and as it happened unfairly. There wasn't a moment of the day when I was not concentrating. I was *trying* with every sinew in my body. I had tried and succeeded in abandoning myself to insecurity. There was no plan in my head. On unfamiliar ground, I put one foot before the other and was happy. I was scared as well; it seemed to me that I might well be one of the many students to be sacked at the end of the first term. There were stories of a class of seventy, whittled down term after term until only ten remained at the end of two years. I refused to think what I would do if and when the worst happened in December.

Two weeks galloped by. Already, I could scarcely speak for self-consciousness. I couldn't even breathe. 'Toothpaste please and a packet of Kleenex,' came out as a scarcely intelligible gurgle. The whole weight of the Academy was thrown behind voice production. We did no acting. We had movement classes with Mrs Boalth, ballet classes, fencing classes with Captain Froeschlen and – a luxury – mime classes with Miss Phillips, which were the closest we came to acting.

The bulk of the time was taken up with voice, voice, voice, breathing, diction, musicality, audibility, control during extreme emotion, posture, rib reserve. It was like being in a nightmare without end. I couldn't envisage that there *could* be an end or that I would ever achieve a state where I would talk without thinking of twenty 'mistakes' I might be making. Miss Morrell, my voice tutor, was grey haired, fair and stern. Each time my turn came to speak a few lines aloud she listened, shook her head dismissively and quickly passed on to the next student. All my life my voice had been singled out for praise. All those years of filling auditoriums that held up to two thousand people had done nothing but iron in a dozen bad habits. Gradually, I let go my home-grown 'techniques' and sank to the bottom of the class. I couldn't even tell *why* other students were right when I was so wrong.

It was fashionable to sneer at 'the RADA voice' partly because RADA had at times been perceived as a finishing school for rich young girls. In fact, there was no such thing as a RADA voice and within the last months the age limit had been raised to exclude sixteen year olds who couldn't think what they wanted to do in life. The long-time principal, Sir Kenneth Barnes, who had still been there to preside over my entrance audition, was yielding to John Fernald, the new principal. He combined the energy and confidence of a successful, practising theatre director with an attitude towards discipline which derived from his other love, the Navy.

RADA was transforming itself into a very tight ship but the emphasis remained on vocal and physical technique, not self-expression. That suited me fine. I was desperate to know the 'how'. We were told that an actor's first duty was to be heard by everyone in the theatre. 'If they can't hear you, it doesn't matter how beautifully you're acting, it's a total waste of time.' Being heard was allied with being understood and that involved not only possessing a tongue that could rap out consonants at the speed of machine-gun bullets but also being master of a diaphragm strong enough to enable one to sustain breath over long passages. 'And then,' we were told, 'you have to have the industry to search out which are the key words in a speech so that you can highlight them while floating over the less important phrases. You don't want to *bore* the audience, do you?' God forbid – in the unlikely event that I would ever again be able to stand up on a stage looking like a normal person and think of ten things while being heard and understood.

I looked up my notes to myself which I had put together when I was an undergraduate – the only papers I'd kept – and actually all this RADA work was related to points I'd thought important, if barely understood then.

What is the secret of acting?

Voice, voice, more voice.

What is the secret of Lewis Casson's diction?

I took heart form the tiny scrap of text that read, 'Sir Lewis is not a Welshman for nothing.' Most important of all the lessons that my idol, Edith Evans, had been taught by her mentor, William Poel – there was a William Poel prize here at RADA. Hitherto I hadn't thought of him as a real person; he'd been a character in Miss Evans's life. He was long dead now but he became a real person to me.

This was grind and drudgery and I embraced it, getting up at six every morning to go through the breathing and the diction exercises and then allowing myself a smidgen of Shakespeare before going to RADA to do more of the same until darkness fell. Not only did I not improve, I got worse. Around me I heard mutinous remarks about the soullessness of this process. Some even said they weren't going to bother with this phase, they were here to act but I thought my soul would take care of itself and the acting would wait for me. I had to find out the *how*.

Chapter Twenty-six

I found digs! I began to feel quite a Londoner. Margot was a third term student; she was beautiful with subtle make-up, hair that practically dressed itself into a chignon and a modest, elegant wardrobe – so far above us harassed and dishevelled beginners. She put it about that there was room for two more students where she lodged. I went to be looked over by my prospective landlady. The Metropolitan Line took me to a part of London that was quite unlike any I'd seen. Dollis Hill seemed very far away and when I got off the train and followed the map to Mrs Styles's house I realised that I was in a bit of the city that must have been almost countryside before the coming of the Underground. The house, a white, rough-cast 1930s semi was on the edge of open land. It didn't seem very big. Where would we all fit in?

I pressed the front-door bell alongside the front window. It was opened by a slim, well-dressed woman, middle-aged with formidably permed, neat grey hair and bright, darting, in-quisitive eyes. 'No flies on me,' said her expression. I was meeting my first authentic Londoner, I realised and I was fascinated. Her terms were reasonable: £2.19s for bed and an English breakfast, dinner and lunch on Sunday, no callers at the house, limited use of telephone, make own bed, in by a reasonable hour at night, use of lounge by invitation. She was brisk beyond belief and I was swept along on a wave of do's and don'ts. This was no motherly Mrs Lewis in Cardiff, but I sensed that she was completely reliable and I needed the quiet bolt-hole she seemed to be offering. Also, more and more, she was intriguing me.

When everything was agreed – on the double (I was to find that every moment of her day was accounted for) – I realised to my dismay that I was to *share* the double room at the back. Margot had the small middle room and Mrs Styles of course had the big front room. True, for a year I had shared a large study bedroom with Audrey at College, but I'd known Audrey for six years at school; sharing with a stranger was something else. It was too late to back out. I hadn't understood because I was too slow and I was embarrassed to admit that now. I arranged to move in. This, I thought, was a real test of my translation from professional person with smart flat and (use of) chauffeur-driven car to humble student. It wasn't very glorious but it was a challenge, nonetheless. The tests in life, I reflected, were difficult because they were so undramatic.

My room-mate turned out to be part of the last intake of Young Things at RADA. She came from Blackpool and she was called Sandra. She was sixteen. She had a mink stole and a generous allowance. Her peroxided, blonde hair hung below her shoulders and she was lavish with lipstick and looked like a slight, baby-version of a Diana Dors or Veronica Lake. We had absolutely nothing in common and I became very fond of her. I was assembling a whole gallery of people who were as exotic and interesting as aboriginals.

How did I strike them at the digs? I fell into the role of 'good guy'. Margot, I gathered, was conducting a liaison which interfered with her student life and this was vaguely disapproved of by Mrs Styles. Sandra was sharp and knew how to stand up for herself. I marvelled at her nerve when she tackled Mrs Styles on the subject of catering arrangements. I don't know which of us was more aghast, Mrs S or myself, when Sandra said pertly, 'I really do think that I need a steak once a week.' I don't think I'd ever eaten a steak and, child of rationing, I didn't understand the significance or desirability

214

of red meat. Mrs Styles was – almost – silenced. Recovering, she said, 'Listen, Miss, steak is a *man's* food. Women can't eat steak. They don't even know how to *cut* it. You have to watch a *man* cutting a steak to see how it's done.' 'I'll have to speak to my mother about that,' said Sandra, as she flounced out of the room.

'I used to give my hubby steak, of course,' said Mrs Styles. I didn't have the smallest feeling about steak, but I was enjoying the drama taking place in the breakfast room overlooking the back garden. Hubby had died, leaving Mrs Styles with two daughters to bring up; one was married and about to start a completely new kind of business. 'Launderette,' said Mrs Styles. New word. I understood that for a considerable outlay one could make a fortune quite quickly by providing people with the use of sophisticated washing machines (like my Auntie Hilda's at home) in a kind of shop where they could bring their dirty laundry. This was so 'London' that I hugged it to myself. The thought of washing one's clothes in public! (My mother had made me promise to post my small parcel of laundry to her at home.)

There was another daughter at boarding school and Mrs Styles augmented her pension by taking in lodgers and 'Temping' (another new word). 'I go to the agency in Baker Street and I take what suits me, where it suits me and for as long as it suits me.' She was fearless. Her life was completely under control. Every so often she and a friend would make a trip 'up West' (another expression new to me) and there was never a sense that she was over-stretched as she easily combined her 'temping' with her immaculate housekeeping which included cooking three massive breakfasts and clearing up, before going for the Bakerloo train to the office and then providing three lavish dinners after her return from work and if we weren't in at the appointed hour we were allowed to steam heat the over-flowing plates. Mrs Styles, after dinner, retired to the lounge to watch a little TV. Her very favourite performer was Liberace and she enjoyed him so much that we were invited to share the pleasure with her. Perched on the edge of the couch of a three-piece suite, I was astonished by him.

Somehow – how? – Mrs Styles had discovered that I was married and in her eyes this gave me a little status. 'It's all right for Siân to be a little late at night, she is a *married woman*.' The first time she made a remark of this sort I was aghast. This was my secret, I'd thought. Certainly, none of my fellow students knew and ostrich-like I refused to consider whether the paper work on my admission revealed to the Academy that I was married. If so, no one mentioned it. I met Mrs Styles's comment with blankness. Sandra and Margot looked puzzled and I pretended I didn't notice. Would they tell anyone? I doubted it; we were all self-obsessed. At this stage we were barely interested in each other as people, each of us an insecure, confused and frightened single entity. I must be the only married female student in the Academy, I thought miserably. This was 1956 and I couldn't deal with the shame of having run out on a marriage to embark on a course of action that could only end some day in divorce.

Divorce. I hadn't stayed around long enough to experience the shock-waves radiating from my grandmother's house and had left my parents to explain as best they could what I was about, and deal with the disgrace. It *was* a disgrace and I felt it keenly. Once or twice I thought I saw the outline of my husband in the shadows across the road from the doorway of 62 Gower Street as I emerged into the darkness of the November nights. I looked over my shoulder as I made for the Goodge Street Underground, and I wasn't sure. If it was him, he never spoke to me; was I imagining things? In fact, I didn't see Don again until we were divorced, years later. I was ashamed of what I had done and glad to be free and ashamed that I was glad and then I put it all out of my mind. There was no point at all to any of the pain and sadness if I didn't fully commit myself to this strange, new life. It was strange and I loved it. All of it.

I was devouring life in all senses of the word. I was living on a very limited budget – a living allowance of £4-0-0 a week from my savings which only just covered my lodgings, my travelling expenses and obligatory theatre-going at the weekend (seeing everything from the Upper Circle) and snacks at the canteen at RADA during the day. Shopping, casual shopping, was a thing of the past, having to have a pair of shoes mended seriously upset the weekly budget. This was the first time I'd had to lead such a proscribed life and it didn't bother me at all. It was a small price to pay. Some of the students were much worse off than I and bar tending or waitressing at night and at weekends. All I had to do was work at acting, look at acting, talk about acting, read about acting and I felt fortunate.

But I was hungry all the time. This was an unexpected consequence of my new life. In Wales I had been beleaguered, over-worked, baulked, frustrated, uninterested in food and emaciated. Mrs Styles was providing me with more food than I'd ever eaten and I wanted more. The canteen sold cheap, fattening, stodgy food and whenever I could afford it, I bought sticky buns and white, sliced bread and margarine. My clothes were beginning to strain at the seams. Was it happiness or insecurity that was changing my shape? I was exercising every day, walking as well and, of course, running up and down stairs, but the regular meals and the buns altered me and during the first term I became – if not fat – for the first time in my life, well covered. I didn't think it mattered and I liked the unfamiliar feeling of well-being and strength I was experiencing as the breathing and posture exercises imperceptibly began to take effect.

Going home to Dollis Hill for dinner I would, if I could find a spare sixpence, buy a chocolate bar at Baker Street. Standing in front of the vending machine I looked at the people on the platform and thought, wouldn't it be wonderful if one of them dropped a fiver into my pocket. It would make such a *massive* difference to the month and I resolved that when, if ever, I became a person of substance again I would do just that – hand a poor looking student a five pound note and quickly pass on without a word. The men around me wore raincoats over sports jackets and flannels. Almost all the women wore hats and gloves and in the early evening the tubes 'up West' were full of well-dressed people in smart clothes on their way to the theatre or to restaurants. The women wore dresses and coats in stiff silk and in cold weather draped stoles made of fur or wool interwoven with metallic threads around their shoulders. Nothing in my wardrobe was suitable for any part of the theatre but the 'Gods'.

But I grew bolder and began to venture further afield on the Underground, becoming better acquainted with this city which had enchanted me.

Chapter Twenty-seven

S unday was my day for walking. London in the Fifties was
shabby. Willow-herb and buddleia flourished on open
spaces that I learned to identify as bomb-sites. The new
buildings, hastily thrown up after the war, were insubstantial
and already looked run-down. Here and there, coffee bars
were opening; they sold weakish coffee with froth on top and
were regarded as infinitely smarter than tea-shops. The tables
and chairs were flimsy with irritating little stick-like legs that
stuck out at awkward angles and tripped one up. Sitting in a
coffee bar was regarded as a bit of an extravagance and I felt
middle-aged as I clutched my winter coat to myself and tried
to shrink into the small space allotted to each patron in tiny,
street-level rooms or mouldy-smelling basements. The floor
coverings were alarming: lino-tiles in aggressively contrasting
shapes and colours or (less often) carpet in brutal combina-
tions of colours; purple with small orange and red jagged
'doodles', reminiscent of temperature charts on hospital beds.

I half liked the feeling of being in an up-to-the-minute place
(there was no such coffee bar in Cardiff), while loathing the
discomfort and especially the interior design which decreed
that no two walls should be painted or papered to look alike
and that ceilings should provide a further, brisk 'contrast' to
the four walls and the floor. Gone were the days when doors
and skirtings and window frames glowed magnolia-like or
snow-white. A nice bright orange seemed to be the favoured

colour. Perched there, dressed to look like my mother, I kept my opinions to myself and wondered if I'd heard correctly and the skiffle group that played at a time when I was safely home ready for bed in Dollis Hill could really be playing *washboards*? My mother still used a washboard, vigorously rubbing dirty clothes up and down the soapy corrugated metal surface of the board propped up in the sink, braced against her ribs. I couldn't imagine what a skiffle group looked or sounded like.

Occasionally, someone from my old life came to London and took me into a London neither I nor my fellows at RADA could afford to penetrate. These restaurants – often hotel dining rooms – looked, I imagined, much as they would have looked before the war. There was no attempt to be 'new' or modern. The best thing a restaurant could provide was a return, or an attempt at a return, to the time of prosperity and plenty and fixed values in food, décor and behaviour. The grander the restaurant or hotel, the more successfully impenetrable the veil that was drawn over the very recent rationing of butter, cheese, sugar and sweets and a shilling's worth of meat per person weekly. Thick, white starched napery and heavy cutlery went a long way towards fostering the illusion that all was as before, before 1939. I felt at home; this was the London I had read about as a little girl and I recognised from my mother's copies of *Plays of the Year 1933*. Steak and red wine were offered as the best treat possible and, indeed, I had never tasted anything so delicious.

When my friends and I decided to eat out – a lavish gesture – we ate snacks at an ABC or consumed 'as much salad as you can eat' at Lyons Corner House or paid 4/6 for a 'proper' formal, three-course meal at the Montmartre in Tottenham Court Road where the food was only a smidgen better than canteen food, but what did we know about such things. The staples were breaded veal escalopes and spaghetti, cooked the only way it ever was in modest English restaurants, *thoroughly* boiled and drenched in thick, ersatz tomato sauce. The Spaghetti House off Tottenham Court Road was a cut above and was saved up for special occasions. Risotto came surmounted by a fried egg and was simply heavenly. When we were in funds we went to Charlotte Street to eat Sunday lunch in the huge German restaurant, Schmidt's, and discovered the joys of dill pickle, sauerkraut and salt beef, and they *were* genuine joys and must have been excellent by any standard, or the restaurant would have joined the other German businesses all over the capital and disappeared once the hostilities had begun in 1939. I always ate everything put before me, sitting up straight, elbows tucked into my sides and appreciating every bite.

Occasionally I was taken to Soho and I remember being shocked when, spending Sunday with my foreign diplomat week-ending in London, and popping into Gennaros before lunch for a drink I heard him say, 'Bring some little things – sausages – olives – salami.' 'Oh, just take a little, *leave* the rest,' he said in reply to my surprised expression. The idea of leaving anything was anathema to me and I thought, 'Oh, well, it's because he's foreign,' as I ate everything in sight.

Some time before I left Wales for good he had taken me to the theatre when I was in London to do a poetry reading at The Arts Council. Terence Rattigan's *Separate Tables* (viewed close-up from the front stalls, a huge novelty) seemed to offer the same reassurance that the catering world did, maintaining that all was as it used to be and all was well. I wasn't totally convinced but I thought the actors were wonderful. Eric Portman was my favourite and there was a *huge* actress (too big, I felt) who was a Terry and consequently must be related to John Gielgud and that was a thrill so I forgave her her size. Margaret Leighton, the leading lady, was rather lovely but spectacularly thin which for me counted against her in the believability stakes. I'd never seen, in life, a person so well dressed, so slim, so *unlikely* looking.

I had seen relatively little theatre in the West End. My mother and father had been to London to see *Waters of the Moon* in 1951 and *A Day by the Sea* in 1953 and although my father had slept soundly through both, my mother had acted

221

them out, scene by scene, when she came home. I *felt* I'd seen both of the N.C. Hunter plays. There were performances which as students we simply couldn't afford to go to. Miss Morrell, emphasising that we had to have plenty of breath and *then* lots left over at the end of a speech, cited the example of the Bolshoi Ballet at Covent Garden when we were in our first term in October of 1955. 'This is the reserve of strength you need,' she said. 'The girls in the corps de ballet in *Swan Lake* exit holding one leg aloft. As they approach the wings, not only does the leg, held excruciatingly high, not drop slightly, it unbelievably actually *rises* slightly.' I passed the beautiful, inaccessible theatre in Bow Street, and stood to look at the photographs and marvelled at the wonders of discipline contained inside.

I was skirting warily around what I could see in the professional theatre, admiring aspects of it, doubting a great deal, listening to other people's opinions, being discreet, aware of the unattractiveness of student superiority. Once only was I completely enraptured and moved to think, 'This is why I'm joining up'. Wandering into a theatre only because there were plenty of available tickets, I'd seen *Waiting for Godot* and it had been the greatest experience I'd ever had in the theatre – except for my first ever visit to a panto – and I think I'd viewed it with the rapture and lack of comprehension of my five-year-old self in Swansea Empire. I didn't understand the 'story' either time but I understood that I'd seen something rare and precious. Faithful to my favourite actress, I felt it would have been even better if Edith Evans had had a part in it. *Godot* apart, it seemed to me that the establishment was firmly in place in the theatre as in the other haunts of the middle class. I had come from a classless society so the minutiae of English life and speech were end-lessly fascinating to me.

My first term came to an end and I didn't feel I'd secured my position at the Academy. I'd been allowed to do one small piece of acting. We were given over to Richard Ainley (of the rough manner), who was the son of the great Henry Ainley, and he worked with us for the whole term on one scene from *A Midsummer Night's Dream*. He gave me Titania and for about seven weeks I prepared her encounter with Oberon, beginning, 'These are the forgeries of jealousy'. I pored over it, every day. Richard Ainley was alarming and unpredictable and he made me look at ways of acting the part which I would never have dreamt of on my own. I knew the play because I had played Helena some years before in the new Festival Theatre in Sophia Gardens in Cardiff, but now I began to think along bolder, more unconventional lines. Richard Ainley must have suggested to me that I capitalise on my height and my Celtic background to play Titania as a *big* woman, deeply in touch with nature, with a maternal distress over the upsetting of the natural order. 'I want *passion*,' he growled, 'not fairy footsteps.' All the pent-up energy of months went into that short scene at the end of term. I didn't know if it was good or very ill-advised. It was certainly committed. Some senior members of staff and the Principal came to see the performance on a wintry afternoon in one of the big studios.

I wasn't sacked. That was my main joy and relief. Mr Ainley, the ogre, gave me a rapturous report 'notice' and so did the other instructors, except those in the Voice Department. I was informed that I'd been given another Scholarship and was told to skip the second term and move into the third. It was the first indication that things were going to turn out well. I hadn't formed any close friendships during this first term. I liked and was intrigued by many of my classmates but the drama of the events leading up to my departure from Wales, the tensions of the audition and my continuing guilt over the failure of the marriage had left me with only just enough energy to get my work done. I needed to be alone. I needed to recoup my strength. But I had become accustomed to working with my group and now I was to be separated from them.

I went home to Wales where the BBC welcomed me back to work part-time as a newsreader and announcer. I had to remember that when I was seventeen I'd lied to the Board and added two years on to my age in order to get taken on as an announcer. This was a bit inconvenient since I was a hopeless liar and I gradually slipped back to my correct age and hoped I would be forgiven if anyone noticed. Saunders called me and said I was to go and see Nesta Harris at the Arts Council. In recognition of the work I'd done over three years of trying to establish a Welsh-speaking National Theatre it had been decided to give me a bursary to study drama 'abroad' and I was going to be allowed to interpret abroad as England. Everything was turning out terribly well and this was a huge help at home. I spent Christmas at the farm and newspaper reports of my 'success' were clipped out, if not remarked upon, and the irregularities of my private life were completely ignored.

Chapter Twenty-eight

I n April 1956 my father drove me to Cardiff Station and we stood in the cold on Platform No. 2. Daily, for the whole of my first term at RADA, we had been reminded of the precarious nature of the acting profession, urged to bear in mind what bad luck as much as lack of talent could do for a career; that most failed. I had absorbed the lesson and my two small suitcases were witness to my continuing, cautious frugality. My circumstances had improved beyond recognition. A new scholarship would take care of my tuition and the Arts Council Bursary would look after my living expenses.

During the holiday the BBC had taken me back as a relief announcer and I'd done a little acting there as well. There was talk that during the coming summer holiday the Arts Council would ask me to play Saunders Lewis's play *Siwan*, a political love story about a Princess of Wales who had been raised and educated by Eleanor of Aquitaine. Herbert Davies was to direct. I was also being approached by BBC TV – fairly new to me – to try my hand at interviewing and presenting. It seemed as though I was going to be able to support myself during my training by working within the profession that I was preparing for. I could see that this was unusual but it did not make me feel in any way special. In everything that mattered to me I was a novice with all to learn and I longed to be on the train and on the way back to London and RADA.

My father, undemonstrative as ever, lifted my luggage on to the rack and nodded, smiling, the smile that never lost its power to de-rail me. Did they miss me, I wondered. I could no longer tell. Their life seemed happy and complete, their circumstances better than they had ever been. I promised to write and waved at my father as the train drew out. He would drive home to the Vale of Glamorgan, to his dog and my mother and her newly acquired (mad) parrot and his piano and his oil painting and the interesting job and the good friends, and was there an empty space where I had been?

Paddington! Now it was like coming home. Dollis Hill was dearly familiar; Sandra was no longer with us and I had the back room to myself. Mrs Styles was as brisk as ever but I fancied she was glad to see me. Margot looked romantic and doomed and even more beautiful. I'd been working on my voice all through the holiday and I'd moderated my eating habits. Now Mrs Styles agreed to help me and promised not to mind if I didn't turn up for my evening meal. She felt sufficiently unthreatened by me to let me use the front parlour as a work room when she wasn't watching television. I felt a great deal more in charge of my life as I travelled to RADA the following morning. Gone were the days when every moment of every day was a trial.

If getting back to London had been good, returning to RADA was heavenly. I couldn't become accustomed to the consolation and liberation of being with people whose beliefs, aspirations and priorities were identical with mine. It was as though a huge weight had been lifted from my shoulders and not a day went by when I didn't celebrate the ease of this life. I had never been much of a 'joiner' but for the first time I understood why people became members of demanding cults and religions or made careers in the armed forces; there was something wonderful about never being at odds with one's surroundings.

My double remove at the end of the first term hadn't made me feel more secure; the 'sack' still loomed as an end-of-term possibility – (maybe my work last term had been a flash in the pan) – but I had learned to embrace this kind of insecurity and the absence of certainty seemed to add to my sensation of lightness and freedom. Last term I had been intimidated by my classmates. As for the Seniors, acting in the Vanbrugh Theatre (in Malet Street, open to the public and critics), survivors of almost two years of winnowing out, they seemed to breathe different air from mine (and of course I reflected that they would have been breathing it properly, which was more than I had managed to learn to do in three months). Now I did at least feel that I had earned a little toe-hold in the Academy and I was sufficiently at home to look about me and take an interest in the other students.

There was one young man who stood out in the busy canteen because amid all the noise and the posturing he seemed to move in a little circle of calm and quiet. One couldn't help looking at him because he never seemed to do anything. I saw him play Dryden's *All for Love* in the Vanbrugh – he was a finalist – and on stage he possessed the same knack of absorbing interest and attention for no reason that I could discover; he wasn't actually *doing* anything. I didn't feel that I knew anything for sure, but suddenly I was certain that Albert Finney was acting really well; as well as anyone I had seen in the West End.

I found myself in a new group of third termers (there were always three groups doing the same work but using different texts) and in the third term there was to be a little acting on stage; not in the beautiful Vanbrugh in Malet Street, gold and red, like a 'real' theatre with proper lights and scenery and a velvet curtain, even a Royal box – we would be allowed there only if we survived to the final term – but in the 'little' theatre in the basement in Gower Street. It was small and shabby and very black, but it was a huge step forward from acting in rooms by the light of day with the traffic of WC1 roaring outside.

We were a mixed bunch in my group, some quite 'mature', which was a new departure at RADA. I didn't want to divulge my secrets so I didn't pry into other people's private lives but I knew that Gerald James had, at Christopher Fry's insistence, given up his job as Youth Employment Officer in Brecon and was, at the age of forty, embarking on this new career and working as a barman to support his wife and two daughters in Wales. He was short and rotund and though his insecurities must have been as great as anyone's, he kept them to himself and watched over the younger ones with avuncular benevolence.

I made friends with Charles Kay and as time went on we began to partner each other in full-length plays. He'd given up a career as a dentist but still remembered the rudiments, which was a comfort to us both when I accidentally knocked out a piece of his front tooth, flapping my hands, heavy with jewellery, behind me while he pursued me across the stage before hoisting me over his shoulder and carrying me off into the wings. I towered over Charles and he must have developed muscles possessed by few actors as he strode about, night after night, in play after play, holding me aloft *and talking* at the same time. He and Edward de Souza had, whether they knew it or not, a steadying influence on me. I couldn't bear to speak of my failed marriage but I felt that if they discovered my story, they wouldn't judge me too harshly.

My girl friends were Thelma Whiteley and Hélène van Moeurs. Thelma was from America and already spoke accentless English (with good breath control). She was calm and direct and wonderfully organised in work as well as in life. She got to know more about me than most and viewed my rather ramshackle life with incredulous amusement. What did I expect from people? I was all too ready for trouble and rather grateful not to be stoned in the street. Hélène, like the other two Dutch girls I knew, was a baroness. A compact and fearless baroness. Like me, she had been an announcer so her English was first class (but I could see that Shakespeare in English was going to elude her for ever). Nothing could scandalise Hélène and she organised her love life, her sex life and her working life with the enviable precision of a general. Towards the end of 1956 we rented a flat together. Fredrik Ohlsson from Sweden made up the fourth in our little group and they provided a refuge for me later, towards the end of my time at RADA, at a time when my life spiralled out of control and I came close to a total breakdown.

But early in 1956 I was still safe in uneventful Dollis Hill. I became more and more fascinated by the students in my group and as the months went by those of us who survived became close in a way that was new to me. As an only child I had been reared to compete and win and I now felt as though I'd used up my entire store of competitiveness. There was none left. But I was preparing for a life in a competitive work; it was considered important to be noticed, to make an impact, but as time went by and we watched each other struggle and fail and advance and fall back, feelings of affection and regard grew and grew and there was nothing but good will. There was, between many of us, a deep, unspoken empathy that left no space for rivalry.

The hours became longer and the work harder ('You will rarely, if ever, have to work as hard as this,' we were told. 'Oh, thank God,' I thought) and I arrived at a depth of happiness previously unknown to me. I remembered, as an undergraduate, spending a week reading Kant's *Critique of Pure Reason* and, remembering the text, I thought now 'we really are doing this *for it's own sake*'. Unbidden came the thought, 'This will not last for ever and you will never again be happy in this way'. I wanted it to go on for ever, preparing to act, learning to act, thinking about acting, reading about acting, watching acting, all so that one could spend the night acting with no object in mind except doing it.

I didn't spend any time trying to decipher a RADA 'method'; there was too much work to do all the time. Voice production remained paramount even after we'd developed into some sort of recognised performers, acting full-length plays in the Vanbrugh. A good notice in *The Times* counted for nothing if Nan Morrell had caught a performance and spotted a lazy tongue or a flabby diaphragm. 'There is no point, Siân, in acting like an angel unless you can act like an angel eight times a week for maybe fifty-two consecutive weeks. *Breathe* and *support*. At this rate you'd be "off" in ten days, and we don't "go off".' 'What a nice performance that was, Siân,' said Hugh Miller. 'Nice, that is, if one were watching from the wings. *Sell it to the paying customers*! They're in the auditorium, all three tiers of it.'

Most of the teachers were unremittingly practical and they hounded us without mercy. Praise was rarely given. We, the girls at any rate, were allowed to stop fencing lessons after a few months but, along with voice production, movement classes went on until the very end of training. Amy Boalth had the awful job of getting me moving in the first place when I was like a block of wood, before I lost my sense of shame and embarrassment. ('The one thing an actor *cannot* be, my dear, is self-conscious.') Mary Phillips, neat, distinguished and quiet was supremely watchful. She taught Mime and in her classes the unexpected happened. She observed small shoots of talent and unobtrusively tended them into startling bloom. From Miss Phillips I learned to be prepared, to wait, not to force the imagination (she also taught me to train my eyes to go for long periods without blinking and that, later, turned out to be very useful). Miss Duff directing a third term play took things at a rush. 'Turn on your actor's keyboard! Come *along*.' Then, all too often, 'Oh dear, *donkeys* all.' I consoled myself with the thought that if I could survive Mary Duff's sarcasm I could survive most things.

The teachers who were actually *in* plays were wonderful creatures, as were those who had worked with great writers or actors. Ellen Pollock, with hooded turquoise eyes, turbanned hair, dark tanned skin and draped in Caribbean colours long before such a look was fashionable, had actually been directed by George Bernard Shaw. Little Nell Carter, who gave us our first-term Shakespeare classes, directing from an ancient prompt copy, had toured in Shakespeare with fabled Victorian and Edwardian actor-managers. John Fernald, the Principal, was of course a very successful director (who'd 'worked with *everybody*'). Young David Giles came to direct plays in the Vanbrugh and Peter Barkworth came from his West End play to brush up on technique and to my dismay he found plenty for me to practise (my least favourite exercise was having to give an informed, emotional reading of a Shakespeare soliloquy while walking round a rectangular table, holding a dainty cup of tea, without spilling tea or losing eye contact with the 'house').

When to my amazement I became reasonably adroit, I progressed to Mme Fedro's Movement class and, like most of her students, was enslaved by her, inspired by her and bowled over by her genuine glamour. She taught movement that enhanced acting – that conveyed feeling and ideas moment by moment. She 'gave' me my first big entrance when, in my final term, I played Magda by Sudermann, a play called *Heimat* (*Home*) in German. Magda was a successful opera singer who, in the play, returns to visit her narrow, oppressive home. The play hadn't been performed since Eleanor Duse and Sarah Bernhardt had both played the title role at the same time in London in the late nineteenth century.

By the time I opened at the Vanbrugh with all the London critics out front and a full house agog to see how I would acquit myself, Fedro had taught me how to walk like the opera star that was Magda, how to assume that I was the most interesting and glamorous person 'in the *whole of London*', she said firmly. Willie in the Wardrobe had shown me how to take off my buttoned gloves and trail my beautiful fur as though I had five more at home, Richard Carey had given me a *real* Sarah Bernhardt fan to wear (and shown me how to use it).

I made an overnight success and job offers flooded in but I was taken back to the class room and slowly and patiently the faults that had slipped by unnoticed in the excitement of a successful performance were laid out, examined and worked on. I was overwhelmed with gratitude for such care and

231

attention. John Fernald, who had directed me, had been concerned only with the play and the part, but he handed me over without a qualm for technical debriefing. I should have been the happiest girl in the world but there was a serpent in my Eden.

Chapter Twenty-nine

A s though there was not enough work to do inside the
walls of RADA, it was the practice to 'loan out'
reliable students to professional and semi-professional com-
panies. We rehearsed on Sundays and any evenings when
we were not needed at RADA. The Tavistock Players had
moved to the Tower in Canonbury, a beautiful Jacobean
house that had once belonged to Sir Francis Bacon. There
was an ancient mulberry tree in the garden and I was
immensely taken by the beautiful, run-down, shabby neighbourhood. As I walked through Islington I thought that one
day I would love to live in one of the broken down
Georgian houses I saw on all sides. Leaving Islington at
sunset, sitting on the top deck of a Number 19 bus with an
uninterrupted view down the hill to King's Cross with the
fairy towers of St Pancras Station silhouetted against the
pink sky, I 'printed' the view in my mind where it remained,
indelible.

I was to play the lead in *Les Justes* by Camus with two
professional actors and, astonishingly, a friend of mine from
my University days. Peter Gyngell, a fellow Philosophy student (and a RADA trained student before that) who had
played Othello, much better than I'd played Desdemona, and
who had been side-tracked into playing *Les Justes* while
preparing to go abroad to begin his new life with computers.
He was an interesting man and *Les Justes* was an interesting

job. Our director was also interesting, all too interesting as it turned out.

Guy was smallish, intense and clever. Ever a sucker for brains, I was charmed at the first meeting. He had graduated from Oxford some ten years previously and I learned that his preoccupation had been documentary film and that he and Lindsay Anderson had together won an Oscar for their first movie, *Thursday's Child*, but now he had assembled a portfolio of plays which he was going to begin trying out, with a view to moving into theatre production. *Les Justes* was the first of these plays and it would be seen by several West End producers. He had cast the rest of the company himself but I was a kind of present from Gower Street for the crucial role of Dora, so I was anxious to prove myself.

I could tell that he quickly came to like his present and the play was a success although it must have been a bit overwhelming; intensely written, intensely acted and intensely directed, not a smile from start to finish, it wasn't everyone's cup of tea. Guy and I began to spend time together, talking and talking in the Tower garden with its mulberry tree and after the show we would drive down to the Embankment in his newly acquired car and sit looking across the river at the OXO sign, drinking cups of tea and eating sausage sandwiches which he bought at the little late-night tea and coffee stall nearby.

Not only was I never in for dinner, I was now getting back to Dollis Hill later and later at night. Guy couldn't believe that I lived in Dollis Hill. He couldn't believe in Dollis Hill. He had just bought a flat in Earls Court, my first resting place in London, though he preferred to say that he lived in Kensington (which was just an inch away) and that, coupled with his snootiness about Dollis Hill, led me to think that he was a bit of a snob. By this time he could have revealed himself as an axe murderer and I wouldn't have turned a hair. I was *fascinated*. And it seemed so sensible and practical for an actress to take up with a director. For once I was using my head as well as my heart and I congratulated myself.

I could tell that Guy, having emerged from a difficult time when he had had to deal with consumption as well as a disastrously unhappy love affair, was not an easy person but at that time I loved a challenge and the fact that he had problems made him all the more interesting and appealing in my eyes. I conveniently forgot that I was a very inconclusively separated, young married woman with a string of failed relationships behind her, who had sworn off men for the foreseeable future and possibly beyond and, needless to say, I kept very quiet about Guy at RADA. I had a feeling that the news of my involvement wouldn't go down well. I didn't know why, I just thought that it wouldn't.

Guy went abroad to make a film and I settled down to a more regular life at Dollis Hill, working hard and doing well at RADA. Charles Kay and I won a verse-speaking prize. It was reported in *The Times* and the following morning we both had job offers, to make a recording in a studio in Soho. Mr Fernald gave us the morning off and we bowled along to W1, hugely excited. The little doorway in Soho didn't look as though it led to much of a studio and we climbed the rickety, narrow Georgian staircase to find ourselves in an almost empty little room with a curtainless window looking on to a ratty bit of back yard. There was a microphone, tied to the back of a wooden chair.

'Okay,' said an indifferent man, 'you for the recording?' We nodded. 'Here's your script,' he said, before disappearing into the next room. I looked at the first of about six pages. 'Hullo Chirpy,' it read – twenty times. I turned over, 'Give us a kiss,' repeated twenty times, took up the whole of page two. The bored face popped round the door. 'This is for the States, so not too Shakespearian. One of you take the intro, then divide it up however. In your own time. Leave decent pauses.' I took the introduction. 'Keeping budgerigars is FUN. Teaching them to speak is a BORE. Let us . . .' And so on. I hardly dared to look at Charlie and for the next couple of hours, leaving decent pauses and not too Shakespearian, we laid down the basis of good budgerigar diction in the United States.

235

Bored face gave us a tenner each as though he was tipping the cleaners and we raced down the stairs and round the corner before giving way to the pent-up hysteria of the morning. So much for the Forbes Robertson or the George Arliss – whichever prize we'd been so proud to win.

I went home at the end of term. My report arrived and to my relief it was good. I did a little work at the BBC as usual, went west to visit Meriel and my cousins and my grandmother, but not to Tŷ mawr this time. John, Meriel's husband had worked long and well at Tŷ mawr, building up the herd and improving and modernising the farm, and they realised that they could and should now move forward and upward, to a farm with richer land and no precipitous hills. Tŷ mawr had been in the family for generations. How would be grandmother respond to the suggestion of a move?

They agonised over the problem for months; my mother thought it too cruel to expect her mother, in her late eighties, to pack up and leave her birthplace where she had loved so long and worked so hard. Meriel, ever more enterprising, thought it worthwhile suggesting. Everyone was astonished when my grandmother, having studied the business proposal and the deeds of the new property further west in Carmarthenshire, looked up and said in Welsh, 'Of course. It's wonderful. When do we go?' These women . . . I thought again, admiringly. My mother misquoted from the Bible, 'What meat does she eat to grow so strong?'

So now I, sentimentally mourning the loss of my birthplace, went to Whitland to visit the new farm and saw my grandmother completely and happily translated to the big inglenook, still awake at 5.30 in the morning, still cooking, still cleaning twenty pairs of muddy shoes each day, still reading the Welsh Bible and the Welsh language paper, *Y Faner*. Her only concession to her great age was that now she slept on the ground floor in the far front parlour. I noticed that Meriel and John and their son, Huw, home from school for the Easter holiday, all deferred to her in the most charming way as they discussed the running of the farm and the virtues of modernising.

Thelma Whiteley, one of my close friends from RADA, was spending the holiday in Wales with me, and my grandmother seemed politely bemused that two great, strapping young women should be idling away their time in London. A diploma in Dramatic Art made no sense to her at all and why should it?

Chapter Thirty

S till in Dollis Hill. More than halfway through my course
and progress had really slowed down. It had been noticed
that I didn't stand straight and the doctor who looked after
the bones of RADA students read me a stern lecture. I was
given exercises and told to persevere with them or else I would
lay up trouble for myself in the future, not least of all, vocal
trouble. Oh, vocal trouble . . . The voice! When I read all
those years ago in Cardiff that acting was 'Voice, voice and
more voice', I had no idea that my life was going to be
completely taken over by voice, voice and yet more voice.
It was still unsatisfactory. I was very good at disguising my
faults but I knew that it just wouldn't do. On with the slow,
plodding, grind.

Guy was due back from location in Indonesia. London
seemed empty without him and late at night on the day of his
return I crept downstairs at Dollis Hill, took the phone from
the hat stand in the hall and, feeling slightly foolish, sat curled
up in the dark in an armchair in the front parlour, dialling his
Fremantle exchange number and settling down to wait. I was
half asleep when the ringing stopped and the familiar, rather
precious, English voice said, 'Yes?' 'I just wanted to hear your
voice say hello.' 'Are you in dreaded NW2?' 'Yes.' 'Be ready
in half an hour, I'm coming to fetch you.' A few days later I
collected my luggage from Mrs Styles, paid my bill in full and
left Dollis Hill for ever.

Collingham Place, Earls Court, and a very different life. Tentatively I played house until I realised that Guy had already made all the domestic arrangements and they were perfectly adequate. I had only to fit in. This suited me very well and I congratulated myself yet again for being smart enough or lucky enough to have fallen in love with a brilliant man who could also buy furniture, order curtains and carpets, equip a kitchen and cook! In Wales, these things constituted Woman's Work and I had never got round to mastering any of them.

My new life stretched ahead in a very agreeable way. Of course, Living in Sin was something to be reckoned with, a new misdemeanour (was it an actual crime, I wondered). Guy wanted no truck with my schoolgirl nerves over what I perceived as an irregular situation, so I kept my worries to myself, said nothing to my family or my friends at RADA and concentrated on the agreeable aspect of our life together. I loved to listen to Guy and he introduced me to a much more sophisticated world than any I had encountered before. Life at Oxford had been very different from life in the provinces and his friends, a good deal older than myself, were, on the whole, establishment figures. I acquired a new reading list and mostly sat around listening and learning.

Things went wrong in a completely unexpected way. I had got out of the way of concealing my ambitions and enthusiasms and chattered away uninhibitedly about plays and parts I wanted to play and parts I was engaged on until one day my seventh sense told me to stop. Months had gone by and Guy had driven me to Wales to pick up my books and bits and pieces of linen and china so that I would feel properly at home in the flat. Our situation had been presented to my parents as a *fait accompli*. They were not entirely happy, and when we drove away from the house I felt that I had burned several bridges. My London life was set and fixed with Guy and I began to feel apprehensive as I realised that Guy's attitude towards the theatre was changing. The habit of a lifetime re-asserted itself and I stopped talking about my working life. He'd made another film and I enjoyed visiting the cutting room in a Soho basement late at night, learning how to handle film and watching him edit. He dazzled me, still.

I was now in my final term, rehearsing *Magda* and knew that it would be a significant test for me. As a final student I was to play in the Vanbrugh Theatre. It was a huge, difficult part and I was only too aware of the pitfalls ahead. The press were taking an interest in the revival and I knew I would be the subject of intense scrutiny. Herbert Davies made plans to come up from Wales to see the play. My parents said they might come as well. I knew that the Welsh press would be there and it seemed the English national press were going to cover it as well. For once I wasn't unduly nervous; the play had learned itself, John Fernald's rehearsals were superbly organised and everything rose to the boil at the right moment. The themes of the play were close to my heart; loss of home, exile, conflict between heart and career.

The reaction, however, took me by surprise. I could have left the Academy at that moment and started a career at the top of the tree. I was offered contracts, plays and movies, all the best agents wrote asking if they could represent me, artists wanted to paint me. I was asked to sit for cover photographs for magazines and endlessly the press wanted to interview me. It was a difficult situation for me as a student, especially since I had accepted the advice of John Fernald, rejected all the offers and decided to stay on at RADA and do another final term to make up for the term I'd skipped over earlier on. I played down the dramatic change in my situation but it wasn't possible entirely to conceal it. From my fellow students I received nothing but generosity. The door was closed on the offers and the excitement. Journalists were discouraged and this suited me; I had no wish to publicise my separation or my relationship with Guy and Guy was becoming increasingly edgy as my stock rose in spite of myself.

Gradually we became bogged down in on-going, far into the night, discussions about the fitness and propriety of a life in the theatre. Guy revealed that he proposed leaving the 'business' altogether and intended making a career in a completely different field, doing something, he hadn't decided what, more worthwhile, of more use to the world. I was aghast. These were themes I had been rehearsing all my life. Every boyfriend, every lover, my husband, Don, had all argued against the suitability, the worth of my chosen career and all had tried to make me give it up. The arguments had varied in skill and intensity but I had never seriously wavered. Now I couldn't face going through it all again. Guy was much cleverer than I was, much, much cleverer. He beat me in every argument, was by turns angry and tender, and I was in torment.

Magda came to an end and with it the brouhaha about comparison with Duse and Bernhardt. I breathed a huge sigh of relief at having come through. After the last matinée I was told I had a visitor. Peering out into the inhospitable cement stairway, I looked down at a very large red face looking up at me. 'I'm Robert Atkins,' said the face. 'I've got just one thing to say to you – *don't* go into the fillums,' and the famous former artistic director of the Stratford Memorial Theatre was gone, leaving me feeling as though I'd been given a very quick award.

I began to rehearse two small parts in *The Silver Curlew*, a musical, in which I was entrusted with a 'point' number (which seemed to define a song that didn't need to be beautifully sung). I was to play an ugly witch in the forest and a fairy godmother with the gift of beauty which I would carry in a little jewelled box as I emerged from a christening cake dressed in a pretty frock and performing a little dance.

Guy was now pressing me to leave RADA after *Magda*. I came to the end of my defences and could no longer justify my chosen life. I had, by now, begun to believe that an actress's life *was* pernicious, that there was no possibility of combining an actress's career with a 'good' life. A psychiatrist friend of Guy's assured me that actresses were scarcely recognisable as normal human beings after the age of forty, when it was too late to hope for redemption. Guy sensed that he'd almost won and the endless discussions lessened.

I confessed my predicament to John Fernald and he was angry. He was enraged. I don't know what I had expected of him but I was too dazed with unhappiness to realise that I was conveying to him Guy's contempt for *his* life as well as mine. He was deeply offended and demanded to see Guy. Meanwhile, I was ordered to concentrate on my work and remember my duty and think of my considerable debt to the Academy. He wrote to Herbert and Saunders and letters began to arrive by each post expressing outrage and completely failing to understand how I could possibly put a love affair before my career.

By now, I was ashamed of everything, ashamed of being in love, ashamed of having a career, ashamed of neglecting my career, ashamed of being unable to make paramount a loving relationship with another human being, ashamed of being too independent, ashamed of being feeble minded. The heavy guns were mobilised and wheeled out to bring me back into line; Dame Sybil Thorndike summoned me to tea and lectured me kindly but forcibly about the nature of Service in the Theatre. Flora Robson was roped in to express sad resignation but to confirm an actress's lonely lot. I couldn't work out what was right and I hung there, in pain.

The situation was slightly diffused by a bout of ordinary physical pain. Driving to a matinée of *The Silver Curlew*, in the throes of a weary argument after a sleepless night, our car struck a lorry in the fog in Paddington – or a lorry struck us. I was aware only of bouncing on to the windscreen and the huge, empty noise of metal striking metal. I came to on a pavement as a voice asked, 'She all right?' 'Nah, don't look it. She's a bit of a mess.'

I drifted off again and the next time I came to on a cold slab, a young man's exasperated voice was saying, 'Oh damn and blast!' as he fiddled with my face. I opened my eyes and peered at him through what seemed to be a thicket of fine, black wires. I lifted my hand to my face and the exasperated one slapped it down gently. 'Lie still. Don't touch. I'm trying to sew your forehead together. You're very lucky you've got eyes, so just shut them for a minute, there's a good girl.' He stitched away silently, confiding to me that my jaw was back in place – he *thought*.

I opened my eyes again. He looked about twelve years old. 'Are you a student?' I asked. 'Never you mind,' he replied and did a spot more embroidery. I came to my senses suddenly. 'What's the time?' 'About two.' 'Oh my God. Excuse me.' I began to slide my legs off the trolley. 'Where are you going?' 'I've got a matinée.' 'Don't be absurd. I'm keeping you in. You're probably concussed and Lord knows what else.' 'Sorry, I'm off.' 'If you leave this building you have to sign a form discharging yourself.' 'Sure thing.'

I was on my feet and fishing for a pen in my bag which someone had put at my feet as I lay on the trolley. 'This is absurd,' began the young man. 'Sorry,' I replied, walking out of the room as steadily as I was able. The nurse, holding out a paper for me to sign, looked at my chest and I looked down to see my cream Viyella blouse stiff and brown with drying blood. 'Is my face clean?' I asked her. 'Ye-es,' she said, doubtfully. I had no wish to look and scribbling my name on the form and calling out 'Thanks a lot,' I left St Mary's, Paddington.

I was feeling decidedly odd but had the sense to button up my coat, hiding the blood, before hailing a taxi. 'Vanbrugh Theatre, Malet Street,' I said urgently. 'I'm in a bit of a hurry.' 'Are you all right?' asked the driver. 'Yes, fine,' I assured him and sank back into the corner of the soft leather seat, wonderfully protected from the outside world which appeared in small foggy bits through the wedge-shaped back window next to my head.

At the Vanbrugh the show was about to begin. 'I'm here, I'm here! Sorry,' I called out before dashing into the dressing room. 'I'll need to see you later!' shouted an angry voice from the stairs. I got into my witch wig and costume and laid about my face with a stick of green Leichner greasepaint. I suppose I was concussed because I didn't actually SEE my face as I got made up.

On stage, bathed in purple and green light in the dark wood, I squatted behind the huge cauldron and bobbed up and down singing my witchy song and it seemed to go quite well. Then I whipped back to my little corner and transformed myself into the Fairy Godmother. This time, it hurt rather to clean off the green paint and wipe the black from my teeth and I noted dispassionately that my face looked odd. The young man's sewing had left a great deal to be desired; great black 'spiders' marched across my forehead and through my eyebrows. My nose was swollen and my lips were a funny shape. There were stitches on my chin. My whole face was turning a strange colour . . . 'Ah well, it can't be helped,' I thought calmly. I dabbed on a little more powder and made off for my place inside the huge christening cake.

'The Fairy Godmother with the gift of Beauty,' shouted a footman (Nick Smith, if I remember rightly). Tum TUM, tum tum, tum TUM, tum tum, went the orchestra. The cake swung open and I tried not to flinch as I stepped into the white and pink light and gritted my teeth as I determinedly set off on a circuit of the stage, keeping one eye on the cradle I was aiming for. 'If I can just make it over there,' I thought, 'I'll have got away with it.' I was so gone in the head I didn't even hear the laughter in the audience. In the wings, someone from Stage Management said, 'For God's sake, *do* something about your face – sequins or something.' I remember only going out between the shows to the chemist around the corner and buying Elastoplast, then down to Tottenham Court Road for purple sparkle dust and glue. Then after my second outing as the witch that evening, I set to work putting Elastoplast across my forehead and gluing purple dust on to the strips. 'Pretty good,' I thought. 'You can't see the stitches at all. Well – just a bit.' I added a few more strips of Elastoplast to my cheekbones and scattered some more purple stuff here and there.

Did anyone sympathise? If so I didn't notice. Certainly no one suggested that I should miss a performance, nor would I

have wanted to do so. Everything hurt, but at one remove. I
didn't even notice how my Fairy Godmother fared on stage
that night and was next fully aware of getting off the tube at
Earls Court. If anyone stared at my face, rainbow bruised and
iridescently decorated, or at my bloody blouse, then I was not
aware of it and not in the least concerned. I felt rather pleased
with myself. Guy was at home. I'd forgotten about him during
the effort of getting through two shows. I couldn't quite bring
him into focus and I certainly didn't want a post-mortem of
the day. Not now. Not at all.

'Bath,' I said, suddenly quite cheerful. As I applied a match
to the wrong bit of the geyser and blew myself across the
bathroom, I lay on the floor and thought, 'Well, it could all
have been a *lot* worse.'

Chapter Thirty-one

T he same divine stupidity remained with me during the coming months and not once did I lament my ruined face, or fear that my career was at an end, or at the least, significantly changed. I came to my senses sufficiently to realise that at home I now occupied the moral high ground for a while. I figured that Guy must feel awful to have been driving the car in which I'd been hurt, grateful that I wasn't going to spoil his no claims insurance policy and *sorry* for me. I was stupidly childish enough to think that maybe if I became a very plain actress I might appear to be more morally acceptable. Nothing much was said at home or at RADA. I postponed my showdown with Herbert and kept out of Mr Fernald's way at RADA. When he passed me in the corridor he shook his head at my bent nose and jagged scars.

At the end of term, Guy decided that we should make a journey to Iona in Scotland. I was thrilled; I'd never been to Scotland and I'd read wonderful things about the islands in the West. Ever optimistic, I thought that everything was going to be all right, after all.

We drove to Scotland. It was a long, wonderful, cold journey. At Oban we took a boat that called at Rhum and Eigg and Muck, before depositing us on Iona. We made our way to the bare lodging house and went for a walk. Night was falling, but full darkness did not come and the lilac light hung between us and the darkening stone buildings, and rough, grey, treeless fields with the black sea beyond. It was the same light that I had seen shimmering on midsummer nights in the Swedish countryside but Iona was a world away from soft, warm, sensual Västeråas. I went to my narrow bed feeling uneasy and all at once isolated.

After breakfast we walked again in the intense cold and as we walked we began to talk and the pit of my stomach seemed to fall away and my throat constricted as I realised that there was not to be an easy conclusion to our debate; I was not going to be able to charm my way to a compromise. We were both raw with misery and Guy was pushing for a resolution. Didn't this place make it easier for me to see how much 'better' life could be? How much better *I* could be in a different world? I longed to capitulate and be gathered up into a warm embrace of approval. The world I was being offered was attractive and I was so in love and terrified as I felt myself free-falling away from the person that I admired, wanted, loved and feared. But I did not in fact have a choice. I couldn't leave the theatre. My world seemed bleak and as cold as charity but it was my world and I had to find a way of living in it.

When he realised that I had made my decision and couldn't do as he wished he grew cold and distant partly, I thought, from pain. He wanted me out of his sight at once. There was no question that we should travel back to London together. I was to leave alone on the first boat and take a train from Oban. I thought my heart was breaking as I watched from the boat and the island disappeared from view. I had expected so much of this place and it seemed wrong that it should have served merely as a setting for an unhappiness that I had brought there.

I sat in the corner of a crowded compartment; eight of us squashed together for hours. Reserve fell away and the other travellers began to chat a little. A hard lump had lodged in my throat, speaking would have choked me. I looked sightlessly out of the window and struggled not to cry out. For eight hours? – nine? I averted my face and forced back the tears that were insisting behind my eyes. It was dark when we pulled into London and still I struggled to retain control of myself until the taxi drew into Collingham Place. I unlocked the door of the familiar flat and, dropping my suitcase on the floor, sank to the ground and wept.

Some time during the night, I shed my coat and shoes and went into the bedroom and, still dressed, climbed into the bed, sheets unchanged since they were our sheets from four long days ago. At daybreak I fell asleep, waking on what day and at what time I didn't know. The clock had stopped, I didn't wear a watch and it didn't occur to me to lift the telephone receiver to ask the operator the time. Tears had given way to fear. I knew there was no going back but what had I done? I was following my instinct but although it was strong enough to have forced me into this situation of extreme unhappiness it wasn't *clever*; it wasn't telling me anything. I was left with no explanations and no certainties.

Self-preservation prompted me to think of food. How many days since I had eaten? But it was no good, I couldn't walk down the stairs and into the street. Instead I lay on the bed and the argument I'd been having with Guy began to repeat itself. I couldn't be sure that he wasn't right. I couldn't be sure that I hadn't taken a fatally wrong step, turning away for good from intimacy and warmth and uncomplicated happiness.

Sitting on the bed, I feverishly picked through the theatre books piled up everywhere. Surely *somewhere, someone* had written *something* that would help me comprehend the nature and the reality of the world to which I had committed myself. Surely it wasn't the monstrous, pernicious, tawdry place of Guy's imagining, or the dark, secret home of the devil as my grandparents had believed. Obviously, it wasn't the place of uncomplicated happiness that I had understood and felt it to be and what was the price of admission? More than I had realised. Worse still, what was the cost of a permanent tenancy and did I have the means to pay it? The questions remained unanswered and exhaustion led me to sleep again.

Waking, I put my coat on, smoothed my hair and ventured out. It was so cold, or was it that I was cold? I picked up a tin of baked beans, then realising that I was going to begin crying again, I quickly paid for it and ran home. No, it wasn't home, not any longer. The tears flowed and I opened the can of beans and ate them cold from the tin. I felt a grim satisfaction that I could eat and cry at the same time. This was a good sign and I undressed and bathed in cold water (I hadn't dared touch the boiler since I'd blown it off the wall), changing into clean clothes and ready then to start living. Leaving all my books and china and most of my clothes, I packed a small bag and after telephoning my parents – in a quiet, and carefully neutral tone – I went to Paddington and caught the train to Wales.

Chapter Thirty-two

My family was tactful. I didn't have to explain that it was all over. It hurt me when well-meaning people who had learned the gist of my story consoled me with praise for having done 'the right thing'. This was not a story about being led astray by a bad person. I wasn't totally sure about the purity of his motives in his dealings with me but Guy was a good person and who was to say what was the right thing to do. I was badly hurt and I kept quiet, scarcely speaking, grateful that I was being given time to recover before returning to London.

On my return Guy had softened sufficiently to find me a flat in Great Ormond Street. I felt better, but not better enough to go back to Earls Court to pick up my things. I experienced a pang of regret only over my complete Charles Dickens which I'd been reading and re-reading since I was little. It seemed better to move on with nothing. I liked the flat, in a modern back extension to one of the big Georgian houses. It was calm, uncomplicated, peaceful. On my first morning there I was awakened at 5 a.m. by the sound of several large vehicles starting up at what seemed to be the foot of my bed. Leaning out of the window which opened on to the little mews behind Great Ormond Street, I burst out laughing for the first time in months as I realised that I was living over a very busy, well equipped garage that sprang to life at dawn. 'Every day?' I asked, weak with laughter. ' 'Fraid so, miss.' I don't know why but I felt immensely cheered and within a week I was sleeping soundly through the noise.

Hélène and Thelma came to inspect my new living arrangements and were cautiously approving. They couldn't believe I'd been so 'stupid'. By now they knew the bare bones of the trouble I had been in at RADA. I loved their breezy dismissal of the anguish and their good-natured incredulity at my 'madness' following the run of *Magda*. I couldn't share their attitude but it was a lifeline to normality. Guy also came to visit. I didn't know why. He said little but he stayed over, sleeping chastely on the floor. During the night I had a dream; the first dream that had ever woken me up and it remained clear and entire in my mind.

Seated in an ornate cage-like lift (the sort I'd seen in France), I was dressed in my blue silk Act I *Magda* dress, playing a cello, very much in the pose of the Augustus John painting of Suggia. It was a brilliant scene: dark blue taffeta silk, gilt everywhere, rich dark shiny wood and the walls on either side of the lift brilliantly lit like the backcloth of an opera. As the lift began its slow ascent my dress began to unravel itself in strips, first the bodice and then the long skirt until, greatly shamed, I was left naked in full view of a large but invisible, silent, audience.

I lay in bed in the early morning sun and went over the dream in my head; 'gilt everywhere', oh Lord, '*guilt* everywhere', 'shame'. This had to stop. Guy woke and I made tea. It was painful, preparing it exactly the way he liked it because I knew, sadly and certainly, that I would never, could never again observe the little ritual or see him again.

A few nights later I was awakened by the instance of another vivid dream, or rather, a recollection of something I had never before recalled. I saw myself in the parlour of the house next to the one I had lived in until I was five years old in the little village of Dunvant, standing in front of a shiny oilcloth scroll which depicted two roads; one a broad thoroughfare with cafés and theatres and dance halls and people having a lovely time strolling down the road until suddenly they tumbled, very surprised, into the flames of Hell at the bottom of the chart. The road from the middle to the top of a scroll was called the Narrow Way and people hobbled and struggled up its rocky surface in awful weather – no cafés or theatres – until they arrived, again rather surprised I would have thought but I couldn't see their faces, on to a level plain in front of a huge rising sun where Jesus Christ (or God, I couldn't be sure which) stood welcoming them with out-stretched arms.

I fancy that my parents weren't best pleased with my daily excursions next door to pore over the Broad and Narrow Way which enthralled me. The neighbours must have belonged to some obscure religious sect and they were delighted by my interest, but I viewed the scroll rather as one would read a horror story. I didn't want to fall into the pit but I hated the rocky path of righteousness and didn't much like the level plain dominated by the over-sized sun either; the only nice bit was the hanging about in dance halls and theatres, but, oh dear, those waiting devils with pitchforks . . . I thrilled to the horror at the bottom of the chart and never tired of peering at the awful details.

I lay looking at the ceiling, wide awake, half amused at the recollection and half appalled. The Broad and Narrow Way was a crude, simpler version of the sophisticated arguments with which I'd been wrestling for so many months, intellectually out of my depth but retaining a small piece of self-determination and just enough backbone to see me through – I hoped.

I missed Guy badly; I missed having a family life with him but I hadn't spent all these years fighting the puritanism which seemed to have been bred into my bones in order to succumb now that I was over twenty. 'Take what you want and pay for it.' I went to work and began paying.

My face had healed, leaving me with deep jagged scars, a broken nose and a rather unstable jaw. It seems unbelievable but still there was never a moment when I worried about my appearance or about its effect on my career. I don't know that anyone believed this but it was the case. My wayward voice began to come to heel! I wondered superstitiously if I was being given some kind of reward for good behaviour when I came to the end of a Shakespeare sonnet and Miss Morrell and I looked at each other and for the first time in almost two years she nodded approval. Not for a single day had I stopped trying to be clear, unaffected, audible, flexible, unforced, musical-where-needed, interesting, intelligible, energetic, durable, strong. All I'd managed was strong, durable, audible and tense, dull, forced, rigid, unnatural and self-conscious. This was happiness, this easy stroll through a sonnet. Miss Morrell had been the bane of my life latterly; even other members of staff had begun to say, 'Well, you know, there's nothing *so* bad about her voice.' I won verse speaking prizes for RADA and within RADA was awarded an embarrassing number of awards. None of this had signified to Miss Morrell and she'd kept my nose to the grindstone. Now suddenly and unaccountably I was through! Everything began to fall into place and my gratitude to my gorgon was limitless.

Deep inside I carried a thick, immovable layer of unhappiness but it was overlaid with pleasure, joy and interest. My friends were wonderful to me. Charles Kay, Edward de Souza and Gerald James, always tactful, never prying, taking me 'out of myself', along with Thelma Whiteley and Hélène van Moeurs and Fredrik. We spent long hours drinking (very little) coffee in Ollivelli's café above the restaurant and Gerald had tamed the greasy spoon café-owner on the corner of Goodge Street and Charlotte Street into letting us occupy the little room for hours on end and even buy meals 'on tick'. Gerald organised trips on the river on Sundays and we went to Kew and to Greenwich. We drank coffee in the Festival Hall café on the first floor looking out over the best view of London I'd yet discovered and on special occasions went back to eat pasta in the Spaghetti House off Tottenham Court Road or a heavy German meal at Schmidt's in Charlotte Street. Edward organised us into more 'as much as you can eat' salad parties at Lyons Corner House in Leicester Square.

Food was still a necessary fuel rather than an entertaining part of life. Our eating habits seemed pathetic to the foreign students, especially to Americans. 'I'm going to die unless I eat some meat,' said an American student, Gay Gadbois, one lunchtime in the canteen. 'Come with me.' Gay looked as though she belonged to a different species: tall, glossy-haired and beautiful, with legs encased for work in shiny American tights and a leotard that never wrinkled. She had the air of one who had been reared on orange juice, cream and abundant meat.

We raced down Tottenham Court Road, I feeling very strange – it had never occurred to me to leave the building during the day. At St Giles Circus she strode into a café that was called a Wimpy Bar. I didn't know what a Wimpy was and refused one when she offered it to treat me – I'd already eaten a cheese roll in the canteen. I watched her as she devoured two hamburgers, flat discs of meat that weren't made of ham at all, squeezed into a large soft roll, ketchup provided in funny round containers shaped like a tomato. I'd never seen anyone so cheered up by a bit of meat and I shared her good mood as we tore back to work. The next time someone from my past life at the BBC took me to a smart hotel, I ordered beef and was appalled at the cutting and chewing involved in my shared piece of Chateaubriand but very impressed by the Bearnaise sauce that accompanied it. A Bearnaise sauce sandwich would have been bliss, I thought.

All these outings and excursions were squeezed into a life filled with work. All day we laboured over mime and move-ment and improvisation, then began rehearsing until at the end of the afternoon we were given a few hours off before the evening performances in the Vanbrugh. I played some good parts in *The Three Sisters* and *The Three Daughters of M. Dupont* and really small parts in other plays and enjoyed those just as much. Even our theatre-going was limited; theatre-going was expensive and we didn't have many nights off. We heard each other's lines even when we were out and grew close and wished each other well. We played old commercial plays like *Cry Havoc* and *Black Chiffon* in halls in Camden near RADA and in the open air in Russell Square where Act One was drowned out by the sound of taxis taking people to the 'real' theatre.

The Caucasian Chalk Circle played the Vanbrugh and also went to the York Festival. I was given the Governor's Wife and Lodovica, the girl in the Hay. The nights were long and fine and we lounged about near the river and I began a flirtation with Fredrik. Gerald shook his head benignly. 'Just you wait my girl, soon, very soon, you're going to be swept off your feet by somebody – like a tornado.' 'I don't think so,' I smiled back at the Welsh wizard. I was only just coming to life again and a massive love affair was not on my agenda. Hans Haas was the curator of the Art Gallery at York. He took us under his wing and gave us a tour and a bit of a picnic. 'Education,' he said apropos of nothing in particular, 'is the impact of quality.' We looked at each other and nodded.

Chapter Thirty-three

T he plan seemed to be to keep me busy so I'd have no time to get into any more trouble. I saw very little of my little flat (so small and so compact that it was actually termed a 'flatlet'). Not only was I acting in the Vanbrugh but I and another student, John French, were loaned out to a wealthy, mildly eccentric English gentleman who presented a Shakespeare play each summer in his beautiful garden in the country, near Newbury. At the weekend, on Saturday, if I wasn't needed at RADA or very early on Sunday morning, Flair, the butler, would pick me up from Great Ormond Street and drive in a stately fashion to Berkshire where Herbie, whose surname I missed completely, was waiting with his wife, Paulise de Busch, heiress to a huge soft-drinks empire ('Every drop of Kia-Ora, dear, is based on some kind of juice from the de Busch factory in Germany,' breathed an awe-struck house-guest cum extra 'walking' lady) eager to feed us sumptuously, deliciously and get on with *Twelfth Night*.

When term ended I was packed off to stay at the country house, spending the week alone with Flair and the house-keeper and awaiting the invasion of house-guests chosen as friends only if they were proved capable Shakespeare actors. It was a charming motley crew of middle-class bankers and lawyers and retired diplomats and my chum (Orsino) was Michael Vowden, who was 'something' in Shell but hated it and wished he'd stuck to acting instead. Herbie in his youth

(he and Paulise seemed quite old to me) had been a member of
the noted F.R. Benson Shakespeare Company. Marriage and
the advent of all that expensive fruit juice had scuppered his
career as a lowly, hard working member of a touring company but he loved Shakespeare and we all bent under his lash
as he re-created the productions of thirty of forty years ago. It
was an agreeable way of passing the early months of summer
and I made my first encounter with the comforts of wealth.
Food was delicious, unlike any that I'd tasted except in France
and Sweden, and comforting little snacks and drinks appeared
unbidden at one's elbow. The famed fruit juice was much in
evidence and I made the acquaintance of a long drink made of
gin and heavenly German ginger beer. And the ice was *round*
and the glasses were beautiful. We sat in the rose-framed
outdoor dining room, protected on three sides, looking out
over the lawns down to the stream with the sun setting
beyond the trees and I thought that my heart might be broken
but I was loving every moment of this soft life.

Flair, the butler, drank. He approached actors taking their
ease in the garden during rehearsal, picking his way cautiously through the summer air with a reviving drink sliding
gently down the wobbly tray towards the reclining house
guest. 'I believe your call is approaching, madam,' he would
intone quietly as the guest snatched the falling glass. On
weekdays when we were alone he would open *The Times*
and fill in the crossword, each clue no sooner read than
solved. At weekends he merely read the crossword, then
ironed the paper before giving it to Herbie.

I didn't much like acting in the open air except towards
the end of the play, when dusk fell and the lights came up
and the performance always drew to a beautiful close no
matter what the deficiencies of the opening scenes. Michael
Vowden was patient and wise when, unusually for me, I
confided my troubles to him as we took walks in the comfortable well-tended countryside of Berkshire. He was one of
the few people who didn't find my preoccupation with good
and evil to be absurd.

As soon as the play was over, my face was finally dealt with. The representatives of Paramount Pictures in London were courting me with a view to putting me under a contract in the United States, though *Magda* was long gone. They sent me flowers and fruit and books on opening nights and occasionally took me to smart restaurants and talked of my life to be in Hollywood. Columbia Films also sent flowers coupled with businesslike letters concerning seven-year contracts. It was assumed by my teachers at RADA that these overtures would be firmly rejected and I was quite happy to comply, never for an instant tempted by the offers. I was in RADA to learn to act in the theatre and I agreed that although I had made a phenomenally good start I needed a great deal more practice and that I would only receive in the theatre. I wasn't being 'pure' or 'good' in this unusual situation for a student, I was taking what I saw as a commonsensical, practical stance. Saunders and Herbert agreed with Mr Fernald and my other advisers. 'But,' said one canny person, 'since they're so keen to do so, why not let them fix her face and her teeth?' The morality of this didn't trouble me at all and I graciously allowed Paramount to arrange a meeting with Sir Archibald McIndoe, the famous surgeon, who still continued to do wonderful work with maimed and burned ex-servicemen.

Sir Archibald was far more intimidating to meet than the movie moguls. He was polite and civil but he was so obviously *somebody* that I was over-awed and didn't make much of a job of explaining *why* I should have my face fixed. He declared that he wasn't interested in prettifying actresses and I didn't have an answer to that, concurring privately that mending my face – which wasn't so bad – came pretty low on a list of priorities that included burned airmen. He said he would be in touch and I was told later that he and Lady McIndoe would be dropping in to the Vanbrugh to see me perform. A week later I was told when to report to East Grinstead where I would be kept for a week and my scars would be re-cut and re-stitched and my nose straightened and my jaw stabilised. Another bout of sublime idiocy took possession of me and I booked myself to make a TV appearance in Manchester two weeks after the operation and promised to be in Wales to do *Siwan* for the Arts Council immediately afterwards, turning up with the part learned so that I could join the production late and open a week later so that I could return to RADA in time for my second final term. Herbert sent me notes on the part and I studied it while rehearsing Viola in the country.

Michael kindly saw me off to East Grinstead and suddenly I was a little apprehensive. When I came to in the hospital the following day, heavily bandaged and none too comfortable, I had a moment's unease about my TV appearance but the happy idiocy prevailed and I thought to myself that everything would probably be just fine.

It was – just – but any sane person would have been distraught at the first sight of the blackened eyes, bruised face and the new lines of (beautiful, even) stitches and the television job a mere six days away. I healed amazingly quickly and looking normal again, took my leave of the great man. He said he'd resisted the temptation to give me a prettier nose and smiled for the first time at my confusion as I struggled to respond to that. No one looked twice at me in Manchester and in Wales my appearance passed unremarked; I looked as I had looked before I took my header through the windscreen. I loved working with Herbert again and acting with Glanffrwd James, Margaret John and Emyr Jones who was fast becoming one of the best young poets in Wales. It was, I realised, a huge relief to be acting in my own language again. Welsh 'placed' the voice differently and I realised that I had never *had* a vocal problem when speaking Welsh. Saunders's words were wonderful, even coming so soon after Shakespeare.

Because I had been allowed to jump a term at the beginning of my time at RADA I now 'owed' a term at the end. It was unfortunate that the correct psychological moment for me to leave was at the end of my first final term when I played

Magda which generated such excitement. It did not occur to me to do so. My gratitude to the Academy was too great and I was glad to do anything to repay my huge debt, so although I had completed the course and *Magda* had won me the Bancroft Gold Medal I put my future on hold and returned to RADA to spend an extra finals term playing *Hedda Gabler* at the Vanbrugh, then on tour in the provinces in England and finally at the Duke of York's Theatre and at the National Theatre in Oslo. Mr Fernald had written out his thoughts on the play and the way he intended to direct it and I read and re-read the play and the notes for weeks before we began rehearsing.

Charles Kay and I played a 'try-out' of a new comedy for a French author before I began the Ibsen. The play didn't work but Charles and I had a hilarious time, he once again valiantly bearing me aloft as he tore in and out of a set of French farce doors. I'd played more with Charles than with any actor I'd known and I was sorry that he wouldn't be appearing in *Hedda* and that he'd be leaving RADA – who knew when we would act together again? In the event it was to be over twenty years before that happened.

Fredrik Öhlsson – large, gentle giant – played Tesman, Donald Burton played Brack and Edward de Souza played Loveborg. The words had learned themselves without my noticing and the three weeks of rehearsal passed smoothly. I had given up my little Bloomsbury home and now shared a large flat with Thelma and Hélène in West Hampstead. Fredrik – Fritte, as we now called him – and I were seeing a great deal of each other and he became a frequent visitor. Hélène took charge of my life, organising everything, making sure I ate proper meals and banishing me to bed early. I loved Thelma and Hélène and deeply appreciated their domestic and organisational skills. I took no pleasure in being 'hopeless' and tried to keep up my end and not be too much of a liability but I think that on the whole they found it more relaxing when I didn't pretend to more efficiency than I possessed.

We opened *Hedda* and the play – and I – did well. Paramount and Columbia pictures were still in attendance, joined now by Sir Michael Balcon who offered me a British film contract at Ealing Films. I was approached about doing a West End play before the end of term and turned down the offer. Out of all the agents that offered their services I was advised to choose Olive Harding of MCA as an agent. She seemed congenial although I did find it odd that on my first visit to MCA at 139 Piccadilly she spent most of our time together talking about Peter Finch whom she also represented. I was also made slightly uneasy by her rhapsodies over the beautiful life of one of her clients who had given up acting in favour of motherhood. She seemed very keen on motherhood; not something I had ever contemplated. I did a lot of nodding and met the men who ran other departments at the agency but I left feeling I almost preferred my Americans who actually said things like, 'I can make you a *star*'. Olive seemed to be saying, 'I can make you retire.' Not a good start but maybe agents were a bit uneasy around actresses. Binkie Beaumont offered me a contract with H.M. Tennant Ltd but I was told not to consider it as Tennants was a graveyard for young actresses who were made to feel less lovely than the young male actors.

Suddenly aware that this desirable life at RADA would shortly end, I began to have a few thoughts about what to do as opposed to what not to do. This pondering took place during a period marked by endless 8.30 a.m. jaunts to Mr Suk, the dental surgeon who was being paid buckets of money by Columbia films to 'do' my teeth. Crowns or caps were all the rage, it seemed, the bigger the better. I went along with everything as usual. First one's own teeth were filed down to little stumps; this was lengthy and noisy but not at all painful, then temporary crowns were stuck over the stumps and one was sent out to face the world with strict instructions not to eat chunks of meat or bite into apples until the finished article was stuck on a week later (and still they came out in apples). I didn't enjoy any of this but sitting there in W1 in the early morning gave me plenty of thinking time. Out of the blue Mr Fernald called me into his office to put to me an unusual proposal.

The new career proposal went a bit like this. A very wealthy man wishes to invest in the Arts. He seeks advice and falls in with the idea that investment in the theatre would be interesting and amusing. 'Theatre' being a bit general, it is suggested that he should invest in a performer and instigate a little human experiment. For example, what would be the outcome if an actress with an embarrassment of offers were to find herself in the position of not having to earn a living? How would she then choose? Would her choices be better?

Douglas Uren was the rich man and he came along to the Vanbrugh to take a look at me and when he subsequently offered me a contract by which he guaranteed me an adequate salary whether or not I worked, I was strongly urged to accept. I had no way of knowing if that really was how the offer came about but I was intrigued by the unusual deal. It was a given at RADA and in many theatre circles that the cinema was not an appropriate place in which to come to rest after a theatre training and it had not occurred to me to question this. When Robert Atkins had said 'Don't go into the fillums' I had wondered why he should imagine I would do anything so foolish. Now I was immensely relieved to be able to put myself out of the running as far as going into the movies was concerned. Being under contract and spoken for would simplify my life no end and also I liked Mr Uren who was distant but friendly. I hoped that I would justify his rather eccentric venture. Why shouldn't I? I was firmly back on track with the hell of heartbreak in the past and my demons quietened, maybe conquered. There was room for cautious optimism.

Chapter Thirty-four

My friendship with Fredrik had blossomed into a romance, which was an old-fashioned way of describing what was for me a new kind of relationship. I wondered at the ease and the enjoyment, the lack of anguish, the absence of scenes and thought it was possible that the fact of our both being obliged to communicate through the medium of a second language was moderating our words and consequently our behaviour. I had moved to Fredrik's flat in the Fulham Road in South Kensington. Thelma and Hélène came to stay at Christmas. We had such a good time that foremost in my mind was the question, 'When will it go wrong?' Fredrik would have to return to Sweden at some point; he had a good chance of working for Ingmar Bergman. He seemed able to envisage me living in Sweden and working in Swedish, and I just couldn't. 'It will be all right,' he promised. I didn't spoil everything by arguing but I couldn't see how.

I had no trouble fitting into Fredrik's life but I did have a problem fitting my clothes into his wardrobe cupboard. My benefactor had decided that I must be made to look more like a successful actress. No one trusted me to achieve this sartorial transformation so, kindly smart Noel Hood, one of my teachers at RADA, was deputed to take me shopping for an entire wardrobe. Equipped with a huge cheque, we set off for Knightsbridge (Harrods and Woollands) and the King's Road which bristled with small, discreet 'Modom' shops staffed by elegant, frightfully grand elderly women who would have frightened me to death had I been alone.

Thanks to Miss Hood, by the end of the day I was, in theory, prepared and poised for any occasion and looked in all the outfits just like my mother would have looked were she to spend a fortune on clothes. Black and grey and violet were the predominant colours. The shoes, the handbags, the three-quarter length gloves were all the plainest and blackest, and the one frivolous item was an incredibly expensive hat; a huge cabbage rose tilted over one eye, a scrap of felt holding it, and a little flirtation of spotted veil just reaching the bridge of my nose ('perfect for easy eating,' I noted gratefully).

Almost immediately yet another American film producer took the hat and me to the Caprice restaurant in Arlington Street. Without a hat one couldn't go to a smart restaurant at lunchtime and the same hat would bar one's entry at night for dinner. My rose clashed or toned in – I couldn't decide which – with the ruched red walls, lit by wall sconces disconcertingly fashioned from raised ceramic hands cut off at the wrist, 'Vivien Leigh's choice,' said my host. 'She *loves* hands.' Sitting up straight in my slinky black frock – wool crêpe, draped everywhere – squinting under a huge errant pink petal, I felt I was right at the centre of things. As usual, I ate everything I was offered and was hugely appreciative and paid no attention to what was being said about my movie career.

My agent began to smell trouble and so did I. We were set on wildly divergent courses (she was mad about films). Even she had to agree with me (though rather shakily), when after a cocktail party outing for a new black, ballerina-length, silk frock with its tiny velvet bolero, small clutch bag and silk shoes, a representative of Revlon rang MCA suggesting that I might be suitable to be the Revlon girl and suggesting an indecently enormous fee, spread over five years. An actress accepting such an offer could kiss goodbye to a 'legitimate career' on the spot. Olive knew this perfectly well and would never have tried to persuade me to make such a mad career move. What shook her, I think, was the ease and *speed* at which the money was rejected. There must have been something mildly unnatural about such aristocratic nonchalance, coming from a sturdy peasant who was, on the whole, biddable. We rubbed along uneasily and my worries grew as the number of *Hedda* performances dwindled.

One day a week I was able to write and present a weekly TV magazine programme beamed to Wales from Manchester. This was television at its scariest; Meredith Edwards and I chatted and interviewed our way through an almost entirely unrehearsed programme, taking a keen, completely uninformed interest in pig farming or double-glazing or trombone-playing. One Wednesday the 'unusual pet' a snake escaped in mid-interview which tested me somewhat and towards the end of that particularly hectic show I glanced up at the control room window to see the director turned away from the control panel, head bowed, having given up the unequal struggle. The public was very tolerant. There was a feeling between audience and performers of all of us being in the same mess together, and a lot of the time it *was* a mess.

Well trained by the BBC, I enjoyed interviewing and talking to the camera and now I was offered the first prestigious interviews 'in depth' on network television. These I accepted and they led to my being offered a more permanent job doing much the same thing. My agent, unaware of my past at the BBC, was puzzled but pleased – television was obviously going to be quite important and she didn't subscribe to the snobbism held in theatre circles towards this new medium. Realising that I was being sidetracked, I rejected all further offers to become a television 'personality'.

I couldn't work out why I felt so confused. The theatre seemed to be changing and changing quite fast. I had spent my life preparing and had now been trained at RADA to be a 'classical' actress, and that was what I wanted to be. The performances I had liked best had confirmed me in this ambition. The Shakespeare production that had most impressed me had been Tyrone Guthrie's *Troilus and Cressida* and my favourite performance was Paul Rogers's Pandarus in that same production, which put him on my private most-loved list along with Edith Evans and Ralph Richardson.

Richard Burton, with whom I played in Welsh as a student in Wales, was now a big star at the Old Vic, along with John Neville. Seeing *Henry V* from the gods I had been aghast, on a Saturday matinée, to find that I couldn't *hear* Richard at all times. Embarrassed and incredulous, I'd sat disappointedly through the play which came and went fitfully, then suddenly, towards the end, Richard walked on to the stage in full Harry rig, gold and blue and resplendent, and there was a collective sigh of appreciation from the audience. Richard just stood there and *was* Henry V. Of course, they could doubtless hear more from the better seats but even in the gods it seemed mean to whinge in the face of such beauty and splendour. All the same . . . what about Hugh Miller's 'Sell it to the paying customers – they're in the auditorium, all *three tiers* of it' and Michael Redgrave's 'To act well and to act well *repeatedly* has to become an obsession'.

I didn't know what to think. Much as I loved Shakespeare, the play I had liked most had been *Waiting for Godot* but there didn't seem to be anything like that about, except maybe at the Royal Court. I'd been going to see the plays that were being produced there by the New English Stage Company, run by George Devine. There was a great deal of talk about 'Working-Class' drama, 'Kitchen-Sink' drama. The massive success had been *Look Back in Anger* and some said that this had changed the face of the English theatre overnight. I couldn't make up my mind what I thought about this. It just didn't seem to me to be particularly working-class or new; rather conventional in fact. And Jimmy Porter, the archetypal Angry Young Man didn't seem to be especially angry. Cross, yes, and at odds with everything but not angry. I'd seen working-class anger during a lock-out at a coal mine and that was a good deal more terrifying than Jimmy's bad temper. I couldn't help feeling that characters speaking with regional accents or 'lower class' accents were perceived to be somehow more 'real' and genuine than characters who spoke with standard English accents. To a foreigner it all seemed to be part of the bottomless English preoccupation with class. Coming from a background where it was dangerous, certainly unwise, to assume that a working-class person was uneducated or illiterate, I was not completely won over by the excitement in Sloane Square.

The Angry Young Man had been popping up in novels since I was an undergraduate in 1953. John Wain's *Hurry on Down* was the book where I encountered my first disaffected young man and *Lucky Jim* had followed in 1956. In life he wore desert boots or sandals, checked, homespun-style shirts – no tie if humanly possible – didn't shave too much if he could get away with it and over his shirt he wore thick chunky sweaters or a shabby sports jacket and the favourite choice for overcoats was the duffel. (Ex-army surplus shops were good sources of Angry Young Man clothes.) I fancy that the English weather prevented the more dramatic American rebel look (Marlon Brando in a singlet would turn purple in Nottingham). Also, it seemed to me that the Angry Young Men, the working-class heroes of English drama, were very specifically English and were the product of a British Act of Parliament, the Butler Education Act of 1944 which reorganised secondary education and introduced the Eleven-plus examination for the selection of grammar school pupils.

In America most people had more 'things' than we did; but they also had bigger problems. Over three-quarters of the population had television sets and washing machines and refrigeration and heating and cooling systems, but there were people who had nothing at all and from a safe distance we read with disbelief that less than a year after the Russian tanks had put down the Hungarian Uprising, Governor Faubus in Little Rock, Arkansas, had used the National Guard to prevent black students from taking up their places at the High School. America was racist. That was a *real* problem. Hungary's revolt against communist rule was a *real* problem. England had a bit of a social problem.

In Britain, thanks to the Butler Act, my generation had been given access to higher education on a scale never before known; most of the students at my university or at RADA were dependent on grants from their local authorities. In England, Equality of Opportunity had, in many quarters, given rise to the misapprehension that we were witnessing the dawn of social equality. Not so in Wales. I remember my mother rather admiring Stafford Cripps for trying to deal with politics in ethical terms, when he suddenly went too far. As Chancellor of the Exchequer he was dedicated to soaking the rich and creating equality, he said. 'That'll be the day,' said my mother, dismissively and switched him off.

London in the late Fifties was awash with young people who had been given admission to a society which hadn't changed since the time when they were excluded from it. They had to come to terms with a society in which the old order prevailed and the class structure stood firm against these post-graduates of the 'école de Butler,' as we were sneeringly referred to. It was a hurtful discovery to find that the admission ticket led only so far, and for a disappointed young man the easiest course was to despise and ridicule the society that so effortlessly shrugged him off. This hero was a hurt misfit who felt he'd been misled, but surely he was offended rather than angry.

There were no Angry Young Women at that time so there wasn't much richness for actresses to plunder. Even the clothes: the skirts so full they were restricting and the petticoats held us all in thrall. The lack of contraception except for married women – upon-production-of-a-marriage-licence – dictated our behaviour (the rituals of communion between the sexes were still quaint). Coming from a truly classless society but not expecting to find one in England, I was not cross or rebellious but I was confused. There was a rush to portray people who didn't belong. I didn't 'belong' but it didn't bother me much and I didn't recognise myself in any of the plays I saw or read.

I was asked to go to the Royal Court for a chat and spent a depressing hour with a group of middle-class people in working-class disguise who told me a lot of things about the importance of the working-class point of view. The concept of the daring, strong, powerful, articulate working-class woman, familiar to me from childhood, was not, I felt, one that would fit in any framework devised in SW1 and to mention such a creature would be tactless. I was glad to get back to Fulham Road to listen to hard working, working-class Frank Sinatra singing Nelson Riddle arrangements.

Chapter Thirty-five

*H**edda* had been going very well and now I looked forward to the challenge of taking her to Oslo or 'Ibsen's own country', as people had begun saying – ominous and somehow more important-sounding than 'Norway'. We planned to do a run-through on board ship and Mr Fernald, who had served in the Navy during the war, was gleefully looking forward to combining two of his great loves – sailing and theatre. All in all we were in a buoyant mood as we left Waterloo Station, I, hatted and gloved like a dowager. Bizarrely I found myself being photographed by the press and waved off by a girl in a Welsh costume.

Our Company Manager (and my friend), Dot Tenham, had been told to brief me on the subject of clothes. I was to wear a hat to all daytime receptions, black court shoes and handbag, gloves to be worn at all times. Hélène, Thelma and I had spent my last night at home unpicking embroidered cherries from my new grey dress, bought specially but hurriedly for smart Norwegian gatherings. 'You look like a fruit bowl,' Hélène said and set to work with scissors and pins to calm the party frock. I had lost interest in clothes but I unpicked enthusiastically for something to take my mind off things.

The Swedish-Lloyd ship bucketed up and down and I made the happy discovery that I was a good sailor at the same moment that I discovered the joys of *smörgasbord*. I had never seen so much food and all conveniently and decoratively laid out for easy and copious eating. We did rehearse on deck during a calm hour or two but I think it was mostly for fun and it certainly didn't distract me from the joys of lurching around the dining room.

What with the food and my ability to take my mind off worrying things, I was quite unprepared for the attention I received in Oslo. I immediately fell in love with the look of the place and I lay in my pretty blue and white room with its painted furniture and gingham cotton curtains, looking at the snow outside, from the soft depths of a bed, warm under a huge and thick, feather-filled something or other. It was like a super – oh, infinitely superior – eiderdown. No, it wasn't like an eiderdown, it was like the smell and taste of dill, novel and simply lovely. London was still post-war grubby and down at heel. Oslo and the air of Norway were unbelievably fresh and clean.

The first hint that I might be under a little pressure came when my dresser, who spoke no English, slammed me in and out of my costumes faster than I had ever before been dressed and undressed. Although it was our first run together, she was always there at my elbow or waiting for me at exactly the right moment and for a while I admired her powers of intuition, until it occurred to me that, as a National Theatre dresser, she had in all probability dressed more than a few Heddas in her time and that this was a play as familiar here as *Hamlet* was in London. Hmm . . .

When opening night arrived, the director of the theatre came round in great good spirits to report 'a packed house, with *seven* Hedda Gablers sitting in the stalls'. Ho hum, I thought grimly, while responding, 'Oh, good!' with all the fake enthusiasm I could muster. My dresser and I looked at my reflection in the long mirror, I nodded a 'thank you' at her and she put her hand on my arm and squeezed gently. Oh God, was she feeling sorry for me? This was no moment to start feeling small so I indicated that I'd go down to the stage now, good and early, and have a bit of a stroll around. She accompanied me to the lift door and I gestured that I'd like to go alone. Punching the button, down I went. Although it was after the quarter-hour call, backstage was silent and in total darkness. I paced up and down a bit, wondering at the cold and the difference in backstage practice between England and Norway. In England the entire crew would be milling about and one would be able to hear the distant hum of a full house. And where were the other actors?

Having completed my private-calming-down-perking-up rituals, I ventured further down to the deserted prompt corner and peered through the curtain to see, to my horror, a completely dark and empty auditorium. I felt that I was inhabiting an actor's nightmare; any minute now someone would call me to begin a play I had never read, let alone rehearsed, and I would be in the wrong costume and then I would WAKE UP! No, waking up was obviously not part of this nightmare and, picking up my skirts, I ran – not to the wretched lift – but out into a passage-way and up the nearest flight of stairs. I would go back to square one and to my dressing room and start the journey again. What *time* was it?

Before I reached my dressing room floor I came upon a brightly lit corridor with busy people – even to a foreigner they were recognisably stage-hands – bustling to and fro, then a reassuringly familiar set of double doors and, slowing down, I strolled through them to encounter a scene of un-Scandinavian, almost Neapolitan panic in full swing. I smiled reassuringly and pretended not to notice the shoulder-shrugging and head-shaking and eyebrow-raising as I walked slowly to my place. The play began and the rhythms of the perfectly constructed piece took over, the inner tumult of not being able to find the stage and the worry at being scrutinised by all those Hedda Gablers fell away and I felt calm and almost passive as the story unfolded.

The curtain fell for the last time and we waited for the applause and prepared to take the curtain call in the one democratic line favoured in the days of *No Star Nonsense* (the title of the book by Peter Cotes). I felt faint with shock when the curtain rose to total silence. After what seemed an eternity we were given a lengthy, conventional and hugely enthusiastic reception. The director of the Folk Theatre, whose family had been taking care of me, rushed backstage, elated at what he called 'A triumph'. 'But they didn't applaud for ages,' I began. He slapped his forehead and explained, 'If they *truly* approve they award you a silence.' Paranoia had taken hold and privately I thought that he was just saying that to make me feel better so I braced myself for a long, difficult reception ahead. As it turned out it was a wonderful party. The Heddas, most of them, came to it and were gracious – as far as I could tell. There was a letter from the most distinguished Hedda of all, Agnes Movinkle, summoning me to have coffee at her house in the morning.

At breakfast, I was told that the notices were nothing short of sensational. ('Don't forget you always get a lot of marks for being foreign,' reminded John Fernald on the phone, but I could tell that he was pleased as punch). Accompanied by an interpreter, I set off to visit the great actress. Gravely she poured coffee and sat looking at me. I thanked her for coming to the play and for letting me visit her. She accepted my thanks and we had a somewhat stilted conversation. Maybe it was the language barrier but I had a feeling that small-talk was not one of her specialities. Finally, she indicated the pile of Norwegian papers on the couch beside her. 'It may be because of your youth that they say you are one of the best. I am not sure what I think about that but I would like you to know – and again this may in part be due to your youth – but I consider that you are one of the most– ' she paused and looked at me, then resumed, '*correct* Heddas that I have experienced.' I wasn't sure if this was faint praise or great praise but I plumped for the latter and said lots of 'Thank you's' before I was released from the Presence and skipped off, feeling pretty cheerful.

The profits from all the performances of *Hedda* were to go towards funding a scholarship in memory of Jan Groth, a Swedish student who had recently died in a tragic accident while at RADA. His parents came to Norway to see the play and our meeting was restrained; they were part happy, happy that Jan's memory was being honoured, part sorrowful.

Back in London we continued playing in far less grand circumstances. The play and John Fernald's production were as sound as a bell and went well, no matter how unpromising the venue. The end of *Hedda* would mark the end of my involvement with RADA and I realised with dismay that I was worried and fearful. It would be difficult to imagine anyone with less reason to be apprehensive, but there it was and I couldn't help it. There were, I had realised, many things about 'the Business' that I had never liked or enjoyed; the competition, the malice, the genuine hard luck stories – sadness at every turn. For two years I'd been protected from all those things and had conveniently forgotten about them. Now I dreaded leaving the safe haven.

Something happened which doubled my fears. One of the broadsheets picked up on the astonishing press that *Hedda* had received in Oslo and reprinted something of it, comparing our reception (and inevitably my part of it) favourably with that received by a far more mature and celebrated company from England that had played there earlier in the year. It was a piece of mischief making but it depressed me. 'Oh, there's the baby Bernhardt or was it Duse? Aiming to be the most popular girl in *Spotlight*, are we?' said a sharp-tongued guest teacher at RADA. Low in spirit, I began to dread seeing my photograph in the press. Flora Robson gave me her recipe for wet-white (to make the hands look beautiful on stage) and pointed out what I already knew, that the periods of riding high, when everything one touched turned, if not to gold then to something shiny, did not usually last long and should be, if not enjoyed, *used*. Easier said than done. I remember the overheard words from my childhood, 'She just isn't cut out for it'. What if they were right, after all?

Chapter Thirty-six

All very well deciding what *not* to do, but what to *do*? Where to go? Which way to jump? The Magic Offer, the one which, when it arrived, would proclaim itself to be the right, the only possible one, did not materialise, but destiny of another sort brushed by me one day off the Tottenham Court Road. It was like being afforded an accidental glimpse of something I was not meant to see just yet. A shutter opened onto a future scene.Without giving it a conscious thought my system absorbed it.

Fredrik, Hélène and Thelma and I were on our way to the Spaghetti House for lunch and Fredrik paused to greet a friend who was accompanied by an actor who had left RADA before I enrolled. So this was the legendary bad boy who had spent the night asleep wrapped up in the Vanbrugh Theatre curtains, who was late to class, who actually drank during the day in the Gower Public House and who was now the shining star of the Bristol Old Vic where he had been the second person in England to play Jimmy Porter but who had already startled everyone with a *really* angry young man performance when he played Hamlet. ('He actually *climbed* the proscenium arch,' spluttered a witness on his return to London.) Peter O'Toole was one of a group of gifted students who were still talked of at RADA (Finney, Pringle, Bedford, Villiers, Briers, the list was long).

Like most women, I have the gift of being able to take in

every detail of an outfit at a glance. O'Toole looked as though he was wearing clothes unlike any I'd seen a man wearing. He had black, curly hair and blue, blue eyes set in a quizzical face. It was the expression of one who could hardly credit the evidence of his eyes. He looked like the Actor in Disney's *Pinnochio*. But that actor was a wolf, surely? We said good-bye and moved on. The wolf wore a green velvet or corduroy jacket, didn't he? And a neckerchief? Or was it O'Toole who wore the jacket and the coloured thing around his neck? I didn't turn to check and we went into the restaurant. I couldn't remember his face, just the wolf's face, an actor's face, though. Actor. Nothing but actor. In the time it took to look at the menu and order risotto with an egg on top, I wondered briefly when it would be that we would marry. Then I never thought about it again.

Not even when, about a year later, we met on the first day of rehearsal of a West End production of *The Holiday* by John Hall. It was still not time. The shutter remained closed as though it had never opened.

Instead of taking an acting job immediately, I left RADA and spent a month sitting still. John Fernald advised me to accept an invitation from the portrait sculptor, Dora Gordine, to sit for a head which she wanted to do of me playing Hedda Gabler. She had seen the play six times and chose to portray a moment from the last act just before Hedda shoots herself. Dora lived in an extraordinary house on a hill looking out on the tops of the trees of Richmond Park. Each morning I left Fredrik at home and caught a bus at nine o'clock so as to be in the studio, on the dais in my wig at ten a.m. Dora, who was Russian, fed me *kasha* seated in my chair and otherwise expected total concentration until six p.m., when I was released. I sat from Monday to Friday for four weeks. John Fernald had been right, sitting for Dora was a demanding but wonderful experience. While I sat silent and still she talked about her youth as a young refugee studying under Maillol in Paris, about winning a five-year commission to sculpt the figures for the new civic centre in Singapore and about spending all her money on semi-precious wood and white hand-woven fabric, returning to Europe by ship with the hold full of her purchases and no place to put them, no money left either.

Meeting Richard Hare was a fantastic piece of good fortune. He proposed, she accepted and together they built their house with materials she'd brought back. 'It'll fall down,' she was warned as she directed the builders herself. It stood and when I was there it was like an enchanted fortress. On entering, shoes had to be removed and one took one's pick from the twenty pairs of carpet slippers in the hall, padding softly across the beautiful wooden floor, perfectly level so as not to jolt the trolley bearing sculptures which were wheeled to the foundry where Dora cast her own bronzes. The first floor was an art gallery with huge windows, veiled with white fabric, and alongside the gallery Dora had built an enormous studio where she worked eight or nine hours a day. Their apartment was on the top floor, high above the trees, a smallish, Russian set of rooms with half-moon doors and custom-made 1930s furniture, all made from Dora's blocks of wood.

She was tiny with the severe countenance of a Bodhisattva. Watching her work with such ferocious concentration taught me something more about the labour involved in achieving anything. 'Education is the impact of quality.' The little tyrant was persuasive. How, I wondered when she showed me the figure, had she persuaded Edith Evans to pose in the nude for her?

Fredrik could no longer delay his return to Sweden and settled me into a little flat in South Kensington. He had accompanied me to Nottingham where I was going to do a season of plays. The fact that I couldn't believe in our future together made the parting, when it came soon after, all the more sad. In my heart I felt that we were saying goodbye for good. Now for almost a year I bounced around at the whim of MCA who were, it seemed, interested only in my future in movies or in the West End. I managed to squeeze in a few things that pleased me and Olive was indulgent.

A while later I was told that this confusing, frustrating time need not have happened. The magical, the 'Right' offer *had* come, unknown to me. Sir Barry Jackson at the Birmingham Repertory Company had asked me to go and play a season there with a view to staying longer and I would have begun by playing Lady Macbeth to Albert Finney's Macbeth. MCA, without consulting me, had rejected the offer saying, 'We don't want her to learn reppy tricks.' When I learned this I was appalled. I left MCA and when they held me to my contract I gladly paid them as well as my new agents 10 per cent until my contract expired.

At the same time as the rise of the Kitchen Sink drama, there was a brief flowering of verse drama and *The Holiday* was part of this movement. Actually, by the time we did *The Holiday*, verse drama was virtually dead so *The Holiday* was more of an ending. O'Toole and I were to make our West End debuts in this play, presented by Donald Albery and playing brother and sister (we did look alike).

Once again, I was playing a part for which I was completely unsuited. It was a hard lesson, knuckling under and working on parts which didn't need anything that I had to offer. Difficult parts were easy – ordinary or bad parts were difficult, I realised. At one point Tony Richardson actually said to me, 'Could you look as though you've just left Harrods?' Well, I could, but I didn't want to and there was something about me that just didn't convince as a middle-class English, specifically Knightsbridge, girl. God, I hated those parts. Margaret in *The Holiday* made and poured tea, mixed and served drinks, was very good to everybody and spoke nicely and dressed quietly.

It was a remarkable company that set out on tour; Colin Jeavons, John Moffat, Nicholas Meredith, Sylvia Syms, Mary Hinton, Jack Merrivale and O'Toole and myself, all struggling with a play that was re-written and re-written, boasting a new title every so often in case that might help. The short, smart, pre-West End tour grew into a lengthy one, on what was called 'the disappearing circuit' as we trailed north into

Scotland where they *hated* us. I felt sorry for John Hall, the author, as he endlessly re-worked the play, but I felt even sorrier for us as our audiences dwindled in the cold north.

John Moffat played the central character of the victim, the outsider who commits suicide and makes everyone feel dreadful on the last page of the play. He was called 'Saxman' for ever such a long time and suddenly, in one of those all too familiar panic measures, word came that his name should be changed immediately to 'Jackson'. Why, I don't remember. Nor did the Company. That night we'd called John's character 'Jackson' for two hours and just before the last curtain, someone appeared centre-stage in the most dramatic moment of the play and said, 'Saxman's hung himself in the garage.' Who? What was that?

There was a long pause as the unfortunate actor's face changed colour and the tiny band in the auditorium stirred themselves into life. 'Who did she say?' 'Who's Saxman?' The S's resounded through the stalls. The whole evening had been rendered meaningless. Rocking with laughter, we all turned up-stage, shoulders heaving, and finished the play with our backs to the audience. It was the last straw. John Moffat's face as he joined us for the curtain was a study. How he disapproved and how he wished he'd been on stage for the fun. Clive Exton, the playwright, was our Stage Manager and he reported the lot of us. Back at the hotel, O'Toole and I ran into a few people who'd been at the play. 'We didn't understand *all* of it,' said a woman, trying to be nice. 'Ah well, y'know – *verse*!' said O'Toole airily and graciously accepted a drink.

Our relationship was, in a way, very proper; we just wanted to spend all our time together. I was introduced to the delights of drink, specifically scotch whisky, and staying up late in bars chatting to the owners We talked and talked and I listened a lot; I wanted to know everything O'Toole had ever done and over the course of seven weeks we covered a great deal of territory. I learned Irish songs and sang him Welsh songs and he played his guitar to me. One morning we woke at dawn, fully clothed, propped against each other where we had fallen fast asleep on my bed with a guitar between us; we were a bit embarrassed as we hastily parted. We were both involved with other people and that was just about the only thing we didn't talk about.

The tour ended with a long journey from Scotland to London. I wondered, but not for too long, how life would be now that we would not be spending all our time together. Not nearly so much fun, I thought. We stayed awake all night talking and when we arrived in London I went home to a new flat I was sharing with Thelma, showered, borrowed a clean frock and went to the BBC in Portland Place where I was to record *Treason* by Saunders Lewis. Two versions: first English and then Welsh. The cast included Richard Burton, Clifford Evans, Emlyn Williams, Donald Houston and myself, playing a 'proper' woman for a welcome change. Richard was hardly ever there. Days went by and he sent messages saying he'd be with us soon. Emyr Humphreys, our director, squared it with the powers-that-be and we made ourselves at home in our studio on the sixth floor, writing letters and doing crosswords and taking long lunch breaks.

Emlyn took me to a restaurant in Wigmore Street and we passed a hearing-aid shop – rather up-market – with a plastic orchid supporting the aid, making it look glamorous and desirable. 'Oh look,' he said, 'privilege to be deaf.'

He began to bring in a typewriter and sat with a glue pot and scissors and coloured paper, re-typing his part and doing mysterious things with paper markers. Only the tap-tap of the typewriter was heard when Wolf Mankowitz put his head round the door, surveyed the silent Welsh gathering and withdrew saying, 'Sorry'.

'Didn't get much of a welcome in *this* valley,' said Emlyn without looking up from his typewriter.

The Commissionaire rang up to say that there was a lady down below for Mr Burton. 'Not here,' said Emyr. Richard was coming to the end of a protracted affair with a famous young actress and evidently she wasn't about to give him an

284

easy exit. Day after day there were phone calls, 'I *know* he's there.' 'I wish,' said Emyr, wearily. Finally the Commissionaire called up to say that the young lady had left a letter for Mr Burton. Emlyn took the call. 'Bring it up,' he said, 'and bring a steaming kettle, too.' Richard, looking a little worse for wear, turned up eventually and was charming and performed wonderfully well in both languages.

I didn't actually talk *about* O'Toole but he was much in my mind and I related some of the fascinating things he'd told me, for instance about his time in the Navy as a National Serviceman.

Me: Did you know that in the Navy – well, in submarines anyway – salt is called 'sea dust'?

Emlyn: Go on, it's not, is it?

Me: And butter is called 'slide'. Isn't that wonderful?

Emlyn: And what other wonderful things did Peter O'Toole tell you on this tour?

I went on to a backbreaking stint of live television, playing a huge leading part each month in what was a version of four-weekly rep but with infinitely more pressure. I rather enjoyed the pressure but began to suffer from boils and abscesses which would develop slowly and painfully during the three rehearsal weeks, then burst dramatically on the day of the dress rehearsal, leaving me weak but free from pain for transmission, and the whole miserable business would begin all over again. The boils, to which I attributed malicious human sensibilities, would occasionally get confused because we went into a small studio, in costume, and performed a short trailer, then, after transmission, we would turn up a few days later and give a repeat performance of the play. The boils didn't know where they were.

Back in London O'Toole and I saw a good deal of each other whenever we were free.

One dreadful night, after a late transmission in Bristol, I revealed a confidence that had been entrusted to me by O'Toole, to a friend of his, a writer who I assumed would have been privy to the secret. He wasn't and when O'Toole heard what I'd done we had a monumental row, standing outside the Royal Court. He was in a towering rage and we parted noisily – and for ever. I walked the length of the Kings Road before I stopped shaking. An actor whom I knew gaped, astonished, as I passed by, sobbing fiercely and walking too fast to be stopped.

We were both due to begin rehearsing new plays. O'Toole was to do his first television, playing Gaudier-Brezska, the sculptor. His play would be transmitted from London. Mine, *The Quiet Man*, was to be transmitted from Cardiff and I stayed with Herbert while I was rehearsing. Herbert sympathised as I told him the sorry tale of how I'd lost 'my closest friend', as I described him. 'Hmm,' he said, looking at me over his glasses, 'and have you told Fredrik about your "friendship"? 'I don't have to. There's no harm in it.' 'Oh, Phillips, Phillips, you're madly in love.' 'Don't be silly. Anyway, I'll never see him again.' And I believed that.

Herbert and I watched *The Laughing Woman* together. O'Toole was breathtaking. We sat silently in the front room, our drinks untouched, until the play was over. It was obvious that O'Toole had scarcely hit a mark from beginning to end and even the cameras were at white heat as they jostled with each other, trying to get in for a close-up of a left ear or a bit of nose. It was live TV at its most thrilling – dangerous, messy and immediate. I could hardly bear the thought that I wouldn't be able to talk to O'Toole about it. But there it was. I'd been really stupid and thoughtless and that was the end of it.

I did my play with Alun Owen, who was giving his last performance before becoming a full-time playwright. He was a good actor and in spite of my sombre mood we had a good time together and the play went well.

My parents were pleased to see me alone, as they thought, running a successful career as a consequence. 'You're better off,' said my mother as we ate our farewell lunch. She was pleasantly flushed as the phone rang all morning with calls from people she knew who had watched the play the night before. I could see that she was a mite surprised that acting was proving to be such a normal, full-time, gainful occupation and I could also tell that she was afraid I might mess it all up. 'It just isn't right for you – being married.' 'What, never?' I asked. 'Oh well – I don't know,' she prevaricated, unwilling to commit herself to anything too sweeping.

I had a feeling that she was probably right. Well, I had no wish to marry and if my childhood picture of myself, living alone but doing what I wanted in life, was coming true, then I could manage that. It wasn't as simple as I'd imagined but who ever said life would be simple?

Chapter Thirty-seven

Lpondon was cold and most of my friends were working out of town. I liked the new flat in Notting Hill Gate, the front room with its big ground-floor window overlooking Ladbroke Square, but I was glad that I was working non-stop. O'Toole was having an enormous success in *The Long and the Short and the Tall* at the Royal Court and each time I passed the front-of-house photographs on my way to rehearsal I thought 'I must go to see the play' – but I didn't. Our falling out had, I reflected, left me with a greater sense of loss and waste than I had ever felt in my life. But I was determined not to fall apart. There was a touch of grimness in my brisk day-to-day life but I was, most certainly, all of a piece. All the same, going to the play was better postponed.

I awoke and wondered why. There was a noise of something at the window. I got out of bed without putting on the light. There was nothing to make me nervous; there was a wide area between my window and the front door steps. Improbably there was a face at the window and a tall figure perilously straddled the gap outside. I raised the window slowly, fearful of upsetting the delicate balance. Two hands plunged in and seized the sash window frame and, with a heave, two long slim feet swung through and to the floor, and over six feet of O'Toole straightened itself cheerily and seemed to sketch a little bow. I wanted to applaud. It was *such* a moment, beautifully executed.

How could I have forgotten that this was going to happen? Like the shutter of a camera, the fingernail of a picture widened to confirm itself, then shut seamlessly as though it had never been. I was a pawn in this scene. As it happened I could see that here was my brother, my lover, my child, my father – and most importantly, my equal partner, who loved and inhabited the world that I also loved. Everything made sense. Everything was turning out right.

'I've got a car. Coming for a cup of tea?'

'It's three in the morning.'

'So?'

'I'm in my nightie.'

'Put a mac on.'

'Why not.'

'Hullo you.'

Index

291